Under The Son

Under
The Son

Living Your Life IN CHRIST

Tony Sheard

Living Word UK

Under the Son: Living Your Life IN CHRIST
Copyright © 2022 Tony Sheard
First Edition, ~November 2022

ISBN: 9798364884985

Copyright Acknowledgements

Thanks

This book is the product of a series of messages given to the church congregation of Living Word Christian Centre, Bath, during the time we pastored there. The church was always encouraging and I gained much from them.

Also, I subsequently taught some of the messages at a leadership conference in Eldoret, Kenya for Bishop Daniel Muiruri. I know that the leaders who were present spent an afternoon going over the truths in them and I am grateful for their feedback and encouragement.

My thanks also go to my wife, Julie, who has been a constant source of encouragement to me during the process of writing this.

Contents

Thanks...7

Introduction...13

Part 1 – Your Life IN CHRIST

Chapter 1:
    Receiving a Letter..19

Chapter 2:
    Our Security In Christ..27

Chapter 3:
    Our Inheritance In Christ.....................................41

Chapter 4:
    Our Position In Christ..59

Chapter 5:
    The Mystery, Power and Strength In Christ 71

Appendix to Part 1:
    Who we are In Christ...83

Part 2 – Your Life Through Christ

Chapter 6:
    His Call, our Response..93

Chapter 7:
    Old Man – New Man..105

Chapter 8:
    The Call to Right Living..115

Chapter 9:
    Walking in Love, Light and Wisdom..................................127

Chapter 10:
    Wives and Husbands..137

Chapter 11:
    Children and Parents..151

Chapter 12:
    Take a Stand..165

Chapter 13:
    Receiving this Letter Today..175

Bibliography...181

About the Author...

Introduction

Memories Are Made of This

It was 1992 and Julie and I were on holiday in Turkey in a place called Dalyan. It is situated in the Mugla province of Turkey, on the river of the same name that flows through it. It is famous for sea turtles on the estuary and a series of Etruscan/Lycian tombs dating from 400BC carved into huge cliffs along its banks.

I well remember that we had to get a ferry across the river while travelling from the airport to get to our hotel up in the hills some way out of the town. It was an idyllic spot, although I remember the beds were hard and the bed covers somewhat sparse. However, the weather was beautiful and we enjoyed our time there as it was different to just soaking up the sun on a nameless beach.

During our stay an opportunity arose for us to do a three day discovery tour of different areas of Turkey, staying overnight and taking in Pamukkale, an area of hot thermal pools formed from carbonate minerals, said to be where Cleopatra once bathed. It also included a guided visit to Ephesus. Being adventurous at the time, we decided to partake, always ready to see more of a country.

Well, Pamukkale was wonderful, but to this day I will never forget my first view over the ruins of Ephesus, standing on the same road that Paul probably walked as he entered the city on his missionary journey, as described in Acts 18 and 19. I immediately fell in love with the city and could only imagine what it would have been like in Paul's time. The remains of the Ephesian library still resonate with me even though it had not yet been built when Paul first arrived. I also remember that we were given a map of the city and I noticed that the site of the ancient Christian church was marked. It was not included in our tour. At the end we were given half-an-hour free time. It was hot that afternoon and Julie decided to stay relaxing at a cafe. However, I was determined to find and photograph the site. When I visited, this was described as the church of John the Baptist although I have subsequently discovered that the first official church structure in Ephesus was called the *Church of St. Mary* and that a further church dedicated to the apostle John was built after his death and subsequently expanded upon during Emperor Justinian's time. My visit involved me jumping over a fence and running along a path until I eventually found the ruins. I considered, even then, that the site was somewhat away from the main, lived in, part of the city and so began my hunger to find out more and also my heart for Paul's letter to the Ephesians grew.

Since then, I have returned once more, with some close friends from America, as an excursion from a Mediterranean cruise. It was still the same and I decided that the more you explore, the more you understand. It is exactly the same with the Word of God.

Ephesians has become one of my favourite books in all of scripture, but then I could say that about so many of them. After Paul founded the church there and spent two years working and growing the family of God's people, he eventually penned a letter to the congregation, to encourage and inspire them, whilst he was incarcerated in prison. Judging by the fact that Jesus, in the book of Revelation, began with the Ephesus church, it was clearly large and significant in the whole area of Asia Minor and Paul had much to share.

The heart of this book reflects my own personal thoughts on what Paul was saying, how it was received, and how we can learn from it and apply it to our daily lives. It is not intended to be an 'in depth' exposition or commentary but my hope is that it inspires you to dig deeper for yourself.

Part 1

Your Life IN CHRIST

Chapter 1

Receiving a Letter

These days, most people don't write or receive letters unless they relate to official business. Nowadays, we tend to communicate with each other by email, Facebook, Twitter, Instagram or any other of the plethora of social media methods which seem to increase each day. All of them tend to be instant and throwaway. Often we do not even read them but press the 'delete' button regularly.

So, for us, it might be difficult to imagine what it would have been like to be the recipient of a letter in the first century AD. Consequently, I feel it is important to paint a picture of the times and circumstances surrounding the city of Ephesus when this letter was delivered, probably by Onesimus or possibly Tychicus, as mentioned in Ephesians 6:21.

Ephesus the City

To have lived in the middle of perhaps the fourth greatest city in the world at the time, and certainly the largest and most influential city in Asia Minor, would have been an immense experience and we should not underestimate its impact on the people.

So, lets briefly consider this city. It had a huge harbour, even though it was beginning to silt up during this time. It was a major export centre, had a 24,000 seat capacity theatre and the population was booming and, perhaps, 'bursting at the seams'. Some estimate that, by then, the population was around one third of a million people.

Apart from being a major religious centre, the home of worship of the goddess Artemis (or Diana to the Romans), the temple of Artemis was one of the seven wonders of the ancient world. It also had a large Jewish colony. The city had obtained commercial eminence in the region and many ships frequented it. As a result, slavery and prostitution were rife and the Ephesian brothel was massive.

In short, Ephesus was situated at a crossroads between East and West and had gained a kind of elite status within Asia Minor, being known as "the Light of Asia".

Paul establishing the Kingdom in Ephesus

It was AD 52 when Paul, with his husband-wife missionary team of Priscilla and Aquila, sailed into the port of Ephesus. In Acts 16:6 we read that the Holy Spirit had previously stopped Paul from going there. Perhaps the time was not right, as only the Lord would know, but now there was a release and Paul did not hesitate to go. The magnitude of idolatry of every kind had reached a new level in Ephesus. It was greater than anything he had encountered before in Corinth or Athens, but it did not deter him.

> [18] ... *Then he took leave of the brethren and sailed for Syria, and Priscilla and Aquila were with him ...* [19] *And he came to Ephesus, and left them there; but he himself entered the*

synagogue and reasoned with the Jews. [20] When they asked him to stay with them, [21] he did not consent but took leave of them, saying "I must by all means keep this coming feast in Jerusalem but I will return again to you, God willing" And he sailed from Ephesus.

Acts 18:18-21

On landing, Paul would have passed a huge slave market. Later, those receiving his letter would have understood that when he used the word "redemption" it was derived from the Greek word *agora* used for the market place where slaves were purchased. There were so many other amazing sights in Ephesus but Paul was not distracted from his purpose for being there as, leaving the others, he headed straight for the synagogue, as was his practice, and began preaching to the Jewish group who were there, perhaps around 10,000 of them in total. Clearly he had an impact on them as they wanted him to stay. Maybe Paul knew the time was not right because, by then, he had understood that the Holy Spirit wanted him to return and really establish a ministry work that would, in due course, effect the whole of Asia Minor.

Later, we learn (Ac.18:24-28) that a man named Apollos went to Ephesus and spoke boldly in the same synagogue. However, Priscilla and Aquila had to help Apollos because he did not know the full gospel at that time. He subsequently went to Corinth.

Paul then returned to Ephesus and his exploits can be seen by reading the whole of Acts 19. After spending three months teaching in the synagogue (Ac.19:8) Paul and his message were eventually rejected by those who did not believe (Ac.19:9) but, undeterred, he still stayed in the city for at least another two years (Ac.19:10).

What we read following that is a huge testament to the work of the gospel. We are privileged to see a documented account of the outcome of the gospel and how much it impacted a wide range of people in the city. Magic practices were huge but so many people deeply believed the truth of the gospel that there was a massive spontaneous burning of magic books valued at 50,000 pieces of silver (perhaps in excess of £1,000,000 today). Also, there were mighty miracles and casting out of evil spirits (Ac.19:11-19).

What we also read is that the word of God spread and before long the church had expanded into the rest of Asia Minor (Ac.19:26).

It is easy to look at Jesus' reaction to the church in Ephesus and judge it, when he declared in Revelation 2:4 that they had lost their first love. However, by reversing this thought we can see that in the beginning the people were so radically and dramatically changed by Paul's preaching that they were recklessly in love with Jesus. This applied to many different culture groups and, judging by everything they put up with as described in Revelation, they stayed committed to their faith.

The Letter to the Church

Paul stayed for at least two years then met with the elders at Miletus as he was heading for Rome. Possibly this was AD 57.

It is thought that he wrote the letter to the church in Ephesus somewhere around AD 62 while he was in prison in Rome. It was five years on, at least, from when they had last seen him.

So, consider this was one Christian church, isolated from any other by many miles, even to Smyrna, probably the closest. Colosse was situated 100 miles away, which would be a couple of hours for us by car, but in those days it would take five days to reach travelling twenty miles a day.

The Ephesian church had become a ministry centre in Asia Minor but it was still isolated and in the midst of a huge city, which did not follow its message. Think what it must have been like to actually receive a letter containing encouragement, teaching and admonition from the leader of the team who had so miraculously changed their lives. I don't know about you but I can still remember the church service I attended on 21 April 1975 at a local mission in Dover, England, and first heard the Gospel. This totally changed my life. I went forward at that meeting, took a card containing a note of repentance and confession of faith. I then took it home, only a stone's throw away, went up to my bedroom and knelt and said that prayer out loud. I know Jesus came into my heart and life that day. So, I am certain that when this letter arrived, perhaps hundreds of Ephesian Christians were reminded of the same experience.

My heart for you as a reader is that these words of Paul become alive. Up until then, the believers in Paul's day only had Old Testament scrolls of the Bible to go on. They also had teaching and preaching from the Elders and leaders under the move of the Holy Spirit among them. However, now for the first time, here was a real-life letter from Paul, the one who had founded the church, speaking directly into their lives and, under the power of the Holy Spirit, instantly becoming the Word of God. For them, it must have been electric as they listened, copied and then began to apply to their lives those words and the principles they contained. It is also widely thought by many scholars that this letter was then passed on to the other churches which had then been established in other areas of Asia Minor. So, one way or another, the Word of God spread.

We also have to remember that they did not have 50 versions of the Bible, books, recordings of teachings, CDs, MP3s, the internet or the plethora of Christian TV stations. For them, hearing the content of that letter was like listening to every single one of the most influential and godly men of our day all rolled into one. It was the most important communication they were ever likely to get. It was precious, holy and vital for their livelihood, both spiritual and natural. They probably held on to every word and, as I said a moment ago, spent months or years going over them, again and again.

In the light of this, we must be challenged to do the same ourselves. The intention of this book is not to do a micro detailed, in depth study, or even a long commentary on each issue. Rather, I want to bring out some of the fundamental thoughts of this letter in the hope that we can all receive it and respond to it in exactly the same way the Ephesian church did. In doing so, we will receive the same power it contains in a fresh new way rather than it being just a scripture which we have heard before.

Authors note:

If you have enjoyed reading some of the background details about Ephesus and how the Ephesian church was formed there are many works and many authors to seek out, some more academic or theological than others. For me, personally, I have found an excellent description of both contained within a book by Rick Renner, *A Light in Darkness*, Volume 1. published by Teach All Nations.

Chapter 2

Our Security IN CHRIST

As I begin to write this section the UK is in the midst of a third lockdown as a result of the impact of coronavirus, a deadly virus, first discovered in China and which, subsequently, has infected the whole world. I have been very impacted to see people's varied reactions to this virus. Sadly there have been many deaths and many lives have been changed forever. However, it has also demonstrated the fragile and superficial way that many people live their lives. This pandemic has been unprecedented and, judging from responses to questions by the media, has shown how many immediately expressed massive fear and anxiety as the norms of their lives have had to change. It has reminded me so much of how poorly the world handles things when everything they are relying on for security is pulled from under them. Thankfully, there have also been some major heroics and communities pulling together showing us what can happen. It has helped me to see the compelling reason that Paul begins this letter to the Ephesian Church, as he does. Today there is hope through the discovery of a vaccine that stops the spread. People are treating this like an answer, so we can get back to normal. All of these things are on the surface of our lives. However, real well-being comes from something much deeper on the inside that keeps us steady and solid when everything else is going on around us.

As Paul begins this letter, bringing assurance and comfort to the Ephesian Church and, through them, to each one of us, it is good to consider again how insecure our lives can be. For the Ephesian church, they were probably quite small and marginalised and held very different views and lives compared to the general population of the city of which they were a part. What is so different today you may ask. The answer is probably "not much", for most Christian believers.

In many countries the Christian population is quite a small percentage of the overall population and we have to get used to the fact that most people do not think and act like we do. Thankfully, I have witnessed a difference in places like the United States, where the Christian population is higher and there is often a tangible difference that can only come through the work of the Holy Spirit. Then again, even in that country a shift is happening in values and, therefore, we have to look again at the first principles outlined by Paul, and really consider where our security lies.

On that basis then, it is important first of all to deliberate on what we ultimately mean when we refer to being secure. It provides us with an interesting insight. Here are a few:

Free from care, without anxiety, having full command of, to rid you of care.
WE Vine, Expository Dictionary of Biblical Words

Untroubled by danger or fear, impregnable, certain not to fail, a thing that guards or guarantees, fixed so as not to get loose or lost
The Concise Oxford Dictionary

Protection or effectual defence or safety from danger of any kind, freedom from fear or apprehension, confidence of safety, something given to secure payment of a debt.
Noah Webster 1828 Dictionary

I am sure most of you could think of a number of other areas that would qualify as security. Thinking about it for any length of time makes us realise that, as humans, we are inherently insecure in our daily lives and we have a tendency to do all we can to increase our security as much as possible because our physical well-being depends on it. That is the reason that the insurance industry is so widespread, because it plays on mitigating against insecurity, in whatever form that takes, in order to give us a sense of safety.

As already suggested, writing through Paul, the Holy Spirit begins to demonstrate that, for the believer, there is an even more secure and powerful place which brings safety and rest regardless of what is happening on the outside. As we consider the Word of God in these scriptures, we shall see the emphasis on the difference it makes to living our life with victory and confidence. That place of rest comes from a deeper understanding of being IN CHRIST.

¹ Paul, an apostle of Jesus Christ by the will of God, To the saints who are in Ephesus, and faithful in Christ Jesus: ² Grace to you and peace from God our Father and the Lord Jesus Christ. ³ Blessed be the God and Father of our Lord Jesus Christ, who has blessed us with every spiritual blessing in the heavenly places in Christ,

Ephesians 1:1-3

We begin with a clear assurance of who we are, "saints and faithful IN CHRIST". God's grace is poured upon us and His peace. In short, we must take on board, right at the start, how God sees us, regardless of how the world sees us, and begin to settle on the inside what we have as believers that is unique and brings us to a place of security. The world's viewpoint would suggest it has everything going for it and we must fully indulge it. Admittedly, some of them we can enjoy. However, we need to think carefully before we jump on board with all of it. So, in the midst of that clamour we need to have an anchor, something sure that we can rely on no matter what. This is where our security lies!

Blessed

We then hear what I believe is one of the most profound statements in the Bible, urging us to receive it and drink deeply in understanding what God is providing. God has blessed us with every spiritual blessing IN CHRIST.

Note that this is past tense. God has blessed us! It is not something to hope for in the future but it is something that we should be enjoying right now because God has already done it for us.

Now, you may not be feeling blessed and happy right now. That may not be your current experience of life. Nevertheless, the Father's blessing has been poured out on you. That word "spiritual" is the same word used in 1 Corinthians 12 describing the gifts of the Holy Spirit. We have every spiritual blessing IN CHRIST. You may feel like a nobody and you may feel like a novice in the life of a believer but the word says that you already have everything you need. It is already yours because you are IN CHRIST.

Chosen

> [4] just as He chose us in Him before the foundation of the world, that we should be holy and without blame before Him in love,
>
> **Ephesians 1:4**

He chose us to be IN CHRIST before He ever created this world. Think about that. He knew you before you were born. You were chosen by God for Him. You were not a random selection. As for God, He chose you for Himself. Of course, He also gave you free will to choose (or not). The big question has always been, as a free agent, will you choose Him? Paul is bringing assurance here for every believer.

You could easily become entangled in the realms of predestination theology at this point. If God has already chosen those for Him then why do we need to evangelise if it is all fixed? A simple way of seeing this is found when the word of God tells you that God is no respecter of persons or, in modern parlance, His choice is not to choose one and reject another. His choice is to choose everybody. The fact that some will ultimately reject that offer is down to their own decision. This verse also enables you to receive a full picture of how He sees you when he chooses you. He sees you as being "holy and without blame before Him in love". This is His heart for you. But note that the scripture here uses the word "should". That is His purpose for you. That is further confirmation that you were not an accident or the product of some primordial soup zapped by lightning, no matter what evolutionists may tell you. No, you were carefully considered by God and this is now who you are. So, if you have made that choice this is a present reality. You must allow this truth to go deep within your being as it alone brings amazing comfort.

Planned forAdoption

> [5] *having predestined us to adoption as sons by Jesus Christ to Himself, according to the good pleasure of His will,*
> **Ephesians 1:5**

God, by His grace, made a decision to create man with a free will. He wanted man to have the freedom to respond to His love and not to be a robot. However, He knew because He is in eternity and not time (a mind boggling concept for most of us in itself) that man would rebel from the place of fellowship and relationship with Him.

So God predestined or planned that when this happened He would not forsake man. Rather, He constructed a way by which man may return to Him just as if he had never sinned. That process is adoption as sons and daughters through the work that Jesus did on the cross. We call this process "the Gospel".

This is the will of God for each one of us and it was His pleasure to do that for us.

Now, we must take this fact deep into our spirits. The Father and the Son planned this before the foundation of the world. As we have said earlier, it was agreed by them before God even began the process of creation. It was before satan rebelled and deceived Eve. It was before Adam rebelled and therefore brought original sin on the whole human race. God's plan was to provide a way to save us through Jesus and then to place us in Jesus and adopt us as one of His sons and daughters to become Christlike even when we did not deserve it!

That statement is a powerful demonstration of the heart of the Father. That He loves you so much, regardless of what you have done, He would sacrifice His only Son for you. Also, that His Son Jesus would willingly say "yes" to that proposal as the only way of "redeeming" you, or bringing you back into a place of fellowship with Him. Jesus willingly took every sin, sickness and mental anguish on Himself so that you could walk free of it and be reconciled to God

> *2 looking unto Jesus, the author and finisher of our faith, who for the joy that was set before Him endured the cross, despising the shame, and has sat down at the right hand of the throne of God.*
>
> **Hebrews 12:2**

That statement is worth a massive shout. You are the joy that was set before Jesus. He had you on His mind when He went to the cross. He thought you were worth all the pain and suffering. He wanted you to experience again the constant life-giving flow of being a part of the family of God.

We need to respond in the same way those first century Christians would have done when they heard this revelation for the first time. They responded to the knowledge about God and who they now were IN CHRIST.

> *15 For you did not receive the spirit of bondage again to fear, but you received the Spirit of adoption by whom we cry out, "Abba, Father."*
>
> **Romans 8:15**

In other words, God planned ahead of time itself to place us in His family. We have to receive that into our life. We are a part of the family of God Himself.

Accepted

> *6 to the praise of the glory of His grace, by which He made us accepted in the Beloved.*
>
> **Ephesians 1:6**

To be accepted IN CHRIST means "graced with grace".

We were accepted in the family as a work of His grace to the praise of His glory. Now, we have a tendency to simplify that term to a most basic saying of "unmerited favour". Of course "grace" includes "unmerited favour" but I believe it is much, much more powerful than we have ever imagined. Basically, it is the process that takes place when the blood of Jesus enters our human spirit at the point when we declare that we confess our sin and ask Jesus into our heart as Lord and saviour. At that very moment, His grace plunges the complete depth of sin that would separate us from the Father, cleanses us with the blood of Jesus and makes our spirit new and whole, literally placing us IN CHRIST in that very moment. Nothing else but His grace can do that. However, the emphasis here is that He is "the beloved". He is loved of the Father and therefore as you are in Him you are also loved in exactly the same way and in the measure that Jesus is loved. You cannot be loved any more than that. There are many instances in the gospel narratives where it is obvious that Jesus knew intimately just how much the Father loved Him. Here, Paul is bringing to our ultimate attention that a full understanding of the extent of that love brings a lasting and deep sense of security in our life, regardless of anything we face on a daily basis.

In summary, you are:
1) Blessed with every spiritual blessing.
2) Chosen from the foundation of the world.
3) Planned for adoption in the family.
4) Accepted in the beloved (i.e. IN CHRIST).

The big issue for each of us then is, "Why and how?" If we are going to feel really secure on a permanent and consistent basis that will last throughout our lives we have to have an answer to that question otherwise it sounds too good to be true. Paul anticipates the query with a further set of IN CHRIST statements contained in verses 7-14 that are designed to enable us to accurately rely on them. What is more, we can live our lives by them as we understand the fulness of what Jesus, the Son of God, has done, both for us and in us.

The importance of this is that we are reminded this is Jesus we are talking about, not an angel, nor a prophet, nor simply a good man, but the Son of God Himself.

⁷ In Him we have redemption through His blood, the forgiveness of sins, according to the riches of His grace ⁸ which He made to abound toward us in all wisdom and prudence, ⁹ having made known to us the mystery of His will, according to His good pleasure which He purposed in Himself, ¹⁰ that in the dispensation of the fullness of the times He might gather together in one all things in Christ, both which are in heaven and which are on earth—in Him.

Ephesians 1:7-10

What is it, then, that the Holy Spirit wants to show us through the hand of Paul in these verses, that will convince us of the truth that we are secure in Him?

Redemption Through His blood

In Him we have redemption, not by any other mechanism. Redemption is a vital word to get to grips with. In this scripture in verse 7 it literally means:

a releasing, for (i.e., on payment of) a ransom.

WE Vine, An Expository Dictionary of Biblical Words

I still remember well the literal translation of the Greek word used for "ransom" from when I studied ancient Greek as a language for one of my courses in secondary school. Basically, it means "to set free for oneself". For us, Jesus ransomed us by payment of His blood and set us free from an eternity of separation from the Father because we were in a prison. It was a prison of our own making due to the basic sin that we all live with. The payment required for us to be freed from that prison is far too big for any of us to be able to pay by our own efforts or ability, ever.

Yet, Jesus came and paid the price freely by taking our sin, nailing it to the cross, and dying in our place, shedding His blood for us, so that we do not have to, because the price was higher than we could ever pay and only He could do it.

It is possible to spend much more time on this basic "gospel" truth. However, I believe that this short summary gives us enough to understand the heart of what Jesus did by His blood. The blood of Jesus is the key that makes everything work. We talk about the blood and some people get squeamish and want to leave all reference to the blood out of songs and preaching but the blood is where the power lies for us. Without the sacrifice of Jesus pouring out His blood for us none of the rest would have been possible. It is the blood that speaks for us. It is the blood that redeems us. Whenever you are feeling insecure as though you will not make it, the blood stands up and says "no, we have accepted His death for us and we are accepted in the beloved."

The blood of Jesus has overcome death for us, the ultimate worst thing that can happen. It cries out for us: "Life! Life IN CHRIST Jesus."

Forgiveness of Sins.

The very thing that has separated us from God, our sin, has been blotted out, or wiped away, in the very act of forgiveness.

Forgiveness is a powerful word as it not only cancels out our sin but, at the same time, also completely removes the cause of the offence. In our natural, finite minds we find that virtually impossible to imagine. We are so aware of mistakes, wrong doing, and evil in our world. Even if someone were caught for offences and goes to prison for the whole of a sentence, thus paying the price, we and he or she are only too aware of the enormity of what has taken place and it is easy to sense the resentment caused and the guilt and shame on the recipient's behalf.

Not so for God because His forgiveness includes a complete forgetting as though that offence had never happened. Paul describes this as "the riches of His grace" (v7). This grace is a treasure for us that no one can take from us.

Therefore, you can stand up strong, secure in the knowledge of who you are IN CHRIST. That enables you to face life and all it can throw at you, knowing you have a destiny and a purpose because of all He has done for you. Your sin, which otherwise would keep you from enjoying all of this security has been completely forgiven. There is nothing against you any more. The most powerful, amazing event in the whole universe has happened to you. You are IN CHRIST.

Can you imagine the Ephesian church celebrating at this information? Until Paul got this revelation of the full extent of what Jesus had done it was a mystery hidden in God but now it has been revealed to the Christian world. Just think of the difference it made to them. What difference does it make to you, right now?

That is your security IN CHRIST.

What will you choose?

From studying this section it becomes abundantly clear that as far as God is concerned He always chooses everyone. That is because He loves us deeply regardless of the life we live. We can see that expressed in John 3:16 in the words "God so loved the world". However, it is also clear that He gave us all free will. We are not zombies and He does not coerce us to do anything. He has reached out to us in love but He wants us to respond and choose to be IN CHRIST by giving our lives to Him, willingly.

This requires a serious decision on your part at this point if you are to enjoy the unconditional truths that follow in this book. You may already have made that choice, but if not and you are stirred to make a decision for Christ right now, I encourage you to say the following prayer in order to seal it in your heart.

Prayer.

Dear God, I come to you in the name of Jesus. I realise that I have a choice to make concerning my life. I believe that Jesus died for my sins and rose from the dead giving me the way to fellowship with you and to live eternally with You. Knowing this I choose to renounce my past and accept the price Jesus paid for me to be total and complete. I choose Jesus to be Lord of my life and to live within me. Jesus come into my heart. I receive and welcome you as Lord and saviour.

Father, I believe right now that I am indeed born again. I am a brand new creation. I stand before You worthy because of Jesus. I am now a child of God. I am truly IN CHRIST.

Amen.

Chapter 3

Our Inheritance IN CHRIST

11 In Him also we have obtained an inheritance, being predestined according to the purpose of Him who works all things according to the counsel of His will, 12 that we who first trusted in Christ should be to the praise of His glory. 13 In Him you also trusted, after you heard the word of truth, the gospel of your salvation; in whom also, having believed, you were sealed with the Holy Spirit of promise, 14 who is the guarantee of our inheritance until the redemption of the purchased possession, to the praise of His glory.

Ephesians 1:11-14

18 the eyes of your understanding being enlightened; that you may know what is the hope of His calling, what are the riches of the glory of His inheritance in the saints,

Ephesians 1:18

Paul has established, for us, the most important principle of what Christ has done for us. Then He provides us with the fulness of what that means because we are now IN CHRIST, we are totally secure! He then begins to expound an important further point to add to this knowledge and shows us that there is always more with God.

Basically, he demonstrates that because we are IN CHRIST we automatically have obtained an inheritance. That inheritance is based on the trust that comes from us believing in His salvation. Furthermore, he assures us that our receiving of the Holy Spirit is the guarantee or, if you like, the downpayment or deposit on the fulness of that inheritance. Then, in verse 18, he wants to make sure that we see the fulness of this by proclaiming that this inheritance is rich and full of glory.

I considered this carefully, knowing that, ultimately, when Paul wrote this letter he was being inspired by the Holy Spirit Himself. I find it fascinating that He (the Holy Spirit) would ensure that we all realise the role that He (the Holy Spirit) is undertaking inside us. The very fact that we have the Holy Spirit is absolute proof that our inheritance is sure!

> *16 And I will pray the Father, and He will give you another Helper, that He may abide with you forever—17 the Spirit of truth, whom the world cannot receive, because it neither sees Him nor knows Him; but you know Him, for He dwells with you and will be in you.*
>
> **John 14:16-17**

So, let us contemplate what we mean by inheritance so we can appreciate what we have obtained. Here are some basic definitions of inheritance:
- Receive property or rank by legal descent.
- Derive genetical characteristics from ancestors (receive by nature).

- Succeed as an heir.
- Receive by gift or divine appropriation.

I am sure that most of this is familiar to you. Some of you may, indeed, have received an inheritance after the death of a relative. I have always thought that what you do with that inheritance is important because you are, in some way or another, carrying on the family wealth or line into the next generation. Personally, I well remember receiving a £500 inheritance from my father when he passed away in 2007, age 76. He had always been a keen painter and photographer so I felt it very fitting that I was able to purchase a SLR camera with that money and have always enjoyed that sense of continuation from him. Of course, if inheritance also means you have inherited your father's big nose or snoring habits that may not always be such a good thing!

So, of course we need to understand, from this, that inheritance has always been vitally important to God. So much so that He wants to assure us that, IN CHRIST, we possess an inheritance for ourselves. In order to understand why this is, and see this in sharper focus, it helps if we go back to biblical times and, in particular, Old Testament passages of scripture which demonstrate how inheritance was vital to the community and how God's inheritance law was very specific for the nation of Israel. It clearly revolved around land and tribes and was designed to ensure a continuation of familial ownership.

In doing so we must appreciate that, in Biblical times, there was no understanding of a 'will' until the time of Herod the Great because Roman laws of inheritance were very different to the Jewish laws, established by God on the plains of Moab just before the Israelites entered the promised land of Canaan.

So, we must first go back to the book of Genesis to follow how God's principles of inheritance are revealed during Abraham's lifetime. In Genesis 12, God calls Abraham. The earth had been in some turmoil since Adam's day and men had gone their own way to the extent that God had cleansed the land in Noah's time. God's purpose and plan for blessing, outlined in Genesis 1:28 looked as though it was thwarted. So God began again with one man, Abraham. God called him out to a land that God Himself promised he would possess and there he would be blessed and be a blessing.

> [1] *Now the* LORD *had said to Abram: "Get out of your country, From your family And from your father's house, to a land that I will show you.* [2] *I will make you a great nation; I will bless you And make your name great; And you shall be a blessing."*

Genesis 12:1-2

God began with one man but His purpose was far bigger. Abraham, at this point, by obeying God's call, was leaving his old inheritance in Ur of the Chaldees and travelling out into the unknown. Yet God had a plan for him. God wanted a nation and for that He needed land. God even appeared to Abraham once he arrived in Canaan land and in Genesis 12:7 said "To your descendants I will give this land" In other words there was a promise of inheritance for Abraham's children even though God knew there would be a period of 400 years when the Israelites were in Egypt as slaves and that promise looked impossible.

The key to this promise can be found in Genesis 15. The whole chapter contains the essence of this promise.

1. In verse 1: God promises a reward for Abraham.

2. In verse 2: Abraham questions this because he has no heir of his own.

3. In verse 4: God promises an heir and then shows him the stars to get his attention and explains that Abraham's descendants would be, like the stars, beyond his ability to count. Abraham believed God and it was counted to him for righteousness. This is a very important point as we shall see in a moment.

4. In verse 7: God then promises Abraham that he would most definitely "inherit" this land. This is the first mention of inheritance in the whole of scripture! However, Abraham, even though he now believes for descendants, still struggles to see how God will be able to give him this land which is currently occupied by many other tribes and he is a foreigner in the land.

5. Then, here is the key. In verses 9-21, God cuts a covenant with Abraham to demonstrate that, as far as He is concerned, this promise is legally binding and unalterable forever and ratified in blood. Abraham, in that day, would immediately recognise this ceremony and it would completely and irrevocably change his thinking and therefore his whole world.

6. In verses 18 and 19: God also told Abraham the extent of this land.

7. Finally, in chapter 17, God confirmed this covenant and told Abraham to keep his part with two physical elements. The first was that every male child was to be circumcised (Gen.17:10-14). Then He said that His covenant would be established through the birth of Isaac (Gen.17:21).

Now, I could spend a great deal more space on the relevance of this covenant principle. However, it is outside the thrust of this book. I, personally, have found that E W Kenyon's book, *The Blood Covenant*, provides a wealth of knowledge on this subject. Nevertheless, we will see the conclusion to this covenant principle in due course through Jesus. Suffice it to say, for now, that although God has the whole earth, Canaan was to be His special inheritance to His people.

I find it interesting that when Moses sent out the 12 spies to check over the promised land in Numbers 13, God clearly said it was the land He was giving them. Regardless of that promise, 10 spies came back and said it was impossible. They clearly had no understanding of the covenant of promise God had given them through Abraham. Only Joshua and Caleb brought a different report because they had a different spirit. As a result the nation wandered about in the desert for 40 years.

At the end of that period the nation came to the plains of Moab right before Jericho. Crossing over there marked an entrance to the land and, in due course, the manna they were eating would cease. At this point, therefore, in Numbers 26 God begins the process of creating the Jewish Inheritance Laws that were intended to apply throughout their generations. He first took a census of the tribes. He then spoke of the distribution of land.

[53]"To these the land shall be divided as an inheritance, according to the number of names. [54] To a large tribe you shall give a larger inheritance, and to a small tribe you shall give a smaller inheritance. Each shall be given its inheritance according to those who were numbered of them. [55] But the land shall be divided by lot; they shall inherit according to the names of the tribes of their fathers.

Numbers 26:53-55

Further pronouncements showed that an inheritance would pass to the eldest son and then to brothers. In Deuteronomy 21 this was extended to include a younger son. Furthermore, if there were no sons the inheritance could go to daughters (Nu.27:1-11). However, there were strict rules that there could not be marriage across tribes and also that the land had to stay in the tribe. Why did God do that?

So that the land was never sold or passed out of the family
The Law of inheritance Wycliffe Bible Commentary

Inheritance is so important to God and we have to receive that for ourselves. The inheritance we have IN CHRIST is forever, for each one of us. He has no intention of seeing us lose it. So let us see now how this idea of inheritance was passed through Abraham to the nation of Israel, then to the land of Israel and finally to us through everything that Jesus did for us as heirs together of the promise.

Jesus as the Heir of the Inheritance

In the Gospel of Mark, chapter 12, Jesus tells a parable which is a reflection of all that has happened for the Jewish nation up to that point. He is showing how the promise of a fruitful and blessed life was being thwarted and inheritance was at the heart of it.

> *[7] But those vinedressers said among themselves, 'This is the heir. Come, let us kill him, and the inheritance will be ours.'*

Mark 12:7

Jesus is talking about Himself in this parable. He is the heir of all God has. He is able to be that because He is a son by relationship. However, Jesus obtains the inheritance and blessings of that relationship through His work on the cross

> *[1] God ... [2] has in these last days spoken to us by His Son, whom He has appointed heir of all things, through whom also He made the worlds; [3] who being the brightness of His glory and the express image of His person, and upholding all things by the word of His power, when He had by Himself purged our sins, sat down at the right hand of the Majesty on high, [4] having become so much better than the angels, as He has by inheritance obtained a more excellent name than they.*

Hebrews 1:1-4

We obtain that inheritance as heirs in the following circumstances.

> *[16] The Spirit Himself bears witness with our spirit that we are children of God, [17] and if children, then heirs—heirs of God and joint heirs with Christ, if indeed we suffer with Him, that we may also be glorified together.*

Romans 8:16-17

If we are children of God then we are also heirs and joint heirs with Christ. This is only possible because we are placed spiritually IN CHRIST when we are born again. We share that divine sonship when we are adopted into the family.

> *14 So that in Christ Jesus the blessing of Abraham might come to the Gentiles, so that we might receive the promised Spirit through faith*
>
> **Galatians 3:14 (ESV)**

This scripture affirms Ephesians 1:13-14

> *13 In Him you also trusted, after you heard the word of truth, the gospel of your salvation; in whom also, having believed, you were sealed with the Holy Spirit of promise, 14 who is the guarantee of our inheritance until the redemption of the purchased possession, to the praise of His glory.*
>
> **Ephesians 1:13-14**

The very fact that we have the Holy Spirit on the inside of us is a sure guarantee that we have an inheritance IN CHRIST. Under the old covenant, physical circumcision was a sign of the promise of inheritance. In the new covenant, we are circumcised spiritually by the Holy Spirit and this seals our inheritance.

Our Inheritance is by Grace.

When the Jewish nation entered the promised land, their inheritance was, by right, passed from one to another in families. Under the new covenant in the blood of Jesus, our inheritance is by the grace of God because of the status we have entered into as children of God and joint heirs with Christ. There is no sense that we have earned this. It comes by grace through faith as we believe the truth of what Jesus has done for us and we accept His sacrifice for us, repent and turn to Him. When we do, His grace flows through to the depth of our being and makes us free.

So what do we inherit?

What do the scriptures tell us that we receive as an inheritance a result of being IN CHRIST?

The answer is all that was symbolised by the land of Canaan and more.

1. You inherit the Kingdom of God

How do we define the Kingdom of God?

> *Suppose someone asked you that question: What is the kingdom of God? How would you respond? The easy answer would be to note that a kingdom is that territory over which a king reigns. Since we understand that God is the Creator of all things, the extent of His realm must be the whole world. Manifestly, then, the kingdom of God is wherever God reigns, and since He reigns everywhere, the kingdom of God is everywhere.*
>
> **RC SPROUL, Articles 2019**

However, clearly, in Jesus this 'territory' is much larger than just Canaan. Jesus is talking about His Messianic kingdom, which is both physical and spiritual. In Matthew 25, Jesus says that we will inherit the kingdom that has been "prepared for you from the foundation of the world". How did Jesus know that unless He was there?

So we must let this fact sink in to our spirits. The kingdom of God is our inheritance. We are in His family and He will not let the kingdom pass out of our hands.

2. You inherit the earth or the land

⁵ Blessed are the meek, For they shall inherit the earth
Matthew 5:5

²⁹ The righteous shall inherit the land, And dwell in it forever.
Psalm 37:29

The earth is a precious commodity as we have been hearing more and more in the last few years. These passages confirm that the earth is being held in trust, for you and me. At the moment you probably only own your belongings and perhaps the house and land that you live in. But the whole earth is yours. Not only that but after the great white throne judgment it will also become the Lord's home when there will be a new heaven and a new earth. Perhaps we need to start claiming some territory of it now, especially in our neighbourhood. Maybe we need to claim authority over what happens in our neighbourhood. After all it is ours. Maybe now is the time to start dreaming about that favourite house you have an eye on.

Also, we need to consider, how are we taking care of our inheritance? Are we ready to stand up and look after what is ours even if the rest of the world doesn't know it or think like that. I could say much more about the environment and what is happening to our planet but I am sure you get the idea.

3. You Inherit Salvation

Speaking of the angels, in Hebrews, the writer has this to say

14 Are they not all ministering spirits sent forth to minister for those who will inherit salvation?

Hebrews 1:14

Salvation is not yours by right. As I have said previously it comes by grace through faith in Jesus. Salvation is also a much bigger concept than just us being born again. We may understand our salvation as being deliverance from sin and death and being delivered from separation from God by Christ's death and resurrection. In scripture it has the connotation of being brought into a spacious environment, freedom from limitation, to redeem, recover property that has fallen into alien hands. It is both moral and spiritual. Salvation opens up something vast that only comes from having that new relationship with Father God.

In fact, there are huge parallels with a phrase that Paul brings in Colossians:

12 giving thanks to the Father who has qualified you to share in the inheritance of the saints in light. 13 He has delivered us from the domain of darkness and transferred us to the kingdom of His beloved son.

Colossians 1:12-13 (ESV)

That has physical links to the Israelites deliverance from slavery in Egypt and finally entering the inherited promised land.

4. You Inherit the Blessing

We previously demonstrated how the basic Genesis blessing over man was cemented in the covenant with Abraham and his descendants. We have also seen that IN CHRIST the blessing of Abraham comes to us. We must see that the favour of God and the joy and happiness that He brings, is our inheritance. It is easy to forget that in the midst of our lives with its ups and downs we are not always protected from such things but we must believe that this is not how it will end up for us. The fulness of his blessing is ours so we can rejoice in Him.

This book of Ephesians begins by reminding us that IN CHRIST we have been blessed with every spiritual blessing in the heavenly places. The inheritance of blessing we have is such a powerful thing. Most people in the world would probably equate such blessings in monetary or material terms. Christians will be familiar with the many warnings from Jesus of pursuing wealth and riches for their own sake and not being generous towards God and others. For that reason I find the following scripture particularly comforting.

22 The blessing of the LORD makes one rich, And He adds no sorrow with it.

Proverbs 10:22

True blessing for the believer comes from God and it will bring a richness beyond worldly values, whether this is actual physical riches or something deeper, regardless of our circumstances.

Whenever you are reading the word of God in future and you see a passage on blessing, stop and consider for a moment and say: "That's talking about me". Blessing is your inheritance and it is vast in its fulness for you.

5. You inherit the Glory

18 For I consider that the sufferings of this present time are not worthy to be compared with the glory which shall be be revealed in us

Romans 8:18

"Glory" is the weight of God's presence, His power, and His majesty and we are destined to share in that by virtue of our inheritance. There is so much more one could say about the glory of the Lord. Here is not the place to expand further but merely to take in that we will possess His presence constantly. It is awesome to look forward to.

6. You inherit incorruption

50 Now this I say, brethren, that flesh and blood cannot inherit the kingdom of God; nor does corruption inherit incorruption. 51 Behold, I tell you a mystery: We shall not all sleep, but we shall all be changed—52 in a moment, in the twinkling of an eye, at the last trumpet. For the trumpet will sound, and the dead will be raised incorruptible, and we shall be changed. 53 For this corruptible must put on incorruption, and this mortal must put on immortality. 54 So when this corruptible has put on incorruption, and this mortal has put on immortality, then shall be brought to pass the saying that is written: "Death is swallowed up in victory."

1 Corinthians 15:50-54

These verses are shouting and rejoicing territory. They promise us immortality. That means we do not have to fear death itself because it is not the end for us. It is one of the fundamental truths of our Christian walk. However, it is clear that, as we review our inheritance, it is not an automatic right. It is only ours because we are IN CHRIST. Yet, this is our ultimate victory.

There is a powerful description of Jesus as high priest after the order of Melchizedek in Hebrews 7. It describes His role as coming "according to the power of an endless life" (Heb. 7:16).

In other words, everything that Christ does for us is through the power of something that lasts forever and does not need renewing year on year. This is a vital point for each of us because we are totally reliant on Christ and His priesthood. In that context we ourselves rise up to be a royal priesthood.

⁹ But you are a chosen generation, a royal priesthood, a holy nation, His own special people, that you may proclaim the praises of Him who called you out of darkness into His marvellous light;

1 Peter 2:9

All of this comes by grace as a result of our inheritance. However, this should not be taken as an excuse to sit back and do nothing, rejoicing in what is to come because it is coming our way anyway. Paul has something to say about this in Corinthians, anticipating what response people may have.

⁵⁸ Therefore, my beloved brethren, be steadfast, immovable, always abounding in the work of the Lord, knowing that your labour is not in vain in the Lord.

1 Corinthians 15:58

Anything you go through now is nothing compared with your inheritance. What is more, Paul makes it clear that the Holy Spirit in you is the guarantee of our inheritance. He works in you now so you enjoy some of the promise and He encourages you to keep going until you receive the fulness of it in eternity.

Chapter 4

Our Position IN CHRIST

We are continuing to move through Paul's letter to the Ephesian church and beginning to understand what it is to live a life IN CHRIST. In doing so, Paul answers a fundamental question that all of us have. "Where do I fit in all this?" Do I have a position IN CHRIST from which I can gain comfort or am I just barely making it?

For us as believers, we do have a position IN CHRIST and a perfect fit, precisely because of the relationship we have with Him as we have given our lives to Him and made Him the Lord of our lives. Nevertheless, it is an important question. When we get born again everything may seem rosy in the garden and we are amazed at the change in us. Then, we soon begin to realise that there is a whole lot more to the Christian life than we ever imagined. We start to see how this new life fits in with our personality, our character and our life experiences to date. We need help to navigate our new life and what that means on a daily basis.

In anticipation of such circumstances, Paul writes the following in Ephesians 1:

16... making mention of you in my prayers: 17 that the God of our Lord Jesus Christ, the Father of glory, may give to you the spirit of wisdom and revelation in the knowledge of Him.

Ephesians 1:16b-17

Paul is praying for the Christians in Ephesus and what he says is fundamentally important for what he is about to say regarding our spiritual position IN CHRIST. Paul wants us to have the spirit of wisdom and revelation. In other words, he wants us to gain true knowledge. He does not want us to be kept in the dark all our lives, struggling to understand the truth and thinking wrong things. It is important we know this.

26 Likewise the Spirit also helps in our weaknesses. For we do not know what we should pray for as we ought, but the Spirit Himself makes intercession for us with groanings that cannot be uttered.

Romans 8:26

This requires wisdom and revelation. True wisdom comes from the Holy Spirit within us speaking to our spirit and enabling us to see a truth that goes beyond worldly or our natural perception. The Holy Spirit is the Spirit of wisdom and His role is powerfully described, both here and in the early chapters of Proverbs. There it demonstrates to us that "fear of the Lord" or, to put it differently, a reverent awe of Him brings wisdom and knowledge.

If someone asked me, I would describe revelation in general terms as "bringing a previously unknown fact into the light of day so others can benefit from it". However, a more accurate biblical definition can be found in *The Moody Handbook Of*

Theology as "that act of God whereby He discloses himself or communicates truth to the mind, whereby He makes manifest to His creatures that which could not be known in any other way".

Paul is well documented for revealing mystery that had been previously hidden in God so that we may have full understanding of what Jesus has done for us. In this scripture that is just what Paul is doing. He does not want us to be ignorant. He wants us to come into the full truth about our position IN CHRIST.

> *18 the eyes of your understanding being enlightened; that you may know what is the hope of His calling.*
>
> **Ephesians 1:18a**

Our outlook on life will be changed if we can really see and take in this truth. So Paul begins to explain what God did in giving us a position in Him.

What God did in Jesus

> *19 and what is the exceeding greatness of His power toward us who believe, according to the working of His mighty power 20 which He worked in Christ when He raised Him from the dead and seated Him at His right hand in the heavenly places, 21 far above all principality and power and might and dominion, and every name that is named, not only in this age but also in that which is to come. 22 And He put all things under His feet and gave Him to be head over all things to the church, 23 which is His body, the fulness of Him who fills all in all.*
>
> **Ephesians 1:19-23**

Many think that either God is irrelevant or, perhaps, acts with a big stick to constantly put us down. That is not the truth and we see here that God worked mighty power. Did He do that against us? No! He worked that power IN CHRIST for us! Jesus took all our sin and pain on the cross right to the pit of hell. This was everything that was separating us from a life with the Father. That power which was worked in Jesus also raised Him from the dead (see Hebrews 1) leaving everything that was against us where it belonged, in hell. Then, He placed Jesus at His right hand. Notice that this is next to Him, not in a position of inferiority, but with Him in power and authority. Ephesians 1:21 then says this was "far above", that means superior to, every name that is named.

Now this is shouting ground for Jesus. It means that He has the ability to deal with and nullify anything that is contrary to a full and victorious life. For example: abuse, sickness, fear and inadequacy. He is above these and is able to change their effect on your life.

The other important element in this passage is that Jesus has power over other supernatural forces, including magic and the occult. This was a great concern in Ephesus where those things were rife, and this is still pertinent for us today. The power of the living God IN CHRIST trumps all competing authorities.

This would have been a very pertinent point for the Ephesian recipients of this letter. They had witnessed miracles at the hand of Paul and a battle with Jewish exorcists (the seven sons of Sceva) in Acts 19:11-17. So much so that many of them denounced their magic practices and burned their books.

19 Also, many of those who had practised magic brought their books together and burned them in the sight of all. And they counted up the value of them, and it totalled fifty thousand pieces of silver. [20] *So the word of the Lord grew mightily and prevailed.*

Acts 19:19-20

Now we have to get hold of the real truth in verse 22 where it tells us that God placed everything "under His feet". You may look at this by first glance and think, "I knew it I am intended to grovel under Jesus." No, read on and we begin to get a glimpse of what is to come. He gave Jesus to be Head over all things and then Jesus gave that headship to the church. That is us, His called out ones, and then He calls us His body. He so identifies with us that in His understanding we are a part of His very being, an intricate part of Him. He describes us as His fulness. In other words He is incomplete without us. We are Jesus in every respect, except for the fact that He is the head and everything we are flows from that.

Paul's identification with the unity of head and body IN CHRIST could well stem from his own conversion experience on his journey to Damascus. Paul was persecuting the Church but Jesus challenged him asking, "why do you persecute me?" (Ac.9:4; 22:7; 26:14) demonstrating the unity that Christ has with his body (the church) and illustrating that Jesus took it personally.

What God did in you

Paul then begins chapter 2 of Ephesians with an honest, and somewhat brutal, assessment of our true position without God. He describes this position as "dead." Without Him we are dead, even if we are physically alive, because this is speaking about our spiritual position. Dead here really means separated from the vital connection, life and relationship with the Father.

That makes us hopeless and totally under the power of the devil and the lusts, or everything we know as contrary to the heart of God. That is important as in those days the Ancient Greeks had a saying "God helps those who help themselves" and I guess this has perpetuated to our modern day. However, Paul is saying this is not the case. We are hopeless, there is nothing we can do to help ourselves to be in a position where God will accept us. Is that not funny because deep down we all can identify with that position of what we are really like underneath? We don't always admit it, we cover it up. So what follows is completely life changing and supremely significant for everyone of us.

> *4 But God, who is rich in mercy, because of His great love with which He loved us, 5 even when we were dead in trespasses, made us alive together with Christ (by grace you have been saved),*
>
> **Ephesians 2:4-5**

I absolutely love this first statement "But God". Those two words fundamentally negate and change what has gone before. In essence it is saying "this is how we were positioned but because of what God has done this is how we are now positioned." I actually carry around a small wrist band that says "But God". It constantly reminds me that whatever I face, God can make it something else. What we see here is that God makes us "alive". This is another powerful imagery of our spiritual state. Alive here shows us that we are now no longer separated. In the very instant that we make Jesus the Lord of our lives, then everything that God did IN CHRIST, He also does in us. In that moment our human spirit is totally recreated by the force of His grace working in us (see: Chapter 2, Accepted). We are placed IN CHRIST.

It is a wonderful description of what God is really like when it says "who is rich in mercy". The reality is that there is no way we can change our position but God did it anyway because He loved us so much. We have to take that on board.

Me, with all my faults, with all my failures, but God still acted because He loved me. There was no way that I could have sorted myself out because the depth of sin and separation made it impossible.

There is a little phrase that follows "together with Christ" So, when He made Christ alive He did the same for you and I.

> *⁶ and raised us up together, and made us sit together in the heavenly places in Christ Jesus, ⁷ that in the ages to come He might show the exceeding riches of His grace in His kindness toward us in Christ Jesus. ⁸ For by grace you have been saved through faith, and that not of yourselves; it is the gift of God,*
>
> **Ephesians 2:6-8**

This is the most amazing statement in this whole book and it takes some believing, but we must. It tells us that IN CHRIST we also are placed with Him in heavenly places (i.e. at the right hand of the Father). That is because of what He has done. That is our true position in this life. Now, our mind is blown away by this because we are so aware of our mortality. God is no longer seeing us from our physical position but rather from our true spiritual position IN CHRIST. Verse 7 lets us know that this is all because He wants to show His kindness towards us from now into eternity. Verse 8 reminds us that this is not because of anything that we have done but it is an absolute gift of God. *The Message* Bible puts it this way for verses **8-10**

> *8-10 It's God's gift from start to finish! We don't play the major role. If we did, we'd probably go around bragging that we'd done the whole thing! No, we neither make nor save ourselves. God does both the making and saving. He creates each of us by Christ Jesus to join Him in the work He does, the good work he has gotten ready for us to do, work we had better be doing.*
>
> **Ephesians 2:8-10** (MSG)

This is a very important connection for us in considering what our position really is IN CHRIST. It tells us that, according to God, our position is:
- Not under His feet.
- Not under the devil's feet.
- It is not a nobody just getting by.
- It is not a poor old sinner.
- It is not an outcast of society.

The reality is that, in spiritual terms, you are sat together with Him. You did not work to earn that but this is your position IN CHRIST now, not in the sweet old by and by when you get to heaven as emphasised in verse **13**:

> *13 But now in Christ Jesus you who once were far off have been brought near by the blood of Christ. 14 For He Himself is our peace, who has made both one, and has broken down the middle wall of separation, 15 having abolished in His flesh the enmity, that is, the law of commandments contained in ordinances, so as to create in Himself one new*

man from the two, thus making peace, [16] and that He might reconcile them both to God in one body through the cross, thereby putting to death the enmity. [17] And He came and preached peace to you who were afar off and to those who were near. [18] For through Him we both have access by one Spirit to the Father. [19] Now, therefore, you are no longer strangers and foreigners, but fellow citizens with the saints and members of the household of God, [20] having been built on the foundation of the apostles and prophets, Jesus Christ Himself being the chief cornerstone, [21] in whom the whole building, being fitted together, grows into a holy temple in the Lord, [22] in whom you also are being built together for a dwelling place of God in the Spirit.

Ephesians 2:13-22

This is a long passage but it serves to emphasise our new nature IN CHRIST:

- We are drawn near by the blood of Jesus (v13).
- We have peace in Him (v15).
- We are reconciled to God (v16).
- We have access to the Father (v18).
- We are fellow citizens of God's household (v19).
- We are becoming the dwelling place of God (vv21-22).

It is like there was an impenetrable wall which separated us from God but Christ has smashed that down so we have access to the Father. I remember some years ago reading a note on this passage, referring to a graveyard in Northern Ireland during the troubles over there. In this graveyard there was a wall, which separated the Catholic graves from the Protestant graves. You could not see it because it was grassed over to look nice, but in reality it was there. Such was the enmity and separation in those days. For us, we really need to grasp the fact that Jesus has broken that wall down. Although that wall is torn-down/broken/abolished we might not realise that we are able to step through. This is important because when we do step through the broken-down wall we have access to the whole package that Christ has won for us.

How do I see my position?

This is very important because I can give you all the facts and proclaim it as truth. It should cause you to shout and rejoice, but unless the knowledge makes a difference to you on a daily basis it will have little effect. So, how do you see yourself in the light of what you have read?

Ultimately we have to live in the fulness of that revelation. All this knowledge should cause us to live and feel differently to how we did before. We need to see ourselves as Christ sees us. We have to rise up as over-comers. It is one thing to be inspired by this chapter, it is another to start to live on the basis that it is so.

To summarise, you don't come to church to get a blessing.

You don't come to feel secure, you don't come to get something from God, you don't come to find out how you fit. All these things are already yours. You come to rejoice and bring others so they might receive what you already have. What is more you will have great success in doing that when others see what Christ has done in you. It is making a difference for you and they can see it. You have to live daily according to this knowledge knowing that it is true. When you do that people will see and begin to desire what you have.

Each of us must catch hold of what we are carrying on the inside of us and reach for our potential. We have an awesome position IN CHRIST which has made a difference to us. Live it, see it, meditate on it, rest in it and enjoy it daily. Then go and show someone who does not have it the difference it would make to them. God remade us for that purpose and we must walk in the fulness of what is ours.

You may feel inadequate to the task but you are adequate, especially when you get hold of this and run with it.

Chapter 5

The Mystery, Power and Strength IN CHRIST

We now come to the last chapter in the first section (Your Life IN CHRIST) of this book. Chapter 3 of Ephesians is probably best reviewed in our study in two sections. The first concerns "The Mystery" of which Paul has gained a revelation, and the second concerns a deeper understanding of the fulness of living IN CHRIST.

The Mystery of being IN CHRIST

First of all, we need to go back and consider again, to whom Paul was addressing this letter? Was it the Ephesian church alone or, through them, to other churches which had sprung up throughout Asia Minor and then to us in the present day?

We must understand that most of these cities had a strong Jewish presence and, as I mentioned earlier, the Jewish synagogue was where Paul often started to preach whenever he went to a new region. We must assume, that by the time of this letter the make up of the Christian churches would contain a mixture of converted Jews to Christ and of "Gentiles" who had come to Christ with little reference to the Jewish tradition. However, Paul's own heritage may give us a clearer understanding of why Paul felt it necessary to explain the mystery he had a revelation of, and why it was so relevant for them to receive.

In that regard Paul is a very different person from many in his day. He, himself was a Jew and also a Roman citizen by right. As a Jew he had been schooled as a pharisee under Gamaliel (Ac.22:3) who was a noted teacher of the Jewish Law. Sat at Gamaliel's feet, Paul describes his upbringing, probably from the age of 12, as

> *[22]... taught according to the strictness of our fathers' law, and was zealous toward God as you all are today.*
>
> **Acts 22:3b**

Research would even suggest that extreme followers of the pharisaical tradition considered Gentile proselytes to the Jewish faith to be subordinate and in some quarters hated and not recognised at all. This is surprising because even King David had proselytes in his heritage. Rahab the prostitute was his great-great-grandmother and Ruth the Moabitess was his great-grandmother. Paul would have been aware of this but the tradition in his heritage probably got in the way. Paul took a dim view of Jews who had converted to "the Way" and championed the Jewish cause by persecuting them.

> *[4] "I persecuted this Way to the death, binding and delivering into prisons both men and women,*
>
> **Acts 22:4**

My point in drawing attention to Paul's upbringing and background is to demonstrate the absolute shock and transformation that he must have gone through upon his encounter with Jesus on the Damascus road as described by him, personally in Acts 22:5-10. This departure was then emphasised further when God called him to go to the Gentiles, especially when you see the reaction of the Jews who were trying to intimidate him before the Roman authorities

> *21 "Then he said to me, 'Depart, for I will send you far from here to the Gentiles.'" 22 And they listened to him until this word, and then they raised their voices and said, "Away with such a fellow from the earth, for he is not fit to live!"*
>
> **Acts 22:21-22**

Overall, it gives us a more powerful insight into Paul's transformation brought about through his conversion on the Damascus road that led to this revelation, given by Christ, of the mystery that is outlined in the third chapter of Ephesians.

Mystery

What is a mystery in the context that Paul speaks about? Our modern understanding is something that is secret, or only reserved for the specially initiated. However, in scripture it refers to something different. Some dictionaries refer to the idea of "uncover" or "unveil". Others refer to "a sacred secret hidden in ages past, now revealed". This latter thought gives us some insight.

I found, perhaps, the most helpful was from W E Vine.

> *In the NT it denotes, not the mysterious (as with the English word), but that which, being outside the range of unassisted natural apprehension, can be made known only by divine revelation, and is made known in a manner and at*

a time appointed by God, and to those only who are illuminated by His Spirit. In the ordinary sense a 'mystery" implies knowledge withheld; its scriptural significance is truth revealed.

W.E.Vine, An Expository Dictionary of Biblical Words

Paul received this revelation from Jesus directly and it obviously blew him away. It was not enough that he could be born again, as a Jew. There was a deeper revelation that he was given.

³ How by revelation He made known to me the mystery (as I have briefly written already, ⁴ by which, when you read, you may understand my knowledge in the mystery of Christ), ⁵ which in other ages was not made known to the sons of men, as it has now been revealed by the Spirit to his holy apostles and prophets:

Ephesians 3:3-5

I find it fascinating to consider this. Paul was so clearly affected by this knowledge, he just knew he could not keep it to himself and everyone needed to know. This knowledge he then describes.

⁶ That the gentiles should be fellow heirs, of the same body, and partakers of His promise in Christ through the gospel,

Ephesians 3:6

This very fact is an important foundational principle that was revealed firstly to Paul (Ac.9:15) and also to Peter (Ac.10:28, 47) and was most likely ratified at the Council of Jerusalem, described in Acts 15.

What is the relevance of this revelation for us? Well, in Paul's day, he was demonstrating to a mixed group of Christians that no matter what their race or culture that, IN CHRIST, they are all part of the same body. Every person has a right to Christ and to enjoy the benefits of the Christian faith. There is no discrimination. In our day this may not be so important but in those early days it was revolutionary. In fact, even in our day it is vital for us to get hold of and let it sink in to our very being. There is nothing that can prevent us from coming to Christ apart from our own personal choice as a human being. That very fact is shouting territory.

Furthermore, Paul rubs it in by exclaiming that this is the wisdom of Christ to the church and every demon in hell, at whatever level, has to deal with that fact because it is the purpose of God for us. We can so rejoice in this because we have access to the Father because of our faith in Him. This is real power at our disposal.

Living IN CHRIST

The last part of this chapter now draws together all the various elements considered in the first section (Your Life IN CHRIST) of this book. It contains a beautiful passage reflecting Paul's prayer for the Ephesian church and provides us with a fuller understanding of what takes place for us as we enjoy life IN CHRIST.

> *14 For this reason I bow my knees to the Father of our Lord Jesus Christ, 15 from whom the whole family in heaven and earth is named 16 that He would grant you, according to the riches of His glory, to be strengthened with might through His Spirit in the inner man, 17 that Christ may dwell in your*

hearts through faith; that you, being rooted and grounded in love, [18] may be able to comprehend with all the saints what is the width and length and depth and height—[19] to know the love of Christ which passes knowledge; that you may be filled with all the fullness of God.

Ephesians 3:14-19

We come, finally, to these last key verses in this first part of our discussion on how we obtain and enjoy our life IN CHRIST. In doing so, Paul first gives the greatest honour to our Father God and then demonstrates we are named as His (i.e., the Father's) "family", both in heaven and earth. It is not surprising that he uses "family" to describe us. After all Paul has just explained the mystery that we are all one IN CHRIST when we receive Him as Lord and Saviour regardless of our race or culture. The use of naming in biblical usage carries with it a sense of this being our true identity. He therefore sees us all as one family, together, IN CHRIST, because this is our identity and this is something we must take in for ourselves. As Christians there is no hierarchy or preference. We all are in that close personal relationship with Him and should respect each other for that.

Armed with that information deep within us, he then asks that the Father, who has immense riches in glory, would enable us to "be strengthened with might through His Spirit in the inner man". This word "strengthened" in the original Greek is the word *dunamis*, usually translated as "power". In this context we could, therefore, translate this as "by the power of the Holy Spirit". Only the Holy Spirit is able to bring might (more of that word in a moment) into our inner man or deep into our spirit, because He applies the personal presence and power of God.

That power is to strengthen us with might. In Greek it is the word *krataiothenai* which means "to become mighty". When researching this word and its context I observed that W E Vine cross-references this Greek word to the Hebrew word *hazaq*.

Hazaq has various meanings including "to be strong, strengthen, harden, take hold of". It also has the sense of something that is impenetrable. I find that very compelling in the context of Ephesians. Once we are IN CHRIST, the power of the Spirit in our lives gives us an impenetrable strength against all that the enemy can throw at us. We really have to receive that and yield to the Holy Spirit working in our lives. We are no longer ordinary people. As God's family we carry something far more precious on the inside of us that will enable us to stand strong, as we will see further when we discuss Ephesians Chapter 6.

Furthermore, as if to press this thought home, Paul then requests of the Father that Christ may dwell in our hearts through faith. This desire is so important for us. We have to believe this. Christ is in our hearts and that is not a temporary thing. The word says "dwell". It has a sense of abiding or being at home in us or making a home in us. Is Christ at home in you? Home is a very important place for all of us. If you think about it thoughtfully, it is somewhere you rest and feel comfortable or, at any rate, it should be. We decorate our houses so we feel more at home. After a hard day at work, or whatever, we come home to enjoy the atmosphere and the presence of our loved ones. It is no different for Jesus. That is exactly what His desire is for us in our innermost being. This is more than just knowing you have salvation. It is a permanent sense of His presence within. Furthermore, the request continues with another statement that we are then "rooted and grounded in love". If you like, this is the heart of the home Jesus creates when He abides in us. If you watch home or property programmes on TV they talk of the kitchen being the heart of the home. Well, for us as believers it is the love of Jesus Himself. What's more, the fact that we are rooted and grounded in His love gives it a sense of permanence. Something which is unshakable. As the psalmist says...

> *³ He shall be like a tree Planted by the rivers of water, That brings forth its fruit in its season, Whose leaf also shall not wither; And whatever he does shall prosper.*
>
> **Psalm 1:3**

That is a powerful expression of what it truly means for Christ to be dwelling in us. When this happens we truly comprehend the vastness of His love. Ephesians 3:18 describes this as "the width and length and depth and height–" Although the dash at the end is not in the original Greek, to me it is totally profound as it feels like Paul is aware that the words he has just written are so inadequate to really describe the fulness of God's love. So he attempts to increase our imagination by including an extra special dimension here beyond the non-spacial fourth dimension of time. Indeed, in recent days scientists have talked about finding a 5th dimension. It seems to me that Paul covers that and any other dimension that we mortals might feel we have found because the love of God is so much bigger we can never fathom it's depths.

It is then fascinating that verse 19 talks about the love of God passing all knowledge. In other words, it is beyond every knowledge that exists in our finite universe. That brings me back to considering the difference between knowledge as a human soulish thing and an understanding of walking in the wisdom of God as a spiritual truth, which brings a deeper knowledge to us than mere human understanding. The first nine chapters of Proverbs are full of how to gain wisdom and the difference it makes. However, perhaps the essence of it can be found here.

> *⁷ Wisdom is the principal thing; Therefore get wisdom. And in all your getting, get understanding. ⁸ Exalt her, and she will promote you; She will bring you honour, when you embrace her. ⁹ She will place on your head an ornament of grace; A crown of glory she will deliver to you."*

Proverbs 4:7-9

With all this knowledge and the deep understanding that the Holy Spirit brings we are then enabled to be filled with all the fulness of God. That fulness is only obtainable IN CHRIST.

Paul then prays in summary at the end of this chapter in verses 20 and 21. In doing so he once again elevates God as he declares that He (God) can do exceedingly more than we ask or think. This is a good challenge for us. What are we able to ask or think of God? Maybe some of us ask big, while others of us are reluctant to do so. Whatever extreme we fall into, God is able to do exceedingly more than that because of His power which is at work in us. We really have to grasp hold of this truth and begin to ask more of Him in our lives because He is able to fulfil that and more. When we do that there will be a raised expectation of God moving in our lives and it will accrue to His glory in the church for all generations forever.

In this first section we have concentrated on everything it means to be alive IN CHRIST. It is all about what Christ has done in us and the difference it makes to us.

In our next section we will be looking at what we do in fulfilment of that revelation. How do we now live our lives to reflect everything he has done in us and who we are IN CHRIST?

Before we do that, I have added an appendix to this section which I recommend you go through regularly, even declaring the truths out loud. These Bible verses speak loudly of who we are and reflect our true identity as people IN CHRIST. Hopefully they will seal within you everything that Jesus has done for you. I have held them dear now for many years and often go back to them, especially when the devil would attack and try to make us feel less than who we truly are. I use them regularly because they give us a solid sense of our sonship with Christ and I commend them to you.

Appendix to Part 1

Who we are In Christ

I've had these statements about who we are IN CHRIST for so long that I can hardly remember from where I first got them. It was probably as a result of my long association with Faith Christian Fellowship, Tulsa, as part of their World Outreach Bible Institute, a number of years ago. I have used them regularly since then. They are currently incorporated as part of Life Church, Bath, UK's foundational course for newcomers called *Kickstart* (*Power for Living*) as part of the session on Sonship, Who I am in Christ.

I AM	Overtaken with blessings	Dt.28:2; Eph.1:3
I AM	God's child for I am born of the incorruptible seed of the Word of God which lives and abides forever	1.Pe.1:23
I AM	Forgiven of all my sins and washed in the blood	Eph.1:7; Heb.9:14; Col.1:14; 1.Jn.1:9, 2:12
I AM	A new creature	2.Cor.5:17
I AM	The temple of the Holy Spirit	1.Cor.6:19
I AM	Delivered from the power of darkness and translated into God's kingdom	1.Cor.1:13
I AM	Redeemed from the curse of the Law	1.Pe.1:18-19; Gal.3:13
I AM	Blessed	Dt.28:1-4; Gal.3:9
I AM	A saint	Ro.1:7; 1.Cor.1:2; Phil.1:1
I AM	The head and not the tail	Dt.28:13
I AM	Above only and not beneath	Dt.28:13
I AM	Holy and without blame before Him in love	1.Pe.1:16; Eph.1:4
I AM	Elect	Col.3:12; Ro.8:33
I AM	Established to the end	1.Cor.1:8

I AM	Brought near by the blood of Christ	Eph.2:13
I AM	Victorious	Rev.21:7
I AM	Set free	Jn.8:31-33
I AM	Strong in the Lord	Eph.6:10
I AM	Dead to sin	Ro.6:2, 11; 1.Pe.2:24
I AM	More than a conqueror	Ro.8:37
I AM	Joint heirs with Christ	Ro.8:17
I AM	Sealed with the Holy Spirit of promise	Eph.1:13
I AM	In Christ by His doing	1.Cor.1:30
I AM	Accepted in the Beloved	Eph.1:6
I AM	Complete in Him	Col.2:10
I AM	Crucified with Christ	Gal.2:20
I AM	Alive with Christ	Eph.2:5
I AM	Free from condemnation	Ro.8:1
I AM	Reconciled to God	2.Cor.5:18
I AM	Qualified to share in His inheritance	Col.1:12
I AM	Firmly rooted, built up, established in my faith and overflowing with gratitude	Col.2:7
I AM	Circumcised with the circumcision made without hands	Col.2:11
I AM	A fellow citizen with the saints and of the household of God	Eph.2:19

I AM	Built upon the foundation of the apostles and prophets, Jesus Christ himself being the chief cornerstone.	Eph.2:20
I AM	In the world as He is in Heaven	1.Jn.4:1
I AM	Born of God and the evil one does not touch me	1.Jn.5:18
I AM	His faithful follower	Rev.17:14; Eph.5:1
I AM	His disciple because I have love for others	Jn.13:34-35
I AM	The light of the world	Mt.5:14
I AM	The salt of the earth	Mt.5:13
I AM	The righteousness of God	2.Cor.5:21; 1.Pe.2:24
I AM	A partaker of His divine nature	2.Pe.1:14
I AM	Called of God	2.Tim.1:9
I AM	The first fruits among His creation	Jas.1:18
I AM	Chosen	1.Thes.1:4; Eph.1:4; 1.Pe.2:9
I AM	An ambassador for Christ	2.Cor.5:20
I AM	God's workmanship created in Jesus Christ for good works	Eph.2:10
I AM	The apple of my Father's eye	Dt.32:10; Ps.17:8
I AM	Healed by the stripes of Jesus	1.Pe.2:24; Is.53:6

I AM	Being changed into His image	2.Cor.3:18; Phil.1:6
I AM	Raised up with Christ and seated in Heavenly places	Col.2:12; Eph.2:6
I AM	Beloved of God	Col.3:12; Ro.1:7; 1.Thes.1:4
I AM	One in Christ. Hallelujah!	Jn.17:21-23
I HAVE	The mind of Christ	Phil.2:5
I HAVE	Obtained an inheritance	Eph.1:11
I HAVE	Access to the Father by one Spirit.	Eph.2:18; Heb.4:16
I HAVE	Overcome the world	1.Jn.5:4
I HAVE	Everlasting life and will not be condemned	Jn.5:24, 6:47
I HAVE	The peace of God which passes understanding	Phil.4:7
I HAVE	Received power, the power of the Holy Spirit; power to lay hands on the sick and see them recover; power to cast out demons; power over all the power of the enemy and nothing shall by any means hurt me	Mk.16:17-18; Lk.10:17, 19
I LIVE	By and in the law of the Spirit of life in Christ Jesus	Ro.8:2
I WALK	In Christ Jesus	Col.2:6
I CAN	Do all things in Christ Jesus	Phil.4:13

I POSSESS	The greater one in me because He who is in me is greater than he who is in the world	1.Jn.4:4
I PRESS	Toward the mark for the prize of the high calling of God	Phil.3:14
I	Always triumph in Christ	2.Cor.2:14
I	Show forth His praise	1.Pe.2:9
MY LIFE	Is hidden with Christ in God	Col.3:3

Part 2

Your Life Through Christ

Chapter 6

His Call, our Response

Many of us will receive a wedding invitation in our lifetime or even some other invite. Very often this comes with an RSVP request at the end of it. Inevitably, the person sending out the invitation would like to know whether or not you will be attending so they can make the necessary arrangements to include you in the celebrations. So, when we receive such an invitation we have to decide, are we going to be there and participate or not?

There is a similar invitation, or even command, that requires a decision from us in relation to everything we have learned so far in the first verse of Ephesians 4.

> *1 I, therefore, the prisoner of the Lord, beseech you to walk worthy of the calling with which you were called,*
>
> **Ephesians 4:1**

Paul is a prisoner in Rome when he writes this verse. However, he does not ask them for some relief from his bonds or that they will use their influence to get him freed. As far as Paul is concerned there is something far more important and urgent that he needs us to know. He has told us about

93

everything we have received and enjoy as a result of being IN CHRIST. We should be in no doubt as to where we stand as a result of saying "yes" to Christ.

Yet Paul urges us to do something with this knowledge and understanding. He wants us to walk worthy of this calling. In other words he is saying that this invitation, this calling, needs a response from us, if we are to fully enjoy the benefits that are on offer and that come with this amazing package. The New Living Testament states that we should "lead a life worthy of the calling." Our lives have to be impacted by receiving the truth that we have received in these first three chapters of Ephesians. We cannot remain unchanged.

Paul knows that calling and position IN CHRIST demands us to take responsibility to live according to the truth of the gospel to which we are called. We are called a Christian so we must live like one to the very depths of our being. I always think that whenever we see a passage of scripture like this we should rejoice because the very fact that the Holy Spirit caused it to be written shows us that it is possible to do.

At the start of this new section then, we have to ask ourselves "will we respond positively to what we are about to read?" If we don't respond, it is clear we will miss out on the joy of Christ in all His fulness working on the inside of us and fine tuning our spiritual lives. It is a challenge we cannot ignore.

If you do not respond to the wedding invitation you will miss out on the celebration, the food and the joy of being there on the day. Of course you can receive copies of the photos taken on the day and hear stories of what it was like, but you will never experience the event first hand, for real, because you weren't there.

In essence, God is saying to each one of us that with this information we have to step up to the mark, be there and count ourselves in. Not to a wedding but, more importantly, to leading the Christian life and walking in the fulness of it. Walking in it goes beyond a mere acceptance of what Jesus has done. The Lord requires us to live it out on a daily basis.

It is not surprising, therefore, that Paul begins to outline some things that we should specifically do as the result of understanding who we are in Him. Importantly, we should note that who we are IN CHRIST always comes before what we do and that is why Paul encourages us to "get this truth under our belt first" to use a colloquial phrase in today's language. It is something we must all receive. Many Christians get their fulfilment in life from everything they do for Him. There is often a drivenness that carries with it a sense that only in the doing will they be accepted. I know this from personal experience and my wife will frequently remind me that "being" is far more important than "doing".

So, we must understand that who we are does not come as a result of what we do. What we do follows out of and is a response to knowing who we are IN CHRIST. That is a bit of a mouthful but it needs to be a constant part of our Christian life.

If we consider Paul's next verses in isolation from what has gone before it makes no sense so, as we investigate further, we must keep on reminding ourselves of the truths established in what has gone before.

On that basis let's take a look at this first section in Ephesians 4 and consider, what changes do we make in our conduct that is a result of walking in these truths?

Heart Attitude

² Be humble and gentle. Be patient with each other, making allowance for each other's faults because of your love. ³ Always keep yourselves united in the Holy Spirit, and bind yourselves together with peace.

Ephesians 4:2-3 (NLT)

We have a tendency to take the condition and attitude of our heart for granted. Yet Proverbs 4:23 reminds us to "guard our heart with all diligence, for out of it flow the issues of life". Another word for "issues" is "boundaries". We can limit or expand our life by how we take care of our heart. We may feel that our heart is just our spirit man that is now alive to God since we came to Christ. However, if you consider it more deeply, particularly in reference to how the heart was seen in the Old Testament, the heart can be described as the centre of man's inward life and the sphere of divine influence. That is why our heart is so important. It reflects the core of our being. It is the real us and therefore impacts on every aspect of our daily lives.

Therefore, the Holy Spirit is commanding us to have a different attitude than the world and we are now able to do so because of who we now are. First, we are encouraged to be humble and gentle. We need to get a better understanding of humility or lowliness as other translations say it. Being humble does not mean any kind of subserviency. We have to move away from the old Dickensian idea of "being ever so humble" while rubbing hands and kowtowing to superiors or bosses. In truth it is a decision to follow after Christ no matter what and to willingly submit to Him and His ways. You choose to follow

Him, not the world. Jesus, humbled Himself to the Father's will but, from reading the Gospels, you would never consider that this made Jesus weak in any way. He was amazingly strong in character as a result of that decision. In fact, humbling in the horse world is a term used for how a wild horse is broken so that it can be ridden by humans. It is not weakened but has its power and strength under control. The same is true of us as we emulate Christ.

With that change we are able to pardon injuries and rule our own spirit. Our love for each other is then able to make allowance for other people's faults. Yes, we have to work on it but as we mature in this we will work together in love to help each other. The Holy Spirit enables us to keep in unity and peace, which seals that attitude.

The reason for this heart change can be seen in verses 4-6. ultimately, it is a "one" thing. There is one body, one Spirit, there is one hope, one Lord, one faith, one baptism, one God and Father of us all.

I started this chapter by writing about weddings and marriage. Marriage is all about becoming one. According to the scriptures, two people come together and become one new person. The Bible describes the process as a mystery. In the same way, because we are all one IN CHRIST, we have entered into something new and can, therefore, see and act with each other in a new way. None of us have an advantage or a position over any one else IN CHRIST. Nor is anyone else better as we are all part of the same. If one rejoices, all of us should. If one is sad, all of us are together (1.Cor.12:26). We all worship the same one Lord and have the same one Spirit on the inside of us. There is one faith which we all share and that is why in Ephesians 4:13 we read that we will all come together in the unity of the faith. Different groups do things in different ways. We call that doctrine. We don't come together in our doctrine because no one group knows it all. However, we do have that one basic faith.

Equipped for Ministry

In Ephesians 2:10, Paul has previously alluded to this next step in our Christian walk. First, he declares we are worked or made anew IN CHRIST. Then he says this will enable us to do good works. One follows from the other. We, therefore, must take a look at how we are equipped by God to do just that.

Before Paul begins to expound this equipping he reminds us of the most important fact of all – that His grace is operating on the inside of us all. It is the greatest gift. It is unfathomable and the releasing of it recreated your human spirit. Again, we see this was a measure of Christ's gift (Eph.4:7). Whenever we read "measure" in the scriptures it is easy to comprehend it as something small and with an absolute limitation. Nothing could be further from the truth. If you delve further into this you immediately see that God's measure is always huge. He gave Jesus, nothing could be bigger than that. He fed 5,000 (or more accurately, including women and children, at least 50,000) people from five loaves and two fishes. Why should we consider that the measure of His grace and faith is anything less. We all have the grace of God in abundant measure.

We then see that when Christ returned to heaven He poured out gifts to men (Eph.4:8). These gifts differ, none are more important than any others. As we are one, the gifts are for our mutual benefit and they enable us to do the work of Christ. I have heard, many times, wise preachers say that the most important gift is the one which is needed right now. In this chapter, however, Paul chooses to highlight five of them and we will see why in a moment.

> *[11] And He Himself gave some to be apostles, some prophets, some evangelists, and some pastors and teachers, [12] for the equipping of the saints for the work of ministry, for the edifying of the body of Christ,*
>
> **Ephesians 4:11-12**

There have been whole books written about these particular gifts so I don't intend to rehearse them further here. Suffice it to note that these gifts are given to fulfil calling and they come with anointing or ability as a result of the grace of God and not because the recipients carry some special gene that makes them superior to every other Christian on the planet. To begin with they are gifts of service even though they carry a sense of leadership. Some think they are high point gifts because they are so visible. No, they are specific gifts for a particular task in the body. They do not reflect position because there is only one position, IN CHRIST.

As with all the gifts, there comes responsibility – that is to always use it wisely under the direction of the Holy Spirit. Here, we see in verse 12, these particular gifts are for the equipping of the saints for the work of ministry, so everyone can fulfil their own gifting. Note, they are not to do the work of ministry, even though it is a ministry in itself. The saints are to do the ministry and these gifts will enable us to do that. I have been a pastor myself and others recognise my teaching gift to the body. I am very aware of the responsibility that comes with that: to hear God, yield to the Holy Spirit, and always aim to be true to the word of God because believers will have a tendency to raise the gift up, when in reality it is just an office which I am walking in, given to me by Christ Himself. This does not make me higher or lower than others in the body. I just have to recognise the purpose for which I am called and aim to always carry that out faithfully. In a way it could be said that I am working myself out of a job so you can work yourselves into yours.

That gifting in itself will edify or build up the body of Christ. Here, then, is an important challenge for each of us. Consider, where does your gifting lie, as you surely have one? In reality we are unique individuals and Christ has given each one a gift that is unique to them which no one else carries. We are here for a purpose and the gifting you carry is absolutely vital to each of us and we cannot manage without it. So, ask yourself, "what am I going to do to fulfil it?" Find out what it is and go for it with everything you have. In doing so you will not only fulfil your call but benefit the body as a whole and cause us all to grow.

There must be an empowering to do that from this, so called, five-fold gifting. Indeed we see the ultimate purpose in our equipping with one of my very favourite verses in scripture.

> *13 till we all come to the unity of the faith and of the knowledge of the Son of God, to a perfect man, to the measure of the stature of the fulness of Christ;*
>
> **Ephesians 4:13**

This is the purpose of all the gifts and in particular those Paul has highlighted. God has an ultimate desire that we all attain to:

a) The unity of the faith.
b) The knowledge of Jesus, the Son of God.
c) Perfect men and women.

d)   The measure of the stature of the fulness of Christ.

Here is that word "measure" again and in this case it is also huge. It is the measure of the stature of the fulness of Christ. I well remember meditating on this scripture and feeling that this is an impossible goal and certainly not attainable this side of heaven. The Lord then revealed to me that He would not have placed this word in scripture and, by the Holy Spirit, caused it to be there, if it was not possible to reach. This is truly what we are all aiming for. This is what brings stability in our Christian walk. It means we do not wander about chasing this or that latest trend, which is a tendency for the world to do, or following fashion, or the latest dance theme, as a reflection of our pop and celebrity culture. Although some of these things can be good in themselves we should not allow ourselves to think they are everything to us or the reason for our existence when that accolade only belongs to God.

15 But speaking the truth in love, may grow up in all things into Him who is the head—Christ—

Ephesians 4:15

This verse encourages us to speak the truth of what we know, in love. Doing so causes us to "grow up in all things". You hear parents saying that phrase "grow up" all the time to their children. Here the Father is telling us to "grow up" IN CHRIST.

This section is then summed up with the following verse.

16 Under his direction, the whole body is fitted together perfectly. As each part does its own special work, it helps the other parts grow, so that the whole body is healthy and growing and full of love.

Ephesians 4:16 (NLT)

This verse refers to all of our gifting taken together. We are knit together as a body by that which each of us brings to the body. We are not complete IN CHRIST on our own, we need each other. As we recognise this, we can then come to appreciate each other more. I am not complete outside of what you supply to it and vice versa. If we are to grow, we all need to do our part. In fact it is essential that we do.

At this point it may be helpful to refer back to chapter 2 and Our Security IN CHRIST to realise that we have been blessed and chosen by God. There are vital truths in that section, which reveal all God has done for us and therefore enables us to relax secure in that knowledge. However, as I said at the end of that chapter, this is a truth but ultimately we have a free will and have to <u>choose</u> to believe that and follow it for ourselves.

In the same way we have to <u>choose</u> to live our life through Christ rather than just bask in the benefits of all that He has done and then go our own way. That is why in Ephesians 4:1 Paul "beseeched" us to do this. That word carries a sense of urging, imploring, even pleading that we do something. Paul has highlighted the deeper results of walking this way but we have to make that decision. Why not join me now in making that commitment?

Prayer

Father God, I have seen and rejoiced in everything you have provided for me IN CHRIST. However, I realise there is a further step I need to make and that is to choose to live my life through Christ. I freely commit to do that now by making a quality decision to live my life that way. In the name of Jesus.

Amen.

Chapter 7

Old Man – New Man

So, we are healthy and growing when we work together and use our gifting for the benefit of each other. Church, in fact life itself, is not just for ourselves, it is for others! We are the supply that will do that.

Jesus calls us to not walk like those in the world. We are in the world but not of it (Jn.17:14-15). That does not mean we have nothing to do with those who are in the world. It means we do not live like they do.

> *17 This I say, therefore, and testify in the Lord, that you should no longer walk as the rest of the Gentiles walk, in the futility of their mind, 18 having their understanding darkened, being alienated from the life of God, because of the ignorance that is in them, because of the blindness of their heart; 19 who, being past feeling, have given themselves over to lewdness, to work all uncleanness with greediness.*
>
> **Ephesians 4:17-19**

Here we find Paul repeating the call for us to live and walk differently. However, this time, in Ephesians 4:17 he exhorts us not to walk like the gentiles "in the futility of their mind". That expression refers to an emptiness or purposeless, the quality of producing no valuable effects. Outside of Christ the world may look good, feel good but in reality it is no lasting good. Outside of Christ there is no lasting purpose even for those who we may recognise as doing good.

Paul then provides us with five traits, or characteristics, of such a lifestyle in order to warn us not to live that way so we are not fooled.

A Darkened Understanding

We read this in Ephesians 4:18. Have you ever noticed someone with a darkened understanding? Somehow it is impossible to get through to them because they will not try to understand or they try but are incapable of understanding. Their mind cannot see what you see. That is because when we come to Christ we go from darkness to light. The gospel passages are full of references to those walking in the darkness who cannot see the light. Jesus Himself is described as light, so we must make sure we take this message on board and that can help us in sharing with these folk. We cannot expect to see it like they do, so don't get offended. That is just who they are. Think of ways to help them in a way that will get through to them. You, yourself, were once in darkness but something got through to you to bring you into the light. By the grace of God they can too. Jesus provides help for us by showing us our true nature as sons of light in the following passage

> [14] *"You are the light of the world. A city that is set on a hill cannot be hidden.* [15] *Nor do they light a lamp and put it under a basket, but on a lampstand, and it gives light to all who are in the house.* [16] *Let your light so shine before men,*

that they may see your good works and glorify you Father in heaven"

Matthew 5:14-16

Once again it is important for us to choose to be light and live that way so we are constantly free from the alternative.

Alienated from God

We have to remember that, increasingly, in the world, the concept of God is not a familiar thing. Many have a problem of just taking on board the concept of God. They are alienated from Him so we have to find ways to help them. To do that we first have to know ourselves who God is, what He is really like and the difference He has made to our life. The world is not going to know any other way than by us sharing with them from our own experience. We cannot expect to talk about God and assume they know. They are alienated, or separated from Him. They have lost touch with Him.

Ignorance of God's Way

Many people have no real idea how God works and what His ways are. Various things are regarded as an act of God when in reality God had nothing to do with them. God gets the blame for all kinds of things He is not involved with. Therefore, we need to be sure that we know His ways and allow His ways to operate in us, then we can help people to see them. If Christ is in you then you need to be following His ways.

Blind or Hardened Heart

Ephesians 4:18, says this is because of "the blindness of their heart". In the core of their being, the heart, they cannot see the truth of Christ. Have you noticed that in people you know. No matter how you share Jesus with them they just do not seem to get it. It is a very real thing. In reality their heart can only be changed if you tell them and God changes them. So watch out for people where you can see their heart has softened towards God. There is then a real opportunity for change. Sometimes a hard heart can be reached quicker than one that is indifferent. It has happened so many times when one incident can open up a life to receive Jesus.

Lack of feelings

Verse 19 indicates that those in the world can get to a point when they become "past feeling" and because of this they have "given themselves over to lewd behaviour" and "uncleanness with greediness".

The Greek word for the effect of "giving oneself over" to something means "ceased to care".

Have you come across those who no longer care what others think about them and feel they can do whatever they please and the world will just have to accept it? That trait is increasingly portrayed in the media, on TV and in films.

In the midst of all these contrary examples Paul then cries out to us and urges us in verse 20 writing: "But you have not so learned Christ."

Another way of saying that is "but that's no life for you". We have to live differently in the light of what we know and whose we are. We have to do this on purpose rather than just hope that things will change for us or one day God will zap us and everything will be okay.

Choosing the New Man

As we highlighted in chapter 2 and alluded to again at the close of the last chapter, we have to choose to live differently. That is making a quality decision to change. In order to assist us in making that choice, in verses 22-24, Paul describes this decision-making action for us in the terms of "old man" and "new man".

> *22 that you put off, concerning your former conduct, the old man which grows corrupt according to the deceitful lusts, 23 and be renewed in the spirit of your mind, 24 and that you put on the new man which was created according to God, in true righteousness and holiness.*
>
> **Ephesians 4:22-24**

What a powerful contrast he gives us so that we are in no doubt which position to choose. He emphasises that this is all about changing our former conduct (verses 17, 22), or you could say the way that we lived without thinking whether it was right or wrong. He refers to this in terms of an "old man" in deceitful lusts. These are not just sexual but could refer to any strong desires. Furthermore, he declares this "old man" is growing corrupt. He is not referring to a slang term for your father or someone who is ancient. He is referring to our former way of life. These are past ways, past hurts, past actions, regrets, good or bad things. In fact, in Romans 6:6 Paul describes this "old man" as having been crucified with Christ, it is no more! It has been done away with and defeated or deprived of power to rule your life. 2 Corinthians 5:17 then states "we are a new creation, old things have passed away."

The issue we are faced with here is that this truth is a reality but we have to do something to bring it into sharp focus for ourselves that will change our perception and our lifestyle. We have to "put off" the "old man". *The Message* Bible states verse 23 very strongly when it says "get rid of it." Jesus has crucified it. There is no longer any power to hold you to that way of life but you have to choose to do it.

I have preached on this passage a number of times and always use a graphic example when doing so. I put on a jacket to demonstrate the "old man" and then take it off and let it go. However, many of us find it easy not to let go even if it is dragging behind us. Or we walk away, then if times get tough we find that "old man" again and pick it up and start wearing it. Or perhaps we put it on a hanger and clean it up so we can wear it again. The trouble is the only thing that can clean that "old man" up is the blood of Jesus. That "old man" will deceive us because it represents old thinking and it will kill us.

I remember one time, a few years ago, I used this example when speaking at a leader's conference in Eldoret, Kenya, for a good friend, Bishop Daniel Muiruri. I forgot that the floors of the church were dirt not concrete or wood and by the time I had finished my jacket was covered in dirt and almost needed cleaning professionally. Everyone laughed loudly as they comprehended the truth of what I was trying to explain. They never forgot that and Daniel still talks about it when I see him, which unfortunately is not too often these days.

So, you have to do this consistently until it becomes a part of you that happens automatically. The more you let go the less power the old life will have a hold on you, whether it is old habits, old hurts or regrets. This action brings about a renewal in your thinking that affects your subsequent action. It is a transformation that happens in your mind and the fruit of it in a person's life is wonderful to behold.

Then exactly the same principle is applied to putting on "the new man". We are reminded in 2 Corinthians 5:17 that IN CHRIST all things have become new. That is the reality. It is new, fresh, clean, wholesome, no history, a clean slate, a blank canvass. This is how you start with Christ. You are created new according to God. Your spirit is new. It is as if it had never existed before. With it comes the power to live this new life to the full and it has the capability of blasting away the now defunct power of the old. Again, however, we are told that it is our responsibility to put on this "new man".

In Kenya I borrowed a lady's beautiful shawl and put it on to show what this "new man" feels like. The "new man" is the real you as God always intended. So you can live according to that new lifestyle everyday. That is possible because of what Jesus has done on the inside of you. I was then able to highlight that it does not look good trying to wear both jackets at once. When you still keep the old jacket on under the new one, somehow things just don't fit right.

It is a little like looking at things through a pair of binoculars. You have the power to change the focus of your life but it is your choice to decide which end of the binoculars you look and live your life by. If you look through the binoculars from the wrong end it gives you a wrong focus. It is then all about you and your needs. It is your world, your issues and your problems. You cannot focus properly on anything as you are seeing it the wrong way.

If you turn the binoculars around and view things the way it was made to function you then begin to see things clearly and can focus in on the truth. The passage calls this "true righteousness and holiness".

The Message Bible has a great way of explaining this:

> ²³⁻²⁴ *And then take on an entirely new way of life–a God fashioned life, a life renewed from the inside and working itself into your conduct as God accurately reproduces His character in you.*
>
> **Ephesians 4:23-24. (MSG)**

Chapter 8

The Call to Right Living

In the first three chapters of Paul's letter to us we have seen what Christ has done in us. We have understood our position as being IN CHRIST. We have also seen, in the early verses of Ephesians 4, the importance of us choosing to be separate from the things of the world that used to dominate us, as a response to this knowledge of Christ in us. Following on from this response, Paul begins to outline that our responsibility is to live in accordance with that knowledge.

In thinking this through we realise and are heartened by the fact that, when we come to Christ, He accepts us exactly in the condition that we have just come to Him. He never asks us to change before He accepts us. However, by the same token that love and grace that he bestows upon us also means that He will not leave us in that state but He will graciously show us how to change and He will help us in that change, through His Holy Spirit.

In the spirit of going through and showing us this process Paul opens up the nitty gritty-subject of God's call to right living in accordance with His will and denying our own previous desires. Normally, we may look at this and think "that's impossible" but remember we are only faced with the possibility of making progress in this area and gaining victory because we are now IN CHRIST. We are no longer in a place where we are easily tossed to and fro following the dictates of our former life.

So lets take a look at what God is saying regardless of whether it seems impossible on the face of it.

1. Speaking the truth

> [25] *Therefore, putting away lying,"Let each one of you speak truth with his neighbour," for we are members of one another.*
>
> **Ephesians 4:25**

This verse includes a quote from Zechariah 8:16.

It is fascinating that Paul does so but it is not surprising as the New Testament is littered with quotes from Zechariah. The context reflects the Jewish nation once again returning to Jerusalem from Babylon and an instruction to finish the building of the temple. The analogy with Ephesians could not be clearer. In Zechariah, God is emphasising how they should conduct their lives as God is restoring and finishing the building. It also has an emphasis that telling lies is something that God hates. So Paul is similarly reminding Christians that God has not changed and always being truthful is a key part of Christian lifestyle. However, he now emphasises both the community and fellow believers because we are all in this together.

Consider further that God is truth and with these commands He is aiming to make us like Him.

I once heard someone say:

"Lying is an attempt to gain personal advantage at someone else's expense. Truth is an attempt to gain someone else advantage at personal expense."

On reflection I think this is only partly correct but it is an interesting thought.

The truth may cost you at the time but the benefits of a clear heart far outweigh the consequences of the alternative.

Psalm 15 even links speaking the truth in your heart to a host of other things in that Psalm and gives an ultimate consequence that if you do these things you shall never be moved.

> *[1] Lord, who may abide in Your tabernacle? Who may dwell in your holy hill? [2] He who walks uprightly And works righteousness, And speaks the truth in his heart;*
>
> **Psalm 15:1-2**

In other words, you shall be able to stand on solid ground because you have not built your life on a shaky foundation. Once a lie begins there is a tendency to continue to lie in order to cover over the first one and so it goes on until you can't remember which is truth and which is the lie. Eventually the lie takes over and you end up with serious eternal problems.

The sad thing is that the world has a tendency to exalt them, calling things "a little white lie" or "being economical with the truth". These are so far from the truth. UK TV even makes a joke out of it with game shows like "*Would I Lie To You,*" where the best results and greatest laughs come for someone who best acts out what is really a lie but presents the scenario as if it were true.

There is a helpful passage in Proverbs 12 that provides us with some godly results from walking in truth

- Verse 17 declares that if you speak truth you declare righteousness.
- Verse 18 says that the tongue of the wise promotes health.
- Verse 19 says a truthful lip shall be established forever.
- Verse 22 says that those who deal truthfully are a delight to God.

So, there are many benefits from speaking the truth. Yet the word tells us to do that in love, considering the other person. Speaking truth is not an excuse to put someone down but to bring benefit to him or her.

2. Develop a right attitude to anger

26 "Be angry, and do not sin".do not let the sun go down on your wrath, 27 nor give place to the devil.

Ephesians 4:26-27

I feel this statement is highly relevant for us in today's society. Anger is everywhere and it spills out in many ways from the extreme of terrorism to the cover up of personal abuse.

There are two specific areas that this passage throws up that are worthy of closer scrutiny.

These verses suggest that there is rightful anger, which is anger without sin. So, let us first consider what this is. In simple terms, there are some things that it is right to get mad over.

Jesus, Himself, was angry with the moneychangers abusing the true temple way of life, which was prayer. Jesus said the moneychangers had made it a den of thieves because they were robbing poor people over their sacrifices. There are some apocryphal accounts from the time that even said, during this episode, that there was literal fire coming out of Jesus' eyes.

Paul is saying be angry but do not let it boil over into sin. Jesus acted rightly but He could have allowed that anger to take Him over and attempt, right there and then, to put right all the other wrongs that were there, but He did not. In fact, He stayed in the temple and quietly taught the people. He did not let the anger get in the way of His real mission in life.

We need to learn from this. We all get angry at times but the word says that we should not let that get out of hand and be allowed to fester over night and keep control of us. Paul describes it as not letting the sun go down on our anger. It does not improve things if we do that, it rather makes things worse. Am I the only one who has both given and received the silent treatment in bed because of unresolved anger or argument?

In fact, in Psalm 4:4, which is the verse that Paul quotes, we are encouraged to take time and meditate on what has happened in our hearts and be still, putting our trust in God to resolve the issues. In effect it is saying think it over and come to our senses, because anger happens when we get out of control. We feel we cannot trust anyone and have to get our own back, so we take matters into our own hand. The word says don't do that. Place your trust in God.

Secondly we have to consider what is the ultimate result of wrong or uncontrolled anger.

Clearly Paul points out that this gives place to the devil to step in and take control of our lives. We, therefore, lose ground in our spiritual walk, because the devil will use the opportunity to gain a foothold. So we need to be aware that this is a tactic of the enemy and where he will take the opportunity to plant a seed that would lead to our destruction if we allow it to grow and take up residence in our life. We then wonder where a bad temper or worse comes from, when in fact we have yielded to carnal disobedience as we have not learned to go back to God, again and again.

3. No more stealing

⁴ Let him who stole steal no longer

Ephesians 4:28a

In some circles, it seems like stealing is an almost expected thing. We tend not to think about it too much and most probably it has become the norm, especially in a business setting. According to the internet 79% of companies experienced theft from employees. In fact it named ten common things that happen at work, which can be regarded as stealing.

- Making personal copies from the printer.
- Using the fax machine personally (now it would be making personal emails on work time.)
- Taking longer coffee breaks.
- Making personal phone calls.
- Running personal errands on company time.
- Making long distance personal phone calls.
- Doing personal things in work time.
- Taking pens, paperclips, folders, staplers, surfing the web.

- Taking longer lunch breaks.
- Starting late and leaving early.

Of course none of us have ever done any of those things, have we? You know, all those statements together bring us up with a start because of themselves, in isolation, they seem such small insignificant things. However, Paul is trying to encourage us, as believers, that our life, and especially our work life changes from one based on what we can get, to one based on what we can give. Our work is not just to raise money for us, but also to have to give to others.

Malachi 3 says that we rob God when we withhold our giving when we should give. However, when we do give our over abundant God opens the windows of heaven to us beyond anything we could ask or imagine. So, this means we do not need to get agitated over the idea of living to give because that is in the heart of God. His way is to reward over and above what we give. We can never out give God.

When we allow Christ to work through us the result is that we become instruments of God towards mankind. If all you are trying to do is get things and resorting to stealing from time to time, you cut yourself off from God being able to bless you. It is that simple. However, if your heart is right He will put you in places to promote you, bless you and get you more pay. If your thinking is that your wealth, or lack of it, is based on what you earn that falls way short of what God intends for your life. He is actually trying to get more to you, not withholding from you. So we have to be diligent in working with Him at all times.

4. Quit corrupt conversation

²⁹ Let no corrupt word proceed out of your mouth, but what is good for necessary edification, that it may impart grace to the hearers.

Ephesians 4:29

More and more these days I feel that this is of huge importance in the mind of God. It was certainly very important in Jesus' thinking when He impressed on the disciples that it was not what they ate and drank that corrupted them but what came out of their heart and was expressed in what they thought and said (Mt.15:17-20).

Our mouth can hold us back from receiving from God. Do we have a tendency to say "Oh we never have anything?" Proverbs 18:21 teaches that "life and death are in the power of the tongue", or what we say. So we have to watch what we say as it will either promote us or bring us down.

Paul talks about corrupt word or conversation. Corrupt has a meaning of being decayed and rotten like spoiled meat. That makes one think. When I speak is it like spoiled meat in the hearers ear? Perhaps that is a good way of thinking to emphasise the effect it will have on both us and others. Instead, our words are meant to be good and pleasant for the hearer and build them up with grace and favour.

If you are thinking that you have been the way you are for such a long time that it would be impossible for you to change then I have good news for you. We are covering all this from a perspective that we are IN CHRIST. We are not on our own we are learning how to live through Him!

I have personal experience of this in my early Christian life. I was eagerly witnessing to a girl at work, shortly after giving my life to Christ. She listened to everything I said and commented at the end. "Yes I hear everything you say, however, how can you do that when you are swearing all the time?"

I did not know what to do as it really convicted me of something I was totally unaware of. I realise now that it was the work of the Holy Spirit reaching out to me. That night when I went home, I got on my knees in my bedroom and repented before Him and asked Him to help me change my ways.

Over a period of time that is exactly what He did. I eventually learned more about the power of the tongue and so I do watch what I say because I know the importance of it. It has become second nature to me. I realise that most people have corrupt conversation because they do not think twice about it. I have learned correct conversation and I do not think twice about that. With God it is possible.

So, as we finish this section here are some important points for us to meditate on and build into our new life In Christ:

- As we speak truth it is health and wealth to us.
- As we watch our anger we live in peace and harmony.
- As we live to give we shall get blessed.
- As we talk right we open up the way for favour

So, think on these things today. Paul provides a helpful way of acting in the future in Philippians.

⁸ Finally brethren, whatever things are noble, whatever things are just, whatever things are pure, whatever things are lovely, whatever things are of good report, if there is anything praiseworthy–meditate on these things. ⁹ The things you learned and received and heard and saw in me, these do, and the God of peace will be with you.

Philippians 4:8-9

You may be struggling in some area. If you are, the Lord has brought these things up on purpose and wants to minister fresh life in you today. Go to Him in prayer and ask Him to intervene in that situation. Take it from me, He will always answer when you cry out to Him. He is waiting for you to do just that because He loves you.

I think it is very pertinent that Paul then, in verses 30-32 of Ephesians 4, emphasises the importance of not grieving the Holy Spirit, who is our helper in changing our lives to be more Christlike because we are sealed by Him in preparation for the things to come. So He encourages us to be kind to each other, walking in forgiveness (which is another huge subject we will not be covering here) because we are the receiver of God's forgiveness. Treating the Holy Spirit right is a key to staying in that right place ourselves. We must understand that the Holy Spirit is a gentleman and He will not go against our will. I was once in a meeting where the minister called certain people forward to be prayed for and the rest of the congregation just broke out in chatting to each other. The minister carried on for a while then remonstrated with everyone because he had sensed the Holy Spirit was grieved and had left. Everyone repented and He returned and there were some awesome healings as a result. It taught me a great lesson in being sensitive to the move of God.

If we yield to the Holy Spirit and go out of our way to please Him we will do well. Our bodies are the temples of the Holy Spirit. He lives in us so the more we go down the route highlighted in these verses, the better it will be for us.

Prayer

I choose to yield to the Holy Spirit now in my life over all the areas I have been struggling with. I choose to do what I have read and turn my thoughts towards you, trusting that you hear me and that the Holy Spirit will work on my behalf to bring me to that place of peace in you.

Amen

Chapter 9

Walking in Love, Light and Wisdom

Before we embark on this next chapter I thought it would be helpful to remind ourselves why we are critiquing these verses in Ephesians. You will remember we began by gaining an understanding of the benefits for each one of us when we come to Christ and find ourselves IN CHRIST. We are now pursuing the commands that Paul provides for living our lives through Christ. As we consider each new term it is easy to feel that these verses are extremely difficult to do, if not nigh on impossible.

We must, however, remind ourselves that with God all things are possible. Indeed we are now reviewing these verses in the very knowledge and revelation that we ourselves are IN CHRIST. Something that may be impossible to do without Him now becomes possible and doable because we are partakers of the divine nature. So let's approach this next chapter with encouragement and joy in our new status, knowing that this new life was designed just for us and determine that we will live it. On that basis let's move on to chapter 5 of Ephesians.

Walk in Love

> *¹Therefore be imitators of God as dear children. ²And walk in love, as Christ also has loved us and given Himself for us, an offering and a sacrifice to God for a sweet smelling aroma.*
>
> **Ephesians 5:1-2**

Straight away we are faced with a strong direction to imitate God. I am sure that many of you are familiar with celebrity comedians and those who have an ability to mimic the voice of a well known person. Those who are very accomplished in this sound really excellent and it is easy to fool us. That is until you hear the real person speaking and you realise it sounds nothing like them in real life. Paul, however is not urging us to just give it a go, knowing that we have no chance of being like the real thing. It is possible IN CHRIST because the Holy Spirit is working in us. In fact Paul adds a caveat to this verse by telling us to be imitators like dear children.

Children have a simplicity of action and we are to be like them in our approach to this. You all will have noticed how easy it is for children to imitate the sayings and actions of their parents. In fact all the habits that in many cases you are unaware of until you see and hear them for yourself. That is a good example of what we are talking about here. Constant presence and association with parents rubs off on the child so they become like them. That is exactly what Paul is encouraging here until we become more like Him. My mother reckons I am becoming more and more like my father (who has now passed away) all the time. However, my wife is always telling me I am just like my mother. You can't win. Is any one else familiar with this experience?

We are then provided with help in this process by an encouragement to walk in love in the same way Christ did in giving Himself for us. We consider Christ's sacrifice for us and are totally overwhelmed but we are then inspired to love like this. As Jesus gave Himself for us, we are to give ourselves for each other. The example Jesus gave us went as far as dying on a cross. That is a sweet smelling sacrifice, or you could say, a pleasant thing. It reminds me of a favourite passage in Paul's second letter to the Corinthians.

> *14 Now thanks be to God who always leads us in triumph in Christ, and through us diffuses the fragrance of His knowledge in every place. 15 For we are to God the fragrance of Christ among those who are being saved and among those who are perishing. 16 To the one we are the aroma of death leading to death, and to the other the aroma of life leading to life*

2 Corinthians 2:14-16

As we have mentioned before, our love is a fragrance to Christ. We should not underestimate the value of our love to Him. With our love we give something off that is awesome even if we cannot see it. The expression of your love could be a crossroads in another person's life. It could draw them into the kingdom of life or confirm for them that they are in the kingdom of darkness. Don't be surprised when people react to you according to the latter. They are only reflecting the kingdom they are a part of and until they come to Christ they cannot help it.

What follows from Paul, then, in the following verses is tough talk, considering it is all in the same breath as walking in love. We cannot ignore this because it is a prerequisite of successfully walking in love and imitating God. For Paul this includes dealing with:

- Sexual immorality.
- Insatiable carnality – never getting enough.
- Filthiness and coarse jesting.

Who said that these issues are only pertinent to our modern society? If you think about it, these matters are all a counterfeit of true love. They have a root in lust and come direct from the devil. Yielding to them leads us away from the love of Christ. It may look attractive, it may even look fun, but the ultimate result is that it draws us away from the true object of our affection, which is Christ.

Today it is almost as if the inference is that everyone is doing this so it is okay. Anyone who thinks differently is marginalised. The media, and especially soaps, push it because then they will sell stories and get bigger viewer ratings. But the word here says do not partake of it or accept it into your life. That may mean you have to give up watching some programs and use wisdom. You have to decide for yourself with the Lord's help.

In the midst of this there is repentance and forgiveness if you realise the wrong you have been involved in. God loves you first and He is trying to get you out of that stuff because He knows there is a better way and you are able to walk in that if you yield to Him and walk in true love.

Walk in the Light

⁸ For you were once darkness, but now you are light in the Lord. Walk as children of the light ⁹ (for the fruit of the Spirit is in all goodness, righteousness, and truth) ¹⁰ finding out what is acceptable to the Lord. ¹¹ And have no fellowship with the unfruitful works of darkness, but rather expose them.

Ephesians 5:8-11

After facing some issues in the previous verses, verses **8-11** are of great encouragement for us. We were once in darkness (Paul even calls us darkness itself) but now IN CHRIST we are light. So we are encouraged to be constant and to walk in that light.

John 1 describes God as light Himself. What does that mean for us. Well a rudimentary research into light reveals the following:

1. Light is the matter, which makes objects visible to the eye. So, if you are walking in the light of Christ then you can begin to see the truth about things which would not have been so obvious when you were in darkness. You begin to see things as they really are.

2. To break out or open or forth, to gleam and shine clearly. IN CHRIST we have broken out of our old life, as we discussed in a previous chapter. We can now see clearly about this life and ourselves in it.

3. According to physics, light is thought to consist of a quantum or photon (i.e. a dense pack of energy). The study of it is called quantum electrodynamics, which has now progressed from Einstein's original theory of

relativity and a simple understanding of a part of the electromagnetic spectrum that humans can see. There is much more on this subject, which is beyond the scope of what we are concentrating on here.

Now, if, like myself, you are a Star Trek fan you will be familiar with the idea of a photon torpedo. So why not see yourself as being like a photon torpedo? You are a pack of energy for God. When you light up and shine your light on the truth, others will see it and be drawn to it.

Pardon the pun, but in the light of this knowledge we make sense of what Paul shares next. He says that the fruit produced by this is goodness, righteousness and truth. The New Living Translation even translates "Spirit" as "light", as follows

9 For this light within you produces only what is good and right and true

Ephesians 5:9 (NLT)

So, these are all characteristics which transform us by walking in the light. We will be able to walk more in the light as we find out what is acceptable to God and begin to apply that on a daily basis in our lives. How do we do that? We do it by reading the word of God because that reveals or sheds light on God and His ways. That reminds me of another powerful scripture

105 Your word is a lamp to my feet And a light to my path.

Psalm 119:105

Fellowship with darkness makes you dark. However, light will expose it. The more you radiate light and walk that way the more you will expose the darkness around. Alternatively, you could say, the more you will see worldly things for what they are.

Walk in Wisdom

15 See then that you walk circumspectly, not as fools but as wise, 16 redeeming the time because the days are evil.

Ephesians 5:15-16

15 Therefore be careful how you walk, not as unwise men but as wise, 16 making the most of your time, because the days are evil.

Ephesians 5:15-16 (NASB)

15 Be very careful, then, how you live – not as unwise but as wise, 16 making the most of every opportunity, because the days are evil.

Ephesians 5:15-16 (NIV)

So what does it mean to walk circumspectly? Well another way of explaining this would be to walk carefully (NASB, NIV), cautiously, sensitively like you would if you were walking through thorny ground. In order to do that in the face of the circumstances of life we need wisdom. However, not any old wisdom but wisdom from the throne room of God that is a mark of the Holy Spirit. We have a tendency to only seek the amazing manifestations of the Spirit. However, He will bring something even more valuable in the shape of wisdom if we yield to that. By doing so it will make you effective in every area of your life, at home, at work, in your marriage (if you are married), and in your choices.

So, how do we redeem the time with wisdom? Well, another way of putting it would be (as the NASB puts it) to make the most of the time you have and use wisdom in how you spend it. Sometimes we waste time, especially by worrying over many things, when we could seek God's help but we don't.

Paul then provides us a number of ways to enable this transformation to take place in the next few verses.

1. Understand the will of God (verse 17). This will give us the wisdom to know what course of action to take.
2. Be filled with the Holy Spirit rather than beer, wine and whisky. Being filled is not a single experience but one of continual application. No, that is not a call to teetotalism but it is a call to wisdom and moderation in natural things and to be extravagant in spiritual things.
3. Use Christian songs and music to keep you focussed and keep you filled with the Spirit. This is wisdom to you. And note that spiritual songs includes impromptu songs in the Spirit which can be in English or in tongues. We should anticipate moving into those things in our worship times.
4. Giving thanks to God.
5. Submitting to one another. This last is significant and we will discuss it in more depth in the next chapter.

As we walk in love and in light and wisdom we will choose to take actions that will cause us to be victorious in the circumstances of life.

Are you ready to choose to walk that way on a daily basis and see the change in you and those around you? As we have stated before it is important to choose this walk IN CHRIST, because it is the way of love and we are, in doing so, declaring our determination to live this way.

Chapter 10

Wives and Husbands

Paul, at this point, begins to open up about the family relationship in a godly marriage. He starts with a conversation about the relationship between husband and wife. It is unfortunate that this discourse has led to more of a debate about the word "submission" that Paul uses than in gaining insight into what he is trying to say. Despite that, I feel it is right to first consider the idea of submission in order that we get a grasp of Paul's approach in terms of family.

Understanding the principle of submission

I realise that providing any kind of insight into submission requires an absolute trust that God knows what He is doing and a yielding to the Holy Spirit's leading. There are so many contrary indications as to what is the truth. Times have changed and with it a different understanding of what is the norm in society. This norm is often dictated by those who shout the loudest from whatever viewpoint they hold. Interestingly, very few now go back to try and understand what God originally intended, so it becomes more difficult to plough an accurate furrow.

In the context of this book we must remember that we are pursuing a life based IN CHRIST so our values and ways will often be at odds with the world. In the last chapter we discussed how to stay in love, light and wisdom. That approach differs from the world's way of seeing things. So as we consider this subject, let us bear in mind that these passages are in scripture because God wants us to look at this differently. Clearly, Paul is under the Holy Spirit's direction to do so.

Let us, therefore, approach submission with the same excitement, knowing that if we all get this right, especially in the realm of a godly marriage, it will lead to success and happiness beyond what many experience.

In my view, as we look at this, an important point is that submission is something that is at the behest of the giver and not the beneficiary. For example in this passage, nowhere does it insist, or require a man to demand that a woman submits to him. Someone chooses to submit for the benefit of the whole. It is a place where one puts all of self, knowledge, opinions, feelings and energies at the disposal of another. Nowhere is this clearer than in a general submission to authority in all its forms, be it employers, civil authorities, spiritual leaders as well as those with whom we have established relationships.

The problem is that in our strange society today, such an act is often seen as obnoxious. How could any woman submit to a man or vice versa? We live in a society where there is a pressing in for everyone to stand up for themselves. So, the idea of submission does not sit easily against it. So, we need to observe what scripture has to say about this process so we can gain a clearer understanding.

a) All Christians should submit to God

> *⁶ But He gives more grace. Therefore He says; "God resists the proud, But gives grace to the humble". ⁷ Therefore submit to God. Resist the devil and he will flee from you.*
>
> **James 4: 6-7**

I find this statement both challenging and encouraging. It is as if James is directing us back to the Genesis incident and indicating a tactic or course of action which would have succeeded when dealing with the devil. Adam and Eve should have submitted to God or recognised that God was the ultimate authority to be followed in the situation they found themselves in. By following a submitted heart to Him they would have been able to resist the devil's advances and he would have left them. Indeed, thinking back to Jesus' own temptation by the devil in the wilderness, this is exactly the tactic that Jesus used and He came out victorious. Truly a great example for us all to follow.

When we make Jesus the Lord of our life we show ourselves willing to follow the process of yielding ourselves to Him and recognise that He has the final say because He knows more than we do. I say it is a process because we all recognise times in our Christian walk where we have gone our own way, harking back to the Genesis tendency, rather than trusting in His ways. It takes time to learn the way we should go, but we are not alone now that we are IN CHRIST. That is why we have to consider some of these issues in Ephesians because it is easy to fall back to an old way of thinking.

b) Submission to governing authorities.

> [13] *Be subject for the Lord's sake to every human institution, whether it be to the emperor as supreme,* [14] *or to governors as sent by him to punish those who do evil and to praise those who do good.* [15] *For this is the will of God, by doing good you should put to silence the ignorance of foolish people.*
>
> **1 Peter 2:13-15 (ESV)**

It is then pertinent that Peter stresses in verse 15 following this that such an action is "the will of God" (in case we were in any doubt). It is so important, regardless of whether we like the government or not. We are commanded to understand and follow the principle, which will cause us to be blessed in life (i.e., to do good). You can see this most eloquently in the honour given to an American president at state functions, regardless of party. No matter which party he represents he is honoured because of the office he stands in. However, this principle is being stretched daily in an increasingly partisan atmosphere in the USA. In Peter's case he was calling on submission even though, for him, it meant doing so with respect to a despotic emperor.

That, of course, does not preclude those who in the past and present stand up against corrupt and oppressive regimes or corrupt practices. Looking back we would recognise Wilberforce, Pankhurst and Mandella in that category.

c) Mutual Submission

> [20] *giving thanks always and for everything to God the father in the name of our Lord Jesus Christ,* [21] *submitting to one another out of reverence for Christ.*
>
> **Ephesians 5:20-21 (ESV)**

On first view, there is a sense that would confirm the state of affairs which is preferred by modern society in that this passage extols mutual recognition and submission where neither party has a sense of authority but willingly submits to the person who has the gifting needed for the situation being faced. However, although one could cite examples where mutual submission is helpful, this is only partly true. When one considers the examples that Paul gives, it is most likely that Paul is advocating that "submitting to one another" involves submitting to others according to the authority and order established by God (see: ESV Study Bible notes to Ephesians 5:21).

Submission is a plan which God has designed to work for our benefit. Men and women are equal spiritually but there are distinctions because each was created with different roles and purposes which has nothing to do with subordination! Submission is something that is first an expression of loyalty to the will and word of God. Submission is not for the weak person. Anyone can be haughty, independent or proud. It takes strength of will to submit willingly and be accountable in that process.

For example, do you submit readily to what God tells you to do or do you argue with Him? So, submission is an act of will. You have to make your mind up to do it and then stick to that commitment. Only then do the benefits come to the surface. As

I said earlier, one human being should never insist that another person submit to them. It should only be given on a basis of trust. It means to retire, withdraw, yield and obey. When we retire our plans we become adaptable to God's plan.

Paul's Approach to Wives and Husbands

So, with this general understanding of what Paul is thinking about in relation to submission let us consider now the specifics of what the Holy Spirit is unfolding about the changed relationship of wives and husbands once we approach the matter on the basis that we are now living our life through Christ.

a) Wives and the Genesis Problem

> [20] *giving thanks always for all things to God the Father in the name of our Lord Jesus Christ,* [21] *submitting to one another in the fear of God.* [22] *Wives, submit to your own husbands, as to the Lord.*
>
> **Ephesians 5:20-22**

This controversial passage has given rise to much debate and different sides taken. Some of this derives from the fact that in the original Greek verse 22 does not include the word "submit." Many, therefore, consider this passage only refers to a mutual submission which is done voluntarily rather than being under the absolute control of another (see the Bible study notes for NKJV relating to this passage). I can see how this can be construed in this way. However, in doing so I feel that Paul gives further clarity on this very subject in Col 3 where he says the same thing.

18 Wives submit to your own husbands, as is fitting in the Lord. 19 Husbands love your wives and do not be bitter toward them.

Colossians 3:18-19.

In this case the word submit, in the Greek *upotassesthe* is most definitely included.

Therefore, if we go back to our original creation we see that in Genesis 1:26 God created man (the species) and said "let them have dominion over the earth. The wording of subsequent scripture shows that God created Adam first and then Eve, as a helpmeet for him to rule alongside in the role that God had fashioned for them. However, when man sinned by taking of the fruit and eating it there seems to be a reversing of function in play. The serpent spoke to Eve but Adam was there and allowed her to take control in the situation. At no time did Adam step in and take his rightful place, protecting Eve, and dealing with the devil as he should have done. Eve was deceived but Adam knew what was happening and allowed it to take place. This, then, makes sense of the words of God to Adam, who probably knew deep down that he had stepped away from his rightful position and caused the result they were both experiencing. Indeed, the Lord called to Adam, not Eve, because he was supposed to be the one in control and with authority over all that God had tasked them. I am in no doubt, also, that Eve stepped in and took control in this situation with the serpent because Adam did not.

God then speaks out plainly how this action will play out in the future in the last part of Genesis 3:16.

16... Your desire shall be for your husband, And he shall rule over you

Genesis 3:16

In other words, God is saying that the action taken and the sin resulting, will turn around the God-ordained plan for mankind. The woman will have a strong desire for control over the man and he will have an overburdening desire to rule over her. This is totally at odds with what God intended and it is a situation that is replicated today. The word used for "desire" in this context is only used once more in scripture and that is when God is dealing with Cain's offering and states that sin is desiring to rule over him but he must not let it (Gen.4:7). Clearly, that desire for control is so strong that Cain ignores God and kills Abel. This should make us sit up and really think through how God intended that we walk in humility together, rather than the situation we often see. It may then help us to see why God is re establishing a godly principle for humans.

b) Wives relating to husbands

22 Wives submit to your own husbands, as to the Lord

Ephesians 5:22

First we must be really strong in facing the fact that this does not say "all women, submit to all men".

The problem is that is how this verse has been interpreted and so receives a modern day spin. Neither does it say that all wives should submit to all husbands. I am certain that this is deliberate. Feminism was rife in Ephesus and, especially, in Corinth. Women were experiencing a level of freedom IN CHRIST that they had never known before. Some historians even suggest that they were asking lots of questions and favouring certain men regardless of the relationship and following them. Paul is pulling the relationship back into the God ordained principle that was always intended.

Wives (note: not women in general) you are to submit to your own husband, as to the Lord. Or you could say, in the same way you submit to the Lord. It is a recognition of authority in the marriage. No one else owes the duty of submission over you than your own husband. In this context we begin to understand the God-given roles in marriage. It is not an excuse for the husband to Lord it over his wife. The wife is doing this because the Lord places this responsibility on her and it is of supreme importance. The decision she makes is similar, if not the same as the decision that any one makes to follow Christ. At that point you let go of your own way knowing there is a higher calling and benefit from going His way.

c) Husbands relating to wives

> [23] For the husband is head of the wife, even as Christ is the head of the church, his body, and is himself its saviour.
>
> **Ephesians 5:23**

The husband's role is to be the head in the marriage. Note particularly that does not refer to all men. Men in general are not the head of women. This is in the context of a godly marriage where the husband is fulfilling his role in the same way that Christ does toward the church. So we need to grasp more deeply this Christ role as it applies to how a man acts in headship.

- Christ is the head of the body, which is the church.
- He is the saviour.
- He is the leader.

He is the one who loves so much that He was prepared to give up His own rights for the sake of ours, was born as a man and carried it through to the extent that He died on a cross to rescue it (Phil.2:6-7)

> ²⁴ *Now as the church submits to Christ, so also wives should submit in everything to their husbands.*
>
> **Ephesians 5:24**

The responsibility of the husband in being head is to demonstrate the same Christlike qualities. That is no small task. When this principle is properly applied by the husband, then it makes it easy for the wife to willingly give herself in submission to him because it is the same as if she were submitting to Christ.

So, rank has nothing to do with value. The husband has to rise up to be the head and he carries the greater responsibility. It is his role. It is not an easy one, yet many husbands fail and don't act like the head. When that happens wives easily take over the position instead of helping him to be the head. Yet there are many women who just long for their husband to rise up and be who they are supposed to be so that they, the wife, can be who she is supposed to be and not some kind of a hybrid to keep both going.

So a wife has to stay strong and close to the Lord because if the husband does, or says, something wrong, then the power of Christ in her life must shine through so it reveals to him what he should be and, therefore, he is convicted of his mistake and so it causes him to put things right.

In that regard you can see, clearly, that it is important for both husband and wife to be yielded to God first. In that way both see the power and peace of God working in any given situation in the marriage.

So, if wives are to submit, what must the husbands do?

> *25 Husbands, love your wives, just as Christ also loved the church and gave Himself for her, 26 that he might sanctify her, having cleansed her by the washing of water with the word, 27 so that he might present the church to himself in splendour, without spot or wrinkle or any such thing, that she might be holy and without blemish.*
>
> **Ephesians 5:25-27**

Initially, it looks like an easy deal on the face of it for the husband. One may think "well that's no big deal". Yet even in worldly terms over the last millennia or two, I wonder how many have really not loved their wife but married for convenience to run the home so he can continue in the lifestyle he desires.

However, in these verses we see the full extent of the kind of love a husband should demonstrate in accordance with the way Christ loved the church:

- He gave Himself for her.
- He made her holy.
- He led her with the word.
- He made her look glorious.
- He made her to be without spot and wrinkle.

28 The same way husbands should love their wives as their own bodies. He who loves his wife loves himself. 29 For no one ever hated his own flesh but nourishes and cherishes it, just as Christ does the church,.

Ephesians 5:28-29 (ESV)

Clearly Paul emphasises his point by repeating this message that husbands should love their wives. Here he encourages husbands to love as they love their own bodies, because then they love themselves.

You could say that Christ loved the church even when she was unlovable because He knew what she would become. He seeks her best constantly so that she always looks good wherever she goes. You may think that's a tall order that requires every bit of faith that you have. Here is the tall cotton, as they say in the States. If you do that to her it is like doing it to yourself. In giving to her it makes you the same because verse 29 declares that as you nourish and cherish your wife you get nourished also.

What follows in verse 31 is the time honoured scripture, repeated from Genesis 2:21, used most often in a marriage ceremony. It states that, in marriage, a husband and wife become joined as one. Therefore, if a husband fails to love his wife, both will suffer, but especially the husband as that is his place.

Paul refers to this unique bonding as a mystery. However, he then links it to the relationship between Christ and the church. In other words, and this is precious news for us, he sees Christ as inseparable from the church. Yet even though this is the highest aim of oneness, Paul still pushes husbands to love their wife and for a wife to mutually respect or reverence her husband. For wives, when your husband is being like Christ he becomes easy to respect. When he is not you have to do it by faith and help him. For example, there are lots of men who have no dress sense. Many men would not be seen dead shopping and it shows. Ladies you have to help in that instance. That does not mean you worship him.

So, as we close this chapter, take a moment to reflect. The power of God operates through those who are submitted first to Him and then to others. Think through this point for yourself. Ask yourself, are there any seeds of rebellion in my character that are holding me back from being submitted to God, or my spouse or my parents, which is preventing the power of God flowing in my life?

If there is, confess that before God and allow Him to change your situation and bring refreshing into your marriage.

Chapter 11

Children and Parents

In speaking about this subject I am being very circumspect as my wife and I have not been able to have physical children, ourselves. We do have numerous spiritual kids. So, the only thing I can do is to go right back to the Word of God, as that provides an insight into so many things that otherwise we would be struggling with.

First, lets take a look at what Paul has to say about children and the relationship to their parents:

> [1] *Children, obey your parents in the Lord, for this is right.* [2] *"Honour your father and mother," which is the first commandment with a promise:* [3] *"that it may be well with you and you may live long on the earth'* [4] *And you fathers, do not provoke your children to wrath, but bring them up in the training and admonition of the Lord.*
>
> **Ephesians 6:1-4**

Steve Motyer, when discussing this passage in his book on Ephesians, provides a unique take on Paul's approach to children by pointing out that Paul addresses children directly. This is at a time when there were no other philosophers or writers providing family advice who even remotely took this position. Clearly, Paul is addressing these children in the church at Ephesus on the basis that they are valuable members of the church in their own right. They are not adults in waiting. They are full members and have a special role and a special need for encouragement.

By using the terms "in the Lord" and "of the Lord" in this passage the relationship with parents is placed on a different level. It is no longer just biological but also spiritual. So, then it helps us to appreciate this new and unique relationship as Paul places some new perspectives on both children and parents.

Paul's very short admonition for children to obey their parents in the Lord might easily be seen as an ultimatum to children, coupled with a veiled threat about living a long life. However, it is important that we immediately see this, with the understanding that everything comes with a sense of deep appreciation and knowledge of who we are IN CHRIST, even as children, and also understanding that this is the position we are approaching everything in this second part of the book, of living our life through Christ.

Perhaps, before we go any further, it is important to go back to some scriptural basics so we can fully appreciate the significance of this parent-child relationship.

> ³ *Behold, children are a heritage from the Lord, The fruit of the womb is a reward,*
>
> **Psalm 127:3**

So we must receive the truth that children have intrinsic value in themselves and they are a blessing because they are His gift. Yet, in the Hebrew the word "heritage" also means "assignment". We know from assignments at school or in any

152

other walk of life that these are treated like a project. We have to plan for it, gather supplies, put it all together and present it. In the same way children are an assignment that the Lord brings.

Another definition of assignments is a legal transfer. I find that thought very compelling. In the very act of being blessed with children God is legally transferring the responsibility for their upbringing to their parents. It seems to me that, in Ephesians 6:1-4, Paul is reflecting exactly that thought.

With that He wants parents to train, invest in and shape them for the future because they are an inheritance of the Lord. He has placed them in your hands and entrusted you to manage them for Him until He returns for them. You have stewardship of them. That is a reward but also a challenge. God wants you to raise them in love, so their cooperation is an easy and automatic choice, not something forced on them.

In Genesis 1:28 man is told to be fruitful and multiply. Now that does not mean that you have the sole responsibility of populating the planet, but you do have the right to have children. He wants to give you joy and a sense of accomplishment in the very fact that you have children of your own. That is important. Also, He believes you will faithfully love them and care for them properly. God has an awesome plan for their lives which is surrounded by and predicated on having an intimate relationship with God.

There is something very significant in developing a relationship with your children because it will often parallel God's relationship with you, and His involvement in your own life comes into sharper definition. Additionally, children have a way of improving your character as they make you look at the world differently. They will bring out patience, love and self control, or lack of it. This, in turn, forces you to make the necessary changes in your own life if you are wise.

In Genesis 17 God promised Abraham that he would establish covenant with him and extended that to future generations. God's heart is to be in covenant with all of us as that future generation. He did not just expect us to get saved and then just leave it up to His children to muddle through and decide what to do. In the same way, God has given us a responsibility to train children and direct them to the path that leads to the promised land – the will of God for their lives. What is more He desires to be intimately involved in that delicate process.

Your goal is to raise supernatural children who know, love and serve God. You may look at your child and say "I need help I can't even get them to wash the dishes without a fight" that's okay it's not too late.

Returning, therefore, to the passage in Ephesians, the instruction is for children to obey their parents in the Lord. Children in this context are IN CHRIST. In that place God tells children to obey because this is right. God commands that position because it is right. They and their parents belong together to the Lord Jesus and grow together in that relationship.

Parents, especially fathers, which is a timely thought in this day where there are so many absent fathers, are then similarly admonished by the Lord to carry the responsibility for not provoking children, and bringing them up in the training, other versions say "nurture" and "admonition," of the Lord. That is they should set aside their own ambitions for their children and train them to be what the Lord wants them to be. In chapter 8, I alluded to the fact that children will copy parents' behaviour be it good or bad. In the interest of helping children to be their own person, therefore, whilst still being in a position to obey, a timely discussion on how the Lord sees godly correction would help in this respect.

Giving Correction

[11] My son, do not despise the chastening of the LORD, nor detest His correction; [12] For whom the LORD loves He corrects, just as a father the son in whom he delights.

Proverbs 3:11-12

True correction is an act of love. Your timely correction now will benefit your child later. Mind you, when your child is experiencing that correction they may not see it that way at the time. It is important, therefore, that correction comes with an explanation or it can just be seen as punishment. There is a big difference between the two!

I am sure most parents can look back and say "I just wish I had done that different or handled that better".

Correction is rooted in love, affection and concern. It is designed to restore honour and focus. It says "I am going to show you the right way because I am concerned about you". That, in itself, demonstrates the importance of knowing the right way before God ourselves. If we do not it is difficult to be able to demonstrate the right way to our children.

Punishment is an action that is undertaken for revenge and to satisfy the need to control. It says "I'm gonna get you boy because it makes me feel better".

Giving correction does not give anyone a right to beat their kids. Bruises are not a sign of discipline, but abuse. Discipline should leave a mark on a child's conscience and not on their body. Remember Ephesians 6:4, at the start of this section, where it says "And you fathers, do not provoke your children to wrath".

Verse 4 seen through the lens of different Bible versions will give us additional insight:

> [4] *Fathers don't exasperate your children by coming down hard on them. Take them by the hand and lead them in the way of the Master.*
>
> **Ephesians 6:4** (MSG)

> [4] *Fathers do not irritate and provoke your children to anger but rear them tenderly in the training and discipline and the counsel and admonition of the Lord.*
>
> **Ephesians 6:4** (AMPCE)

We are, today, preparing our children for the future and that is important. Most times children just see correction for today, what is happening in the next minute. But you are training them for adulthood There is nothing worse than a person who was not properly prepared as a child to function in this fast-paced society we live in.

So let's consider some things we need to take responsibility for if we are to present our children to God as a blessing and reward for Him.

Teaching and Training

> [18] *Here am I and the children whom the* LORD *has given me. We are for signs and wonders in Israel from the Lord of Hosts, Who dwells in Mount Zion.*
>
> **Isaiah 8:18**

Despite the hassle you experience when getting children to brush teeth, bathe, keep their clothes clean or eat their vegetables don't forget that, in the process, God desires to use them as signs and wonders in the earth today. On that basis you have to assume responsibility to train and prepare them to be just that. They don't have to wait until they are older they can start right now.

That requires training. Training can never be assumed. I once heard this phrase "Just because you live in a garage doesn't make you a Rolls Royce".

> [6] *'And these words which I command you today shall be in your heart.* [7] *"You shall teach them diligently to your children, and shall talk of them when you sit in your house, when you lie down, and when you rise up.*
>
> **Deuteronomy 6:6-7**

In other words, you be the example to them. Proverbs 22:6 states that we are to "*train up a child in the way he should go and when he is old he will not depart from it.*"

I find that pertinent in the way God Himself trains us in our Christian walk. In this context, train means to mould character, to instruct by exercise, and to drill.

I guess some of the oldies among us will immediately remember how Captain Von Trap, in the film *The Sound of Music*, used a whistle as he drilled his children. Well, it's not quite like that but it will mean a certain amount of discipline This brings us to taking on board the difference between training and teaching. For example, you can teach the importance of personal hygiene by explaining about it. However, who knows just teaching and expecting someone to get it and do it is a different thing? It is clear so many children, and, therefore families, these days, appear to lack training. That is the discipline of reinforcing the teaching.

Good old fashioned training is important. For example, showing manners to those in authority, developing good hygiene and showing proper table manners to name just a few.

All these things should be taught and followed by training in the home and not learned on the street. If parents do not do that then they will get into trouble.

A good example of this can be found in 1 Samuel 3:12-14 where God speaks to Samuel concerning Eli because Eli had not disciplined his sons (described in 1 Samuel 2:12-25). Basically God said He would intervene in that situation because Eli knew what was going on and did nothing about it. That is a key observation. If you do nothing to stop something wrong when you know it to be so, it has an effect on the whole household. You can see that from the story lines of some of our well known "soaps". If you turn a blind eye it is as if you yourself open up that negative door. God holds you responsible as a parent.

Nurture and admonition

Ephesians 6:4 also encourages parents to bring children up in the nurture and admonition of the Lord. This in itself places focus on God and we are wise to develop our plans for raising children on that basis. I want to discuss three types of parenting in this regard. Only one of them involves trusting God.

a) Isolation

If you, as a parent, are fearful of what goes on in society you might try to isolate your children from contact with others aside from school and church. You may not allow them to play in the neighbourhood "just in case". So the children get stifled and become dysfunctional due to the parents fears.

We are all aware of the problems out there today so it is not surprising if you as a parent feel some of those things. Nevertheless, don't look to isolate them. Instead use the situation from outside and the negative influences to teach them the best way from the Word of God. In that way you are quietly weaving the truth and the best way into their thinking.

As a result children will then be equipped to make correct decisions by what you have instilled in them.

b) Passivity

Some parents give up hope of influencing children amid what goes on in society and so they cave in under pressure and allow their children to be influenced by others. These parents neither plan purposeful training, nor plan for their children's future. These are the bunch that says great-sounding things like

"I'm going to allow them to decide what they want to do" or "I don't want to interfere with their lives".

The problem with this is that children then suffer because of poor choices they make, influenced by other children who are also making poor choices. So you can't give up or cave in just because it's easier to quit. As a parent you must point them in the right direction.

3) Nurturing

Parents who determine to train or nurture their children God's way don't allow the cares of the world to govern their lives. Remember Mark 4 and the sowing of seed and how some seed do well until the cares of the world come and then choke them so that, like seed sown on thorny ground, they fall away.

Parents who take active responsibility for their children don't isolate them but instead select the other children they allow their kids to associate with so they grow up with similar values. In that way they help them make the right decisions in life.

Honouring Parents

In Ephesians 6:2-3 Paul makes a direct quote from the Ten Commandments of Exodus 20:12 concerning honouring fathers and mothers. It carries with it a promise of being well and living long on the earth. It follows a command from Paul for children to obey parents in the Lord.

My wife, Julie, and I have first hand experience of this as our parents have grown older, as I am sure many of you reading this will have found out also. Sometimes, honouring is not convenient, especially when parents live a distance away, or are in care homes with dementia. However, there is a blessing in honouring them that goes beyond the physical looking after them. God is clearly watching our heart and our attitude, especially when following this principle can stretch us if it interferes with our own lives. Our experience is that blessing flows from the Lord and cannot be understood in any other way. I am certain that much of our success, or failure, in this area comes out of the way in which we have been brought up.

We have to look very carefully at these verses because this could easily be misconstrued. At first sight we could see that it means all children should obey whatever a parent says or asks for. But that cannot be right. Some children are brought up in non-Christian families where parents may be encouraging a child to do all kinds of things that are not right. What we see here is not a blanket admonition for children to obey parents. If your parents had told you to run under a bus and you had obeyed you would not be here today.

In fact there is a little clause in that verse which sets everything straight. It says "In the Lord" Provided your parents are doing things "in the Lord" then its right to obey. If they are teaching you to steal then that is not "in the Lord", so don't obey. Personal rules of the house may not be laid down in scripture but as long as they don't violate the word they should be followed. For example, where is the scripture that says "thou shalt brush your teeth"? It ain't there but it still is a good rule to be obeyed. You can't say "well the Bible doesn't tell me to do it so I wont". That probably would be disobedience and it would create some spiritual problems as well as causing your teeth to decay. Nevertheless, if you are a Christian in a non-Christian household there is still a requirement to honour even if you are choosing not to obey because it would violate your relationship with the Lord.

You can honour but not obey. Or, you can obey but hate the relationship and be in so much fear you only obey because of what the consequences may be. So, obedience and honour relates to how Christ treats the church.

Then, if you are in a home where parents are not Christians they may put pressure on you to obey things that are not right.
In cases like that where it is not right to obey you can still honour your parents. Romans 13:7 says "Give honour to whom honour is due". In the context of Paul's letter it is unlikely that any children would be a part of a non-Christian home but the principle applies.

It is the same way you should give honour to those in government even if you totally disagree with their politics. The Bible tells us to do so and so we should.

Prayer

Father God, I thank You that my family is established on Your promises.

Thank you that my children are godly, holy and submitted to Your will for their lives.

I thank You that they love Your word and make it their final authority.

I declare their names are written in the Lamb's book of life and that angels are encamped about them every minute of the day.

Today, I choose to build my own house on Your word by treating my children as an inheritance and a blessing from You. I will do my part to train and teach them, as you would have me do. In Jesus name,

Amen.

Chapter 12

Take a Stand.

¹⁰ Finally, my brethren, be strong in the Lord and in the power of His might. ¹¹ Put on the whole armour of God, that you may be able to stand against the wiles of the devil.
Ephesians 6:10-11

In Ephesians 6:10, Paul reaches the point where he is begins the conclusion of his letter by writing "Finally". Perhaps we must, therefore, at this point, make a summary of what we have so far covered. We have searched the scriptures and seen our security, our position, our place and our inheritance IN CHRIST. We have then considered what our response should be to that deep understanding within. We have grappled with the kind of life this encourages us to lead. Then we have understood the powerful truths that these convey.

With the word "Finally", Paul introduces two key elements to the Ephesian church (and, in turn, to us) for us to keep hold of in the midst of everything else that may assault us as we aim to follow the principles we have learned:

- Be Strong.
- Take a stand.

Primarily these key elements are aimed at dealing with the devil but they can equally apply to any and every area of our Christian life. Your potential, your destiny, your decisions in life to fulfil the purposes of God in your generation are all reflected in these two statements. So lets consider them carefully.

First, it is a reminder to us of Ephesians 3:16 where Paul is asking God that we be strengthened with might. Here, he assumes that we have followed that and can, therefore, be strong. But that strength is in the Lord, not in anything else. When we are dealing with the devil and the issues of life, every other area may let us down. So, we must, in the midst of everything place our strength and trust in the Lord Himself. Nothing else will bring victory. We may feel weak but He is our strength.

It may be that Paul was reflecting on his own life experience in this regard, which he recalls in 2 Corinthians 12:7-10. Paul was constantly besieged with a messenger from satan, someone trying to stop him at every turn from fulfilling his destiny. He called this "a thorn in the flesh". What you or I today might refer to as a "pain in the neck", not some kind of sickness. Paul clearly struggled with it for a long time and even asked God to deal with it. The Lord's reply was:

> [9] "My grace is sufficient for you, for My strength is made perfect in weakness."
>
> **2 Corinthians 12:9**

We cannot underestimate the power of God's grace operating in us. As we rely heavily on His grace, when it seems like nothing else is working, we will find that His strength will begin to work in us and success will come. After this encounter we do not hear Paul talk any further about it, so we can only assume he began to obey the Lord's words himself and victory came.

He then encourages us to stand wearing the whole armour of God

> *11 Put on the whole armour of God, that you may be able to stand against the wiles of the devil.*
>
> **Ephesians 6:11**

The ESV says "*against the schemes of the devil.*"
The NLT says "*against all strategies and tricks of the devil.*"

It is important that we put on the "whole armour" of God, not just a few parts of it. Paul takes this phrase from the Greek word *panoplia* that refers to the complete equipment of a fully armed soldier and it fits in well with the Roman weaponry of the day, equipment that the Ephesians would have been familiar with.

In that regard Paul is highlighting that, since defeated by Christ on the cross, the devil only has schemings and tricks to deceive us and he has some clever strategies in that regard so always wearing our armour is a vital defence against him. Just because he is always scheming does not mean he will succeed. Yes, we have to take him into account, but we do not live our lives like he is hindering all our steps. He does not have the power to do that. We must let that sink in. Paul also reminds us strongly in verse 12 that our enemy is not flesh and blood, even though he may use people against us, ultimately they are not the source of our challenges in life. He makes it clear that the offensive against us lies, well and truly, in the various ranks of the fallen demonic world.

¹² For we do not wrestle against flesh and blood, but against principalities, against powers, against the rulers of the darkness of this age, against spiritual hosts of wickedness in the heavenly places.

Ephesians 6:12

The answer to all of this is the whole armour of God that enables us to stand, and having done all to stand. I am sure in this respect Paul is reminding us of everything we have learnt to enable us to be IN CHRIST.

Firstly, it is useful to remind ourselves that ultimately every knee will bow to Jesus (Phil.2:9-11), including the demonic realm. Then we recall Ephesians 2:6 that, in reality, in the Spirit, we are sat with Christ in heavenly places. We are IN CHRIST, therefore all of these demonic influences are under our feet, as they are under His feet, provided we constantly wear the armour. The devil is the ruler of darkness but we are to walk in the light. When we received Jesus we moved from darkness into light. As long as we determine to stay in the light we will not be ruled by these demons. Determining to live our life in that way is everything we have considered in this letter.

³⁸ For I am persuaded that neither death nor life, nor angels nor principalities nor powers, nor things present nor things to come, ³⁹ nor height nor depth, nor any other created thing, shall be able to separate us from the love of God which is in Christ Jesus our Lord.

Romans 8:38-39

Let's then consider what it means to "wrestle" in this context.

Ultimately, it means to actively engage in one-on-one combat. It implies close-up, hand to hand fighting, grappling or struggling with one's opponent, trying to immobilise them, pitting your strength against theirs, looking for opponent's weaknesses.

In short this whole passage is instructing us how to engage in combat with the real enemy. It is a reminder that there are circumstances when we must recognise, and engage in such spiritual warfare. We cannot afford to ignore it. It implies a contest and a struggle. However, that struggle comes from a place of victory IN CHRIST. At the end of the day, it is not a fair fight because the devil is no match for Christ or us when we are firmly placed in Him. The wrestling is not in the physical. It is spiritual warfare so we have to apply spiritual principles in the battle. How many of us would like to fight in a physical battle that, if you use the right equipment and do the right things, you will always win? I am sure that we would all like that and indeed Paul is showing us, here in Ephesians 6:14-18, what our spiritual equipment is and how to use it. So we are not ignorant of what is at our disposal.

Each piece of our spiritual equipment is linked to a physical piece of armour as an easy way of remembering it but let's not get bogged down and make heavy work of each piece of equipment. Keep it simple by considering it this way:

Know the gospel, know the truth, know you are saved and righteous. Use your faith with the word of God. In this you have everything to do battle.

Take a stand

The reason that this forms our chapter title is because Paul, clearly, considers that taking a stand is the primary key for us. The word is mentioned in one form, or another, four times. Let's consider again this whole passage.

> *[11] Put on the whole armour of God, that you may be able to stand against the wiles of the devil.[12] For we do not wrestle against flesh and blood, but against principalities, against powers, against the rulers of the darkness of this age, against spiritual hosts of wickedness in the heavenly places. [13] Therefore take up the whole armour of God that you may be able to withstand in the evil day, and having done all to stand. [14] Stand therefore, having girded your waist with truth, having put on the breastplate of righteousness*
>
> **Ephesians 6:11-14**

The word "stand" appears four separate times in this passage. Each time there are different Greek words. So we are provided with a progressive sense of the fulness of what we are to do in standing.

- In verse 11, "*that we may be able to stand against*". This is the Greek word *stenai* meaning to hold at bay aggressively or to stand in front of and oppose.
- In verse 13, "*that we may be able to withstand*" This means to resist or be found standing after an active battle. It derives from the Greek word *antihistemi*, with which we are familiar as a form of medication today (all the words for stand in verses 13 and 14 are derived from this same root). It carries the sense of standing our ground and withstanding the enemy.

- In verse 13, "*having done all to stand*", once again uses the word *stenai* with a sense of giving everything to the cause.
- In verse 14 "*Stand therefore*" is from the Greek word *stete* which means to take your stand in preparation for the next assault or battle.

In short Paul is demanding that we take a stand from the fact he repeats it so many times. Clearly he does not envisage us giving up or withdrawing once we are wearing our armour.

When you have done all that, our armour is in good use. Also, it is vital to note from these definitions, that standing is an active word. It is not passive but something that we enforce consistently. It means to stand like flint with no backing down. It reminds me of the action Jesus took in Luke 9:51 when He knew it was time to face the cross. So He set his face resolutely for Jerusalem. No devil in hell was going to stop Him going to the cross for you and I in order to bring us salvation. The thing is, the devil did not know what He was really going to do. 1 Corinthians 2:8 says "*had they known they would not have crucified the Lord of Glory*"

This brings us to the important thought. "how long do you stand?"

The answer is until victory comes. Remember, in that regard you are not standing passively and doing nothing. Verse 18 proclaims that you are to "pray always with all prayer and supplication in the Spirit" which is an active part of standing. It implies a consistency. In other words asking God for answers. It is in the Spirit, not a flesh thing and it requires perseverance.

Perseverance is an area we often lack as people and especially as a church, corporately. We do not see, as we

171

should, the importance of a prayer meeting or the spiritual power that emanates from it. It is a key to progress and success for us. Be glad and rejoice when someone tells you they are praying for you. Rejoice because you are not on your own.

The result is hinted at by Paul at the end of that passage. It is a bold proclamation of the gospel. It demonstrates you are an ambassador for God. i.e., a representative of a ruling authority. Spiritually mature men and women. That's who you are. Take your stand and pray, knowing who you are IN CHRIST. You will prevail. Do not be caught out. Do not be unaware of what is going on in the spiritual realm in which you live. Do not shrink back for a moment. Take your stand and pray constantly and victory is yours in life.

Chapter 13

Receiving this Letter Today

At this stage, if you have followed everything so far, I would first recommend reading through the whole of the Ephesians letter again, just to cement it firmly on the inside of you. Then, I think, it is important to consider and be fully persuaded that you are, indeed, IN CHRIST, because there is no comparison with having that sense deep within your spirit.

Once you have done that it is important to remember being IN CHRIST and living life through Christ are contemporaneous. In other words, they constantly work together. Neither take precedence. Living a life through Christ is not always an easy road to take. We come up against many pressures and circumstances in life that can be difficult to face. So, it is important to remember that we do not face that alone in our personal journey. Times of adversity will always reveal what is already inside us. That revelation will either take us through to victory or will create worse situations for us as we muddle through on our own. It is for this reason that I consider this book to be so important. It provides an anchor of truth for us which we should be able to automatically fall back on when in times of trouble. In fact, the more we make it part of who we are, the more we will reflect, looking back, how much it has underpinned our decisions, even though we may not have been aware of it at the time.

We are sons and daughters of the most high God and we must never forget that in times of difficulty. He is always someone we can go to and rely on to see us through.

Perhaps it may help if I give a somewhat personal testimony of my experience, while writing the original notes and preaching the messages, that form the basis of this book. Looking back I realise that I put all this together in a period during which my wife and I, would describe as our *annus horribilis*, to quote our late British Queen from 1992.

During 2007 we were sensing a change was coming. The gracing on us for pastoring the church in Bath under our care was lifting and we did not know what to do. I felt I was in a wilderness time and it was not fun. Then in May and October respectively we both had a parent die from cancer, unexpectedly.

During that time, I remember going to a conference in Switzerland, organised by my ministry organisation. One of the speakers preached a message along the lines that we needed to realise we are all in a different season in our journey. In the middle of it I still remember shouting out:

"Okay, well I am in a winter season. What does spring look like?"

Fortunately a number of fellow ministers helped me and prayed through with me. I recount that so you can see the depth of what I was going through. I did not know what to do. As I had heard from the Lord to start the church ten years before, I felt that somehow I had to keep going and it was just the devil getting to me.

I have since realised that the Lord was leading me into a new season and all I needed to do was trust Him, because He was already there. A number of, seemingly disparate, events helped me to see what the Lord was doing. Foremost among them was doing all the research for the several messages I gave on the letter to the Ephesians which form the basis of this book. In doing so, I realised once again, even though I already knew it, that I was indeed, IN CHRIST. So, no matter what happened I was secure in Him. It was a safe place to be regardless of what was going on. I honestly had not thought about the significance of that before. But now I can see how relevant it was and how God always leads you to read and study the word of God you need at any given point. That in itself is life changing.

Additionally, completely unrelated, I read a book called *The Oz Principle* by Roger Conners, Tom Smith and Craig Hickman, published by Portfolio, a member of Penguin group USA. The book used the OZ Principle, The Wizard of OZ, that is (not the slang term for Australia). I though it was all about getting results through better organisational skills, so I needed it to sort things out to take the church forward. However, reading it and reporting back to my Trustees that I had seen the answer was not to be found by some strategic goal, like the wizard, but actually on the yellow brick road itself. I was taken aback when my Trustees all suggested that this was not about the church but me personally. It gave me much to think about for my future and was so much in line with what I was studying in Ephesians.

I then recall that later in the year I attended a men's meeting called "Excel" at Abundant Life Church in Bradford, as it was then called. During worship we sang a new song I had not heard before called "Send Me". It carried lines of "I will go for you, send me" and others similar. In the midst of it tears began to flow from my eyes and I knew I was singing it from the heart but at that time I did not know the significance.

Perhaps it was all God needed to propel me into the next season as He saw my heart and my steadfastness IN CHRIST. Later, in November I received an unexpected invitation to go to Nigeria and preach at a conference for someone I had met earlier in July when I spoke for the first time for Sesan Emmanuel Aina and his church in Slough, Living Word International. We are firm friends now but how that came about is another story. We decided that I should go, even though it was at an inconvenient time in December. I flew to Lagos and found myself speaking to, what was and still is, the largest congregation I have ever had the privilege of addressing in the course of my ministry.

During that time I was assigned a small team to drive me around and experience life in Nigeria. There was a great deal of congestion in Lagos. Cars were either at a standstill or travelling at about ninety miles an hour, or so it seemed to me. It could have been scary. But I remember, on one occasion, after I had been taken to an old slave trading station, which had a massive impact on me, just relaxing in the back of the car and feeling at peace, despite my circumstances and surroundings.

In the middle of all that I sensed the presence of the Holy Spirit all over me and tears flowed as before. I just knew that God was showing me that His favour was on what I was doing and this was where He was leading me. I went home and Julie and I decided to take a step and close the church we had started and for me to change my course and become an itinerant minister. We did this at the start of 2008 even though I had no place to speak. I now recall how good the Lord was as

I took that step, because, seemingly completely out of the blue, I was invited to go to Pakistan and preach with Dr Will Pantin for Great Joy in the City Ministries. In February I headed out there and have been another three times since and recently spoken on two subjects for their Chosen Academy Bible School, on line.

This has followed with subsequent overseas ministry trips to Russia, Kenya, Ghana, Zimbabwe and the USA, in addition to our constant trips to Romania, in support of pastor Ovi Starlici.

In the dark times of the previous year, I had never imagined how God would be using me. Nevertheless, I now realise that in those dark times I was still living in the security, inheritance, position, and power and strength of being IN CHRIST. Everything I have done, both before and since, is in the deep understanding that I am living my life through Christ, and there is no better way to live.

My heartfelt desire is that you experience the same.

Bibliography

Connors, R., Smith T., Hickman C. (1994), *The Oz Principle: Getting Results Through Individual and Organisational Accountability.* Hoboken, New Jersey, USA: Prentice Hall.

Kenyon, E.W. (2020), *The Blood Covenant: The Hidden Truth Revealed at the Lord's Table.* New Kensington, Pennsylvania, USA: Whitaker House.

Motyer, S. (1994), *Ephesians: Crossway Bible Guide – Free to be One.* Reading, Berkshire, UK: Crossway Books.

Renner, R. (2017), *A Light in Darkness Volume 1: Seven Messages To The Seven Churches.* Tulsa, Oklahoma, USA: Harrison House.

Vine, W. E. (1940), *An Expository Dictionary of New Testament Words.* Edinburgh, UK: Thomas Nelson, (also available online).

About the Author

Tony Sheard is an accomplished and passionate speaker with a heart to bring fresh purpose and direction in the Christian world today and, especially, to help build the local church and transform lives to be all that God has for them.

Tony was born in Yorkshire and, with his wife Julie, currently lives just outside Bath in the UK.

Having spent a number of years as a speaker in various churches throughout Europe and the USA, Tony and Julie became the first European Directors of Jesse Duplantis Ministries, steering the office successfully through 5 years of pioneer growth.

During this time they received a call from God to Pastor and formed Living Word Christian Centre, which they led together for 10 years. Tony longs to see people fulfil the destiny and purpose on their lives. He is determined to see the Holy Spirit move powerfully as signs follow the preaching of the Word.

On the prompting of the Lord, he stepped out of Pastoring and formed Living Word UK as an outreach of LWCC in order to carry this message to the world. That is, together with a compassion to support those who need help, which is a vital part of the ministry. Tony has a heart to come alongside churches and work with them as they fulfil the vision of God in their communities.

Tony is chair of Trustees of Kenneth Copeland Ministries Europe, council member of Churches in Community International and has developed coaching skills working one on one with ministers. He regularly supports pastors with strategic planning and helps ministry training.

Other books by Tony Sheard

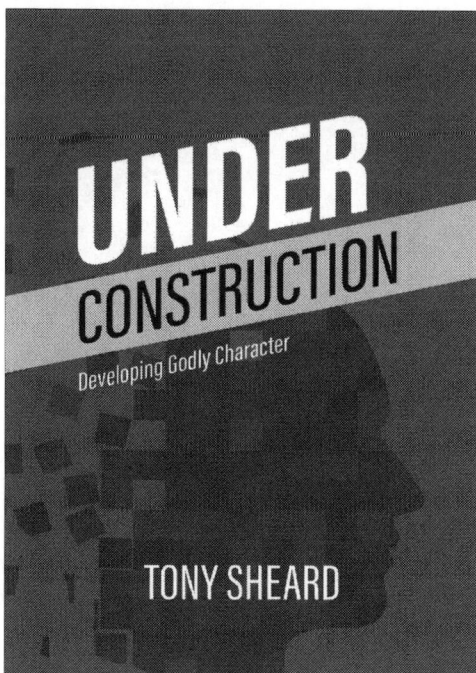

Available to order online, in paperback, from Amazon...

www.amazon.co.uk/dp/B08JVKGSG5/Under-Construction

Available to order online, for Kindle, from Amazon...

www.amazon.co.uk/dp/B08JZCPK6Q/Under-Construction

Printed in Great Britain
by Amazon

16275934R00108

Preface

This book covers the use of vSphere Replication and VMware Site Recovery Manager to make your vSphere environment recoverable in the event of a disaster. All the concepts and tasks covered in this book are for vSphere Replication 6.1 and VMware vCenter Site Recovery Manager 6.1.

What this book covers

Chapter 1, Installing and Configuring vCenter Site Recovery Manager (SRM) 6.1, introduces you to the architecture of SRM and also guides you through the process of installing and configuring SRM to leverage array-based replication.

Chapter 2, Creating Protection Groups and Recovery Plans, teaches you how to configure protection for virtual machines by creating Protection Groups and creating an orchestrated runbook with the help of Recovery Plans.

Chapter 3, Testing and Performing a Failover and Failback, teaches you how to test the recovery plans that were created and also perform a Planned Migration, a Failover, and a Failback using them.

Chapter 4, Deploying vSphere Replication, guides you through the steps required to deploy vSphere Replication Appliances and vSphere Replication Servers.

Chapter 5, Configuring and Using vSphere Replication 6.1, teaches you how to add target sites and enable replication on virtual machines and recover them. It also teaches you how to configure vCenter SRM to leverage the vSphere Replication engine.

Chapter 6, Using vRealize Orchestrator (vRO) to Automate SRM and vSphere Replication, guides you through the process of deploying and configuring vRealize Orchestrator. It also teaches you how to install vRO plugins for SRM and vSphere Replication and has instructions which will help you to locate SRM and vSphere replication logs and use them for troubleshooting issues.

What you need for this book

If you were to follow along with each chapter by practicing the tasks in a lab, then you would need two ESXi hosts, two vCenter Servers, two SRM instances, and two storage array nodes with replication configured between them. This might sound like a lot of hardware, but all you need is a VMware Workstation or VMware Fusion and a Virtual Storage Appliance such as HP Store Virtual (LeftHand networks). You could get a trial license for HP Store Virtual by registering for one at HP's website. For the suggested lab architecture the ESXi hosts, vCenter Servers, vSphere Replication Appliances, SRM Servers, and the storage nodes will be virtual machines that are hosted using the VMware Workstation/Fusion.

Who this book is for

This book is a guide for anyone who is keen on using vSphere Replication or vCenter Site Recovery Manager as a disaster recovery solution. This is an excellent handbook for solution architects, administrators, on-field engineers, and support professionals. Although the book assumes that the reader has some basic knowledge of data center virtualization using VMware vSphere, it can still be a very good reference for anyone who is new to virtualization.

Conventions

In this book, you will find a number of text styles that distinguish between different kinds of information. Here are some examples of these styles and an explanation of their meaning.

Code words in text, database table names, folder names, filenames, file extensions, pathnames, dummy URLs, user input, and Twitter handles are shown as follows: "Every virtual machine will have a swap file (.vswp)".

Any command-line input or output is written as follows:

```
c:\windows\system32\cmd.exe /c d:\demoscript.bat
```

New terms and **important words** are shown in bold. Words that you see on the screen, for example, in menus or dialog boxes, appear in the text like this: "The **Ready to complete** screen will summarize the settings; review them and click on **Finish** to initiate the test."

> Warnings or important notes appear in a box like this.

> Tips and tricks appear like this.

Reader feedback

Feedback from our readers is always welcome. Let us know what you think about this book—what you liked or disliked. Reader feedback is important for us as it helps us develop titles that you will really get the most out of.

To send us general feedback, simply e-mail feedback@packtpub.com, and mention the book's title in the subject of your message.

If there is a topic that you have expertise in and you are interested in either writing or contributing to a book, see our author guide at www.packtpub.com/authors.

Customer support

Now that you are the proud owner of a Packt book, we have a number of things to help you to get the most from your purchase.

Downloading the color images of this book

We also provide you with a PDF file that has color images of the screenshots/diagrams used in this book. The color images will help you better understand the changes in the output. You can download this file from http://www.packtpub.com/sites/default/files/downloads/DisasterRecoveryUsingVMwarevSphereReplicationandvCenterSiteRecoveryManagerSecondEdition_ColorImages.pdf.

Errata

Although we have taken every care to ensure the accuracy of our content, mistakes do happen. If you find a mistake in one of our books — maybe a mistake in the text or the code — we would be grateful if you could report this to us. By doing so, you can save other readers from frustration and help us improve subsequent versions of this book. If you find any errata, please report them by visiting `http://www.packtpub.com/submit-errata`, selecting your book, clicking on the **Errata Submission Form** link, and entering the details of your errata. Once your errata are verified, your submission will be accepted and the errata will be uploaded to our website or added to any list of existing errata under the Errata section of that title.

To view the previously submitted errata, go to `https://www.packtpub.com/books/content/support` and enter the name of the book in the search field. The required information will appear under the **Errata** section.

Piracy

Piracy of copyrighted material on the Internet is an ongoing problem across all media. At Packt, we take the protection of our copyright and licenses very seriously. If you come across any illegal copies of our works in any form on the Internet, please provide us with the location address or website name immediately so that we can pursue a remedy.

Please contact us at `copyright@packtpub.com` with a link to the suspected pirated material.

We appreciate your help in protecting our authors and our ability to bring you valuable content.

Questions

If you have a problem with any aspect of this book, you can contact us at `questions@packtpub.com`, and we will do our best to address the problem.

1

Installing and Configuring vCenter Site Recovery Manager (SRM) 6.1

In this chapter, we will cover the following topics:

- What is Site Recovery Manager (SRM)?
- Laying the groundwork for an SRM environment
- Host presentation (Zoning) at the protected and recovery sites
- Installing SRM on both the protected and recovery sites
- Pairing SRM sites
- Installing the Storage Replication Adapters
- Adding array managers and enabling array pairs
- Configuring placeholder datastores
- Creating resource, folder, and network mappings
- Virtual machine swap file location

Introduction

With today's IT infrastructures, be it virtual or physical, disaster recovery is of prime importance. Any business should be able to continue operating with reduced downtime for its sustainability among the competition. It also has a legal obligation toward customers to whom it sold its services. Two of the major factors used to market or sell a service are its High Availability and Recoverability.

Recoverability is the guarantee that the service offered and its data are protected against failures, and High Availability is the guarantee that the service offered would remain operational and the failures are handled in a way that the user of the service would not even know that there was a failure.

There are many ways in which businesses plan and implement disaster recovery. Although important, much of these decisions depend on the budgetary constraints. What turns out to be the most important is the existence of a disaster recovery plan. Gone are those days when you had to wait for a long period of time before all your critical applications were made available at a recovery site. With a lot of automation and scripting, businesses now expect better Recovery Point Objective (RPO) and Recovery Time Objective (RTO).

So what exactly are RPO and RTO?

RPO defines the amount of data an organization can afford to lose when measured against time.

RTO defines the amount of downtime the organization can afford for its services before it becomes operational again.

Both RPO and RTO are defined by time. For example, an organization can have an RPO set to 4 hours and RTO set to 1 hour. This means, it can afford to lose up to 4 hours of data, but it can only afford a service downtime up to 1 hour.

RTO only defines the amount of time a service can remain unavailable but doesn't account for the data loss. This is where RPO pitches in. It defines how much data loss can be afforded.

For example, if you were a company hosting an online document format conversion service, then setting a lower RTO value is very important because the customers will prefer access to the service, rather than to the historical data. The RPO value will determine how much historical data you will have to kee

Both RPO and RTO help an organization to determine the type of backup and disaster recovery solution to meet the business requirements.

What is Site Recovery Manager?

vCenter **Site Recovery Manager** (**SRM**) is an orchestration software that is used to automate disaster recovery testing and failover. It can be configured to leverage either vSphere replication or a supported array-based replication. With SRM, you can create protection groups and run recovery plans against them. These recovery plans can then be used to test the **Disaster Recovery** (**DR**) setup, perform a planned failover, or be initiated during a DR. SRM is a not a product that performs an automatic failover, which means there is no intelligence built into SRM that would detect a disaster/outage and cause failover of the **virtual machines** (**VMs**). The DR process should be manually initiated. Hence, it is not a high-availability solution either, but purely a tool that orchestrates a recovery plan.

Site Recovery Manager(SRM) architecture

vCenter SRM is not a tool that works on its own. It needs to communicate with other components in your vSphere environment. I will walk you through all the components involved in an environment protected by SRM.

The following are the components that will be involved in an SRM-protected environment:

Protected Site	Recovery Site
Platform Services Controller (PSC)	Platform Services Controller (PSC)
vCenter	vCenter
SRM Instance	SRM Instance
Array Managers	Array Managers
Storage Replication Adapter (SRA)	Storage Replication Adapter (SRA)

SRM requires both the protected and the recovery sites to be managed by separate instances of vCenter Server. It also requires an **SRM Instance** at both the sites. SRM now uses **PSC** as an intermediary to fetch vCenter information.

The following are the possible multiple topologies:

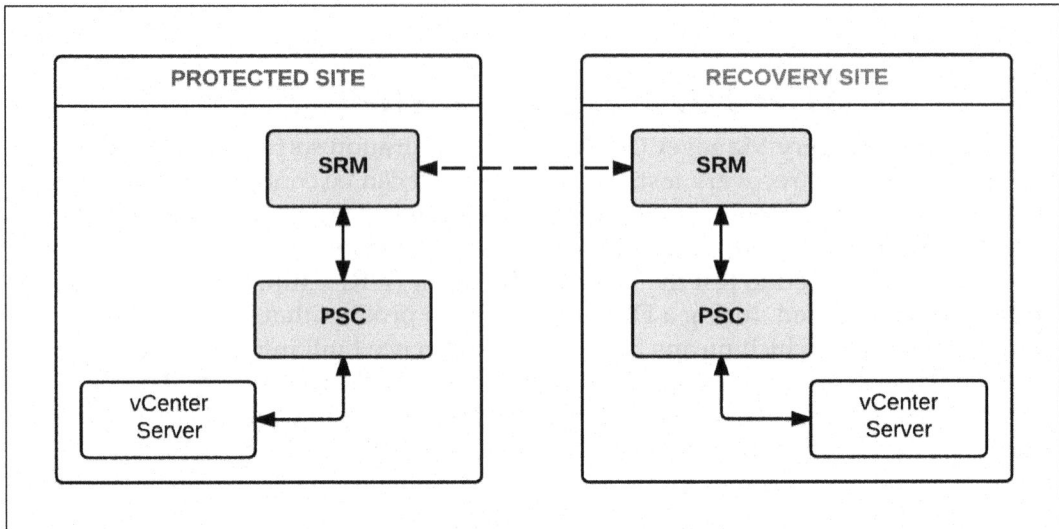

As mentioned previously, SRM cannot work on its own. This is because it is only an orchestration tool and does not include a replication engine. However, it can leverage either a supported array-based replication or VMware's proprietary replication engine, **vSphere Replication**. We have separate chapters covering vSphere Replication.

Array manager

Each SRM instance needs to be configured with an array manager for it to communicate with the storage array. The **array manager** will detect the storage array using the information you supply to connect to the array. Before adding add an array manager, you will need to install an array specific **Storage Replication Adapter (SRA)**. This is because the **array manager** uses the installed SRA to collect the replication information from the array:

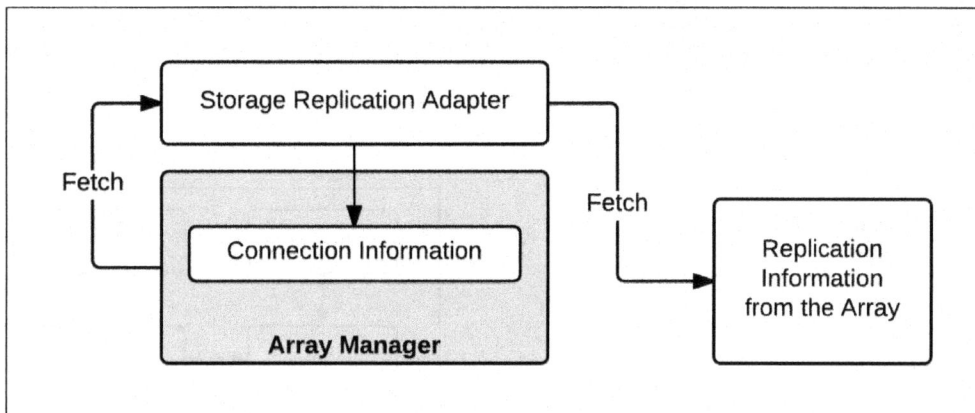

Storage Replication Adapter (SRA)

The SRA is a storage vendor provided component that makes SRM aware of the array's replication configuration at the array. SRM leverages the SRA's ability to gather information regarding the replicated volumes and direction of the replication from the array.

SRM also uses the SRA for the following functions:

- **Test Failover**
- **Recovery**
- **Reprotect**

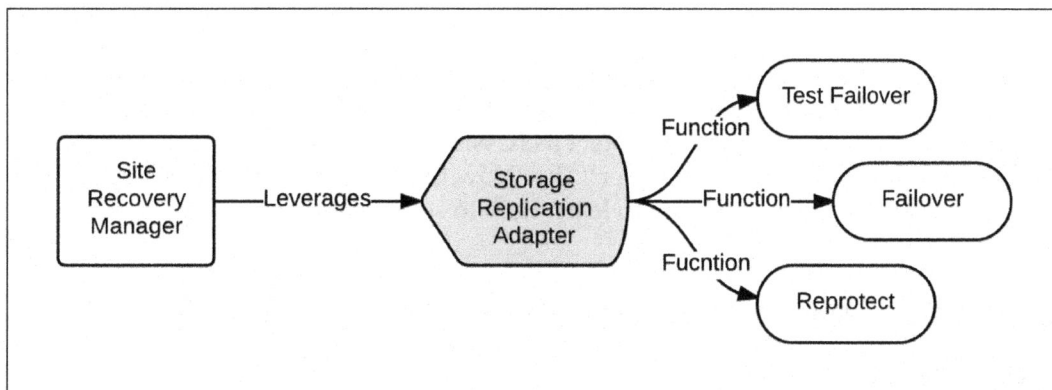

We will learn more about these functions in the next chapter. For now, it is important to understand that SRM requires an SRA to be installed for all of its functions leveraging array-based replication.

When all these components are put together, a site protected by SRM would look as depicted in the following figure:

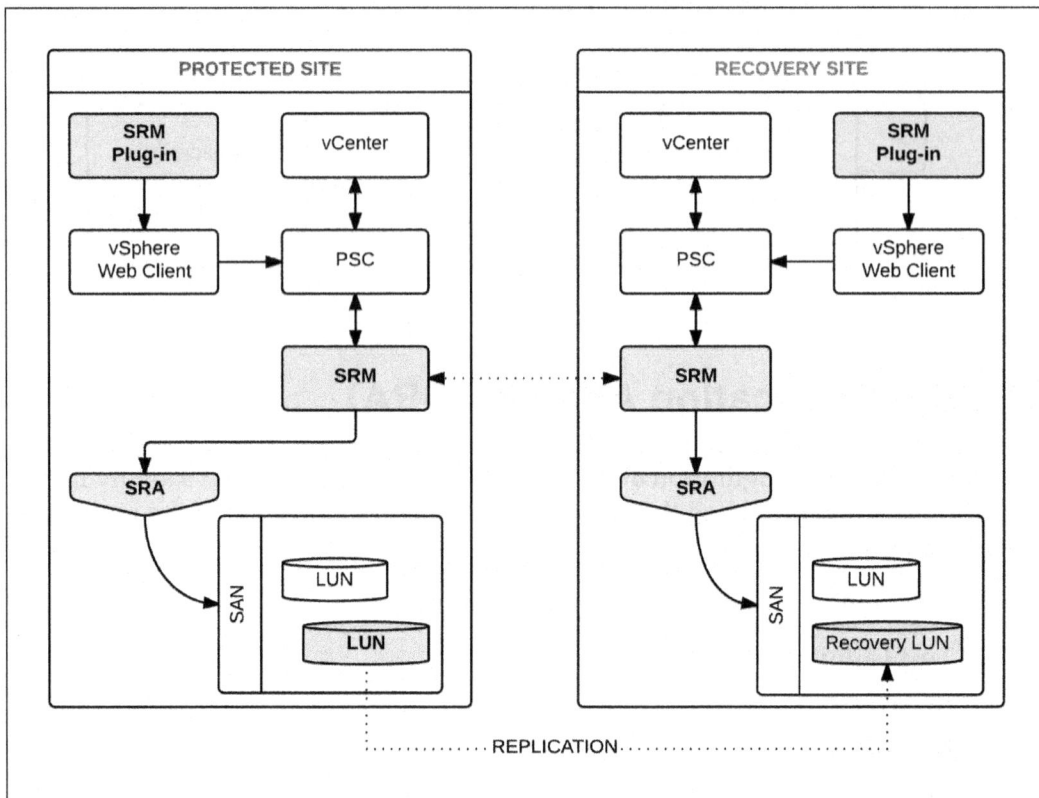

SRM conceptually assumes that both the protected and the recovery sites are separate, regardless of their geographical location. But such a separation is not mandatory. You can use SRM to protect a chassis of servers and have another chassis in the same data center as the recovery site. Now that we have a brief understanding of the SRM architecture, it is time to learn how to setup these components.

Laying the groundwork for an SRM environment

You will need to perform a set of configuration activities to lay the groundwork for an SRM environment so that it can be used to test or execute the recovery plans.

Here is an outline of the tasks that need to be done to form an SRM environment:

- Preparing the storage for array-based replication
- Host presentation (zoning) at the protected and recovery sites
- Installing SRM on both the protected and recovery sites
- Pairing the SRM instances
- Installing the SRA
- Adding the array managers
- Enabling the array pairs
- Creating resource, folder, and network mappings
- Creating placeholder datastores

Preparing storage for array-based replication

The first thing that you will need to do is to make sure that your array is supported by VMware and licensed for array replication by the array vendor. Array Replication is a licensed feature from the storage vendor.

Now, to enable replication, you have a couple of approaches that you can employ:

Approach-1	• Identify the VMs that you want to protect
	• Identify the VMFS datastores the VMs have their files on
	• Identify the LUNs corresponding to the already identified datastores
	• Enable replication on the identified LUNs
Approach-2	• Identify the VMs that you want to protect
	• Plan the sizing of a datastore large enough to hold all the identified VMs
	• Create a LUN large enough to host the datastore
	• Present the new LUN to the hosts running the identified VM and create a new VMFS volume (datastore) on it
	• Migrate the VMs that you want to protect onto the new datastore
	• Enable replication on the new LUN that corresponds to the new datastore

- **Approach-1**: This is used in scenarios where the array does not have the spare capacity to provision a separate LUN for host-protected VMs. This approach adds an administrative overhead if the VMs are spread across multiple datastores. It also contributes to the wastage of replication bandwidth and storage space, since the LUNs that are replicated will also contain unprotected VM data.

- **Approach-2**: This is used in scenarios where you have ample spare capacity. This approach is the best as it reduces the complexity and avoids the wastage of replication bandwidth and space, unlike Approach-1. However, this approach will have an impact on the size of the LUNs required at both the protected and replication sites.

Host presentation (Zoning) at the protected and the recovery sites

If you are involved in a new implementation, then you will have to plan how the ESXi hosts are zoned to the array at both the protected and recovery sites. This means that LUNs should be correctly zoned at the Fabric:

- At the protected site array, zone the ESXi hosts to communicate with the array, and make sure that the LUNs housing the VMs to be protected are assigned to the ESXi hosts

- At the recovery site array, zone the ESXi hosts to the array, but do not map the replica LUNs to the hosts yet

Installing SRM on both the protected and recovery sites

VCenter SRM has to be installed at the both the protected and recovery sites for the disaster recovery setup to work. The installation process is identical regardless of the site it is being installed at; the only difference is that at each site, you will be registering SRM installation to the vCenter Server managing that site.

SRM can be installed either on the same machine that has vCenter Server installed or on a different machine. The decision to choose one of the installation models depends on how you want to size or separate the service-providing machines in your infrastructure. The most common deployment model is to have both vCenter and SRM on the same machine. The rationale behind this is that SRM will not work in standalone mode, that is, if your vCenter Server goes down, there is no way to access SRM. Like vCenter Server, SRM can be installed either on a physical or on a virtual machine.

Another factor that you would want to take into account is the installation of the SRA. SRAs have to be installed on the same machine where you have SRM installed. Some SRAs would need a reboot after they are installed. So, it is important to read through the storage vendor's documentation prior to proceeding to make a deployment choice for SRM. If the vCenter downtime is not feasible, then you will have to consider installing SRM on a separate machine.

Nevertheless, it is important to make yourselves aware of the software and hardware requirements of a software installation before it is actually installed. This is to make sure that you don't run into compatibility or supportability issues during the course of using the product. To understand the requirements for SRM, refer to page 13 of the *Site Recovery Manager System Requirements* chapter, in the *Site Recovery Manager Installation and Configuration* guide for SRM 6.1.

This guide can be accessed at the following URL:

```
http://pubs.vmware.com/srm-61/topic/com.vmware.ICbase/PDF/srm-
install-config-6-1.pdf
```

The following flowchart depicts the processes involved in installing vCenter SRM:

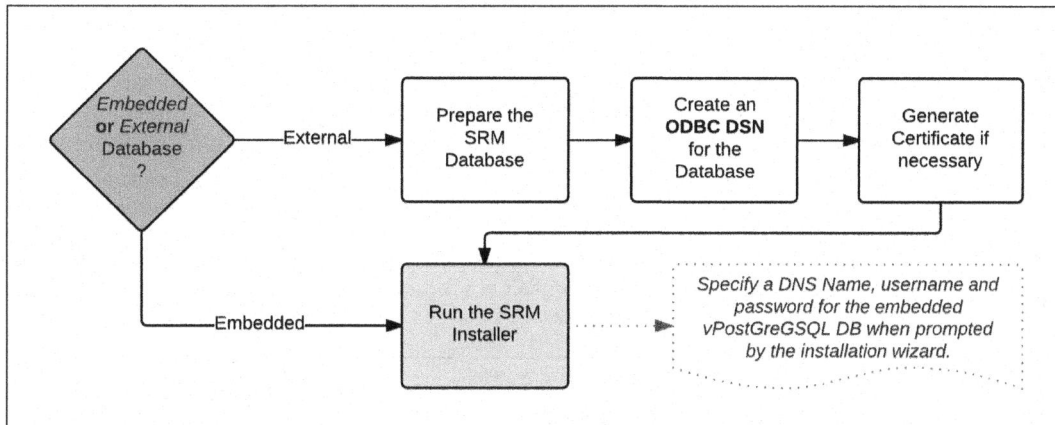

Performing the SRM installation

Let's assume that the SRM database and the 64-bit DSN have already been created. We will delve directly into the installation procedure using the SRM installer.

Before you begin, you will need to download the SRM installation bundle from VMware's website. It can be downloaded by navigating to www.vmware.com and then to **Downloads | vCenter Site Recovery Manager**. You will need to log in to your my.vmware.com account before you cloud download the executable.

The following procedure will guide you through the SRM installation wizard:

1. Double-click the downloaded executable to load the installer.

2. On the welcome screen of the installation wizard, click on **Next** to continue.

3. On the **VMware Patents** screen, click on **Next** to continue.

4. Accept the license agreement and click on **Next** to continue.

5. On the **Installation Prerequisites** screen, click on **Next** to continue.

6. Choose a destination folder for the installer to put the files. The default location is `c:\Program Files\VMware\VMware vCenter Site Recovery Manager\`. You can change this by clicking on the **Change** button. For now, I have chosen to leave the default in place. Click on **Next** to continue.

7. On the **vSphere Platform Services Controller** screen, supply the FQDN or the IP address of the PSC and its **Single Sign-On (SSO)** credentials:

VMware vCenter Site Recovery Manager	☒

vSphere Platform Services Controller

Register Site Recovery Manager with a vSphere Platform Services Controller

Provide the Platform Services Controller address.

Address:	VCSRMSITEA.vdescribed.lab	FQDN or IP address of the PSC and its SSO Credentials
HTTPS Port:	443	

vCenter Single Sign-On administrative credentials are required to perform administrative operations in this Platform Services Controller.

Username:	administrator@vsphere.local	(case-sensitive)
Password:	••••••••••••	(case-sensitive)

NOTE: If prompted, you must accept the certificate for the installation to proceed.

InstallShield

< Back   Next >   Cancel

The details supplied here correspond to the PSC of the vCenter site that you intended to protect. Click on **Next** to continue.

8. You will be prompted to accept the PSC certificate. Click on **Accept** and then on **OK** to close the **Certificate Information** window.

9. On the **VMware vCenter Server** screen, choose the vCenter to register the SRM instance with and click on **Next** to continue:

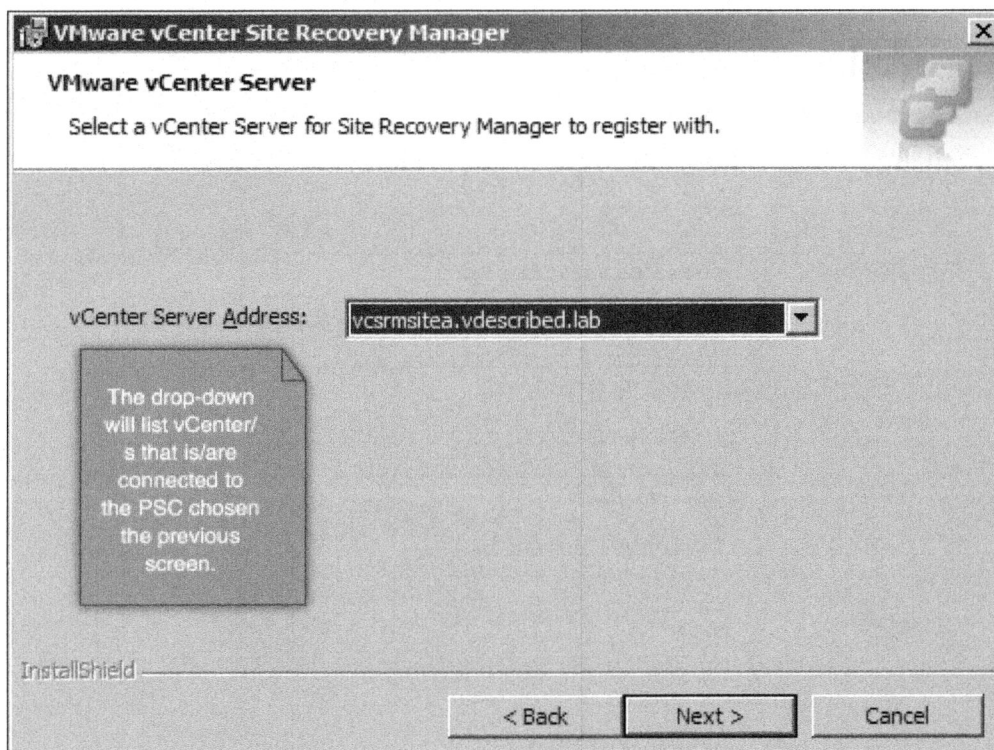

You might get a list of more than one vCenter if there is more than one vCenter using the same PSC, or if the PSCs are part of the same SSO domain—Linked Mode for example.

10. In the **Site Recovery Manager Extension** screen, supply a **Local Site Name**, **Administrator E-mail**, and local host IP address. **Listener Port** by default is set to **9086**. The local site name could be any name that can identify the vCenter sites in the SRM GUI. The local host IP address is the IP of the machine on which SRM is being installed. It is possible that the machine on which SRM is being installed has more than one network interfaces configured with different IP addresses. The local host option will let you choose the interface you want SRM to be available on:

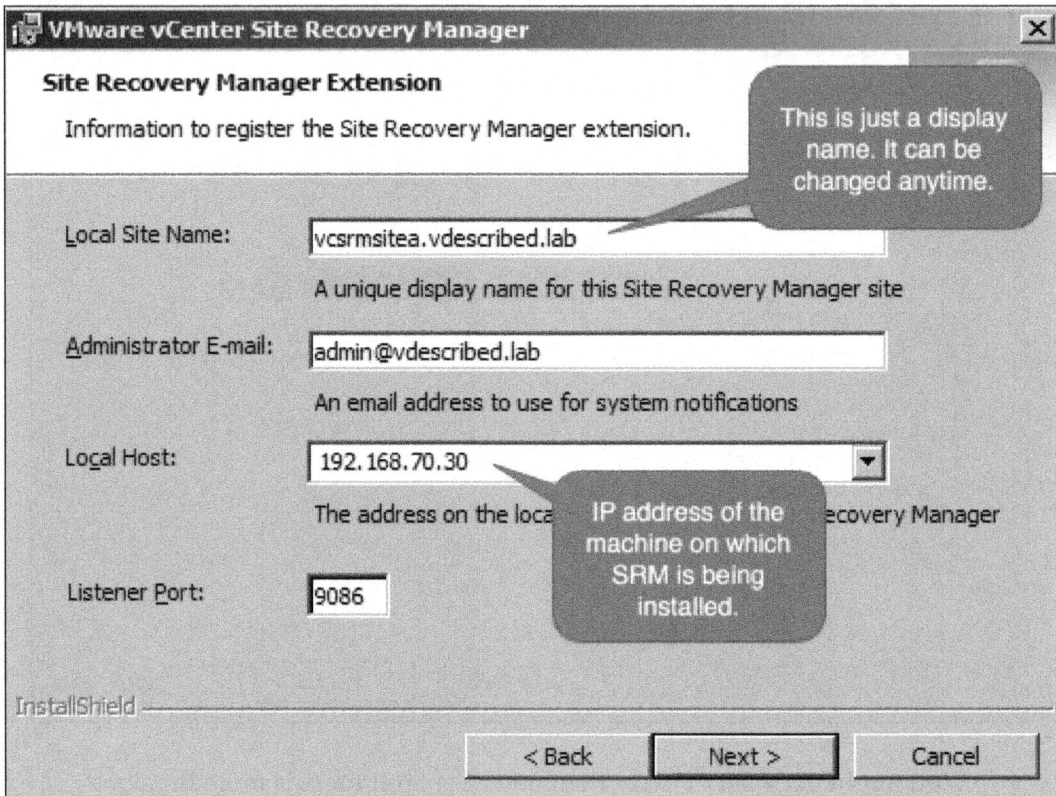

11. On the **Site Recovery Manager Plug-in ID** screen, choose the **Default Site Recovery Manager Plug-in Identifier** option. The **Custom Site Recovery Manager Plug-in Identifier** option is used when you need to share a single site as a recovery site for more than one protected site. You will learn more about this in the *Setting up a Shared Recovery Site* topic of this chapter:

12. In the **Certificate Type** screen, you can either let the installer generate a certificate or you could supply a certificate file generated by a certificate authority.

The options available are:

    ° **Automatically generate a certificate**
    ° **Use a PKCS#12 certificate file**

Make your choice and click on **Next** to continue.

The first option will let the installer generate a new certificate. Use the second option if you already have a certificate file from your certificate authority. VMware recommends using CA signed certificates for all of its products.

13. On the next screen, supply the details (**Organization** and **Organization Unit**) for the certificate generation and click on **Next** to continue. You will be prompted for this information only if you have chosen to automatically generate a certificate.

14. On the **Database Server Selection** screen, you have a choice between an embedded database server and an external database:

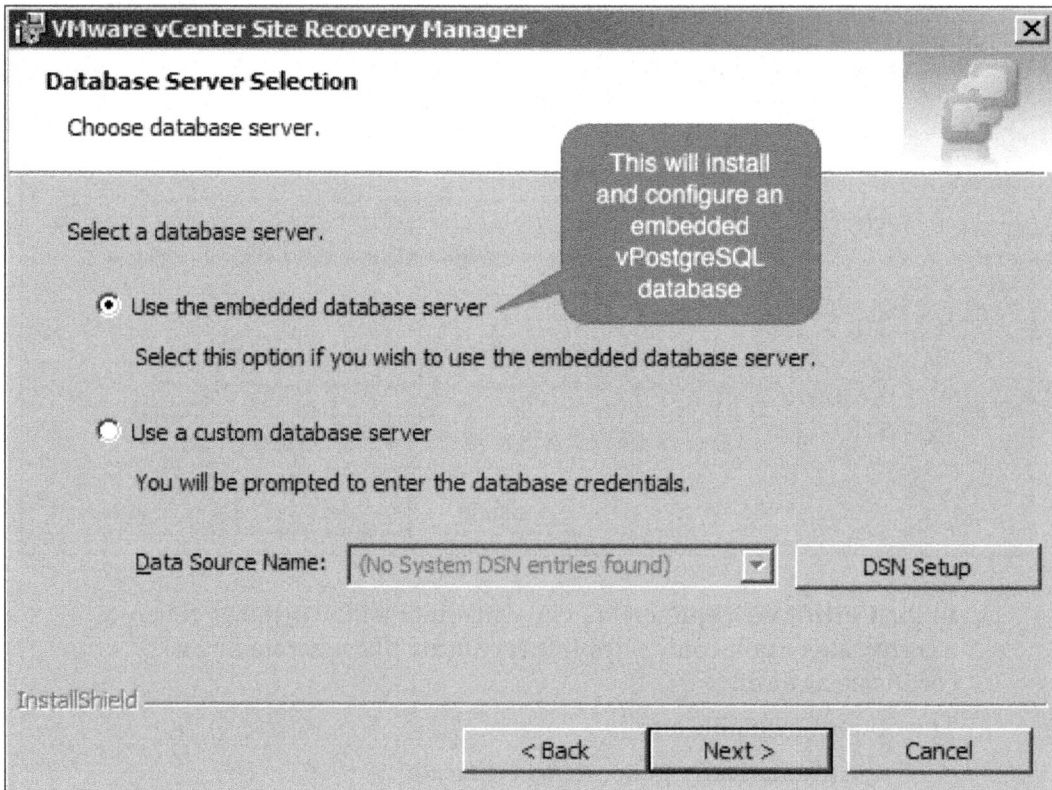

VMware vCenter Site Recovery Manager

Database Server Selection

Choose database server.

This will install and configure an embedded vPostgreSQL database

Select a database server.

(•) Use the embedded database server

Select this option if you wish to use the embedded database server.

( ) Use a custom database server

You will be prompted to enter the database credentials.

Data Source Name: (No System DSN entries found)   DSN Setup

InstallShield

< Back   Next >   Cancel

The embedded database is a vPostgreSQL database and an external can be SQL or Oracle.

15. If you choose the embedded database server, then on the next screen you must specify a **Data Source Name**, **Database User Name**, and **Database Password** for the embedded database:

If you choose to use an external database, for instance SQL, then you will need a 64-bit DSN pre-created and the valid credentials for the database connection. It is not a recommended practice to expose the database server's sa credentials. Hence consider using a service account.

16. The **Site Recovery Manager Service Account** by default will use the local system account. However, the best practice is to use a separate service account for this.

17. On the **Ready to install the Program** screen, click on **Install** to begin the installation. The account should be a member of the local Administrators group.

18. Once the installation is complete, click on **Finish** to exit the installer.

Pairing SRM sites

Once SRM is installed on both sites, then the next step is to pair these sites together. The pairing process establishes a connection between the vCenter Servers at the protected and recovery sites, which in turn makes the SRM instances at both sites become aware of its counterpart at the other site (protected/recovery). Without the sites being paired, we cannot proceed with further configuration of the DR setup.

Here is how the sites can be paired:

1. Connect to either of the protected/recovery sites through vCenter Server using vSphere Web Client.

2. Navigate to the inventory **Home** and click on **Site Recovery**:

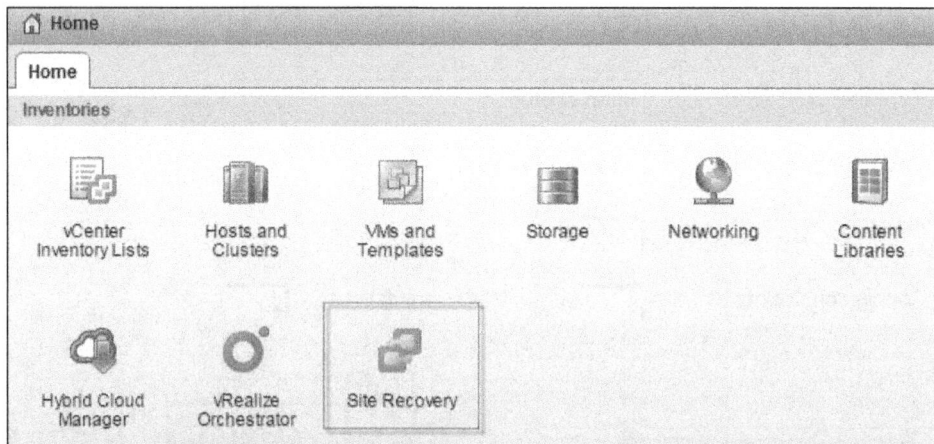

3. At the **Site Recovery** home page, select **Sites** from the left pane and navigate to its **Objects** tab.

4. The **Objects** tab will list the current SRM site. Click on the pair a site icon ▦▦ to bring up the **Pair Site Recovery Manager Servers** wizard:

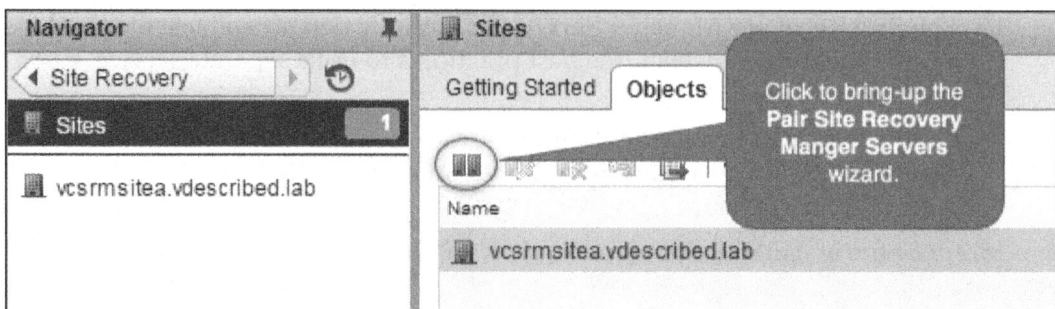

5. On the **Pair Site Recovery Manager Servers** wizard's **Select Site** page, supply the FQDN or IP address of the PSC that corresponds to the secondary site and click on **Next**:

6. On the **Select vCenter Server** screen, select the intended vCenter and supply its SSO credentials. Click on **Next** to continue:

7. You will now see a certificate security alert for both the sites. Click on **Yes** in both dialog boxes to continue.

8. Once done, you will see both the sites listed:

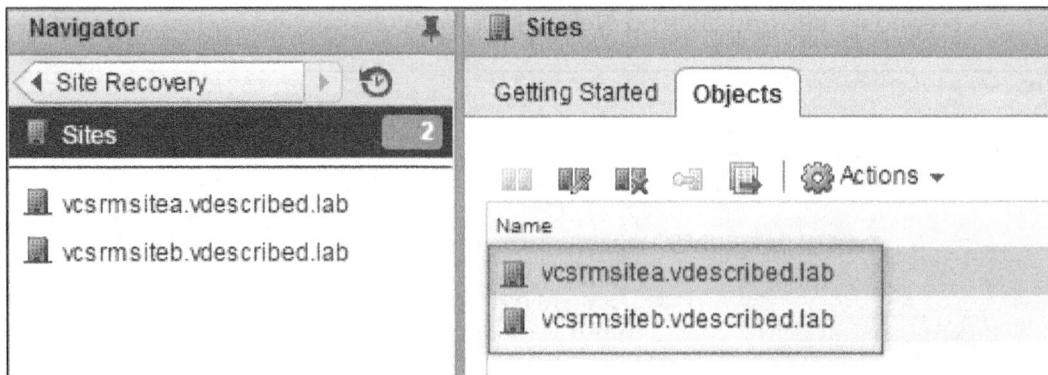

9. Now, select the site that you just added and click on the 🔑 icon to bring up the **Login Site** window, prompting the credentials for the vCenter managing the second site:

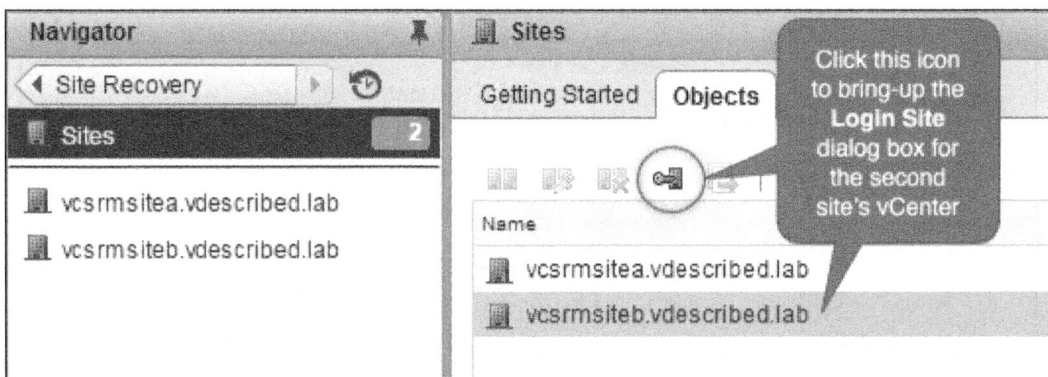

10. On the **Login Site** window, supply the vCenter credentials and click on **Login**. This completes the site pairing process.

The paring is done only from one of the sites. This is because the pairing process establishes reciprocity by configuring the connection in the reverse direction as well. But when you open the site recovery solution at the remote vCenter Server, you may be prompted to enter the administrator credentials of the other site.

Installing the Storage Replication Adapters

Once you have SRM instances installed and paired, the next step is to install the SRAs. SRAs are coded and provided by the storage vendors. VMware certifies the SRAs and posts them as the compatible ones for the SRM.

Downloading the SRAs

The certified versions of the SRA can be downloaded directly from VMware's website. Keep in mind that most vendors publish the updated versions of the SRA at their website before it is certified by VMware. Since SRA is a vendor-supported component, you could choose to install the latest version available from the vendor, if that is known to fix a problem that you are dealing with.

Here is how you can download the SRA:

1. Go to VMware's website `www.vmware.com`.
2. Under the **Product Downloads** category, navigate to **Downloads | vCenter Site Recovery Manager**.
3. Once you are on the download page for vCenter SRM, click on the **Go to Downloads** hyperlink listed against **Storage Replication Adapters**.
4. At the **Download Storage Replication Adapters for VMware vCenter Site Recovery Manager** page, you will see a list of all the certified SRAs. Click on the **Download Now** button corresponding to the required SRA.

Installing the SRA

The SRA component, once downloaded, has to be installed on both the sites. In most cases, the SRA installation is pretty simple and straightforward, but this can be different from vendor to vendor. You need to refer to the vendor documentation for the installation procedure.

Adding array managers and enabling array pairs

Once you have installed the SRA at both sites, you will now need to add an array manager at both sites. An array manager is required to discover the replicated LUNs and perform other storage operations initiated by SRM.

Here is how you can add an array manager:

1. Connect to either of the protected/recovery sites through vCenter Server using **vSphere Web Client**, navigate to **Home | Site Recovery**, click on **Array Based Replication**, and select its **Objects** tab:

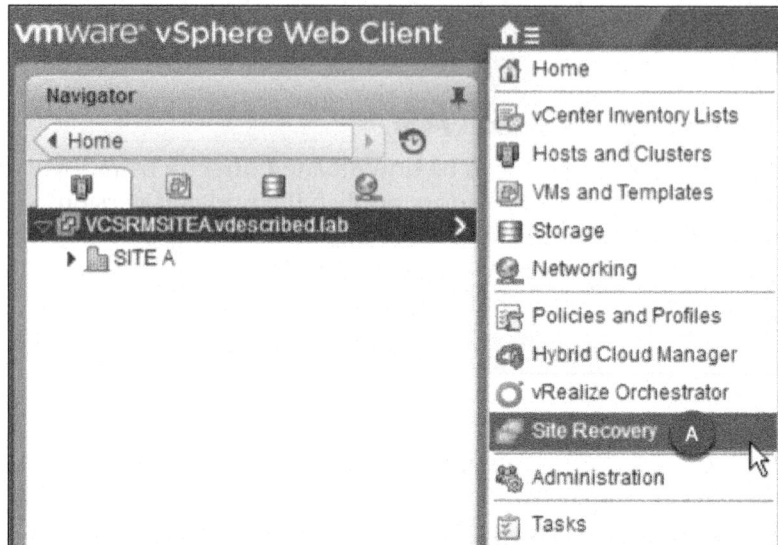

2. Under the **Objects** tab, click on the icon to bring up the **Add Array Manager** wizard:

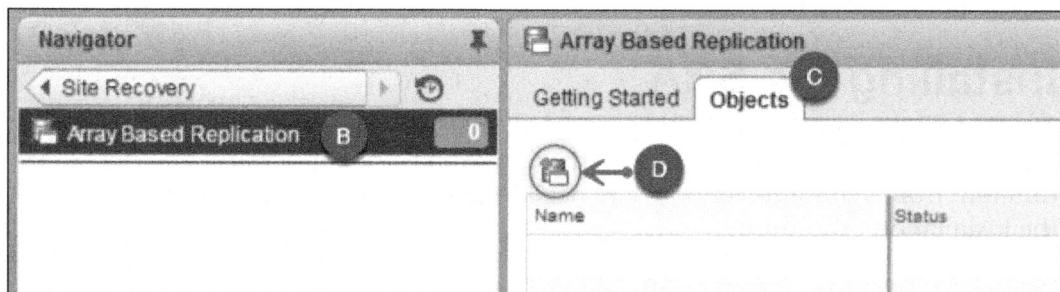

3. The **Add Array Manager** wizard presents two options:

   ° **Add a pair of array managers**: This is used when you want to go through the process of adding both the protected and recovery site array managers and enabling the array pair. Use this method during this initial configuration.

- **Add a single array manager**: This is used when you want to add the array managers as separate steps. This can be handy when you want to remove and re-add the array manager corresponding to a particular site.

4. Select the **Add a pair of array managers** option, and click on **Next** to continue.

5. Select the site pair to configure the array managers, and click on **Next** to continue:

6. The **Select SRA type** screen will list the discovered SRA installed on the SRM servers at both the sites. You will not be able to proceed further if it cannot find the SRA at the paired site:

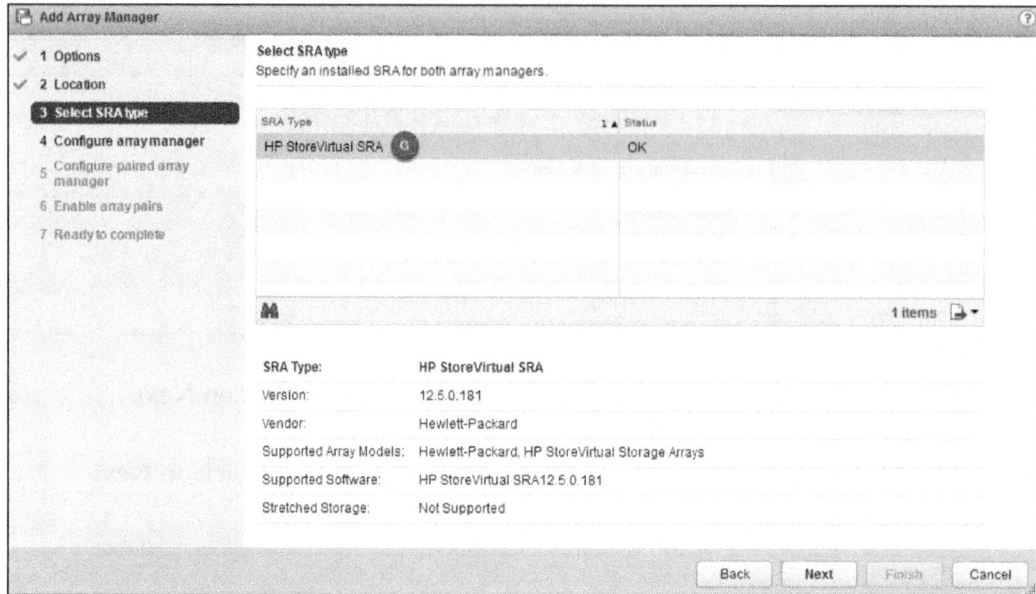

This will be followed by two configure array manager screens, one each for the protected and recovery sites.

7. On the first **Configure array manager** screen, enter a **Display Name** and the login information required by the protected site's SRA to connect to its storage array. Click on **Next** to continue:

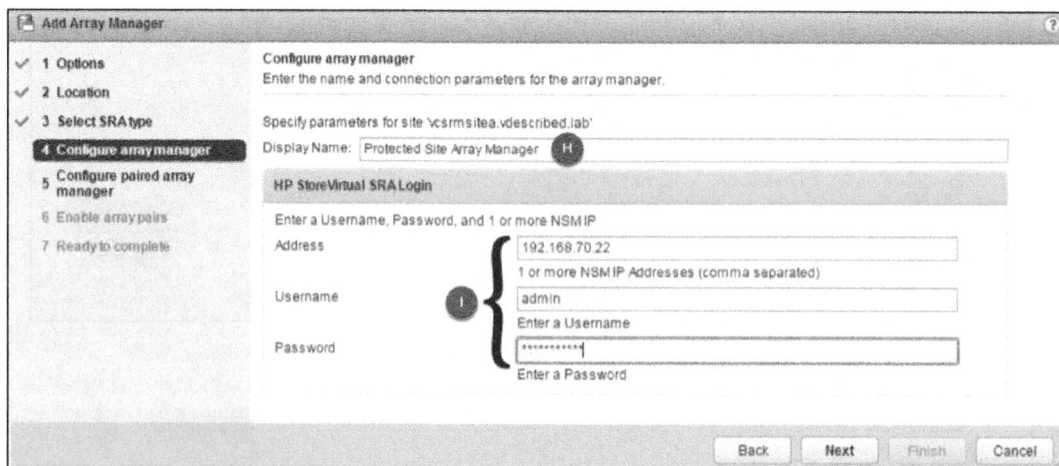

8. On the second **Configure paired array manager** screen, enter a **Display Name** and the login information required by the recovery site's SRA to connect to its storage array. Click on **Next** to continue:

9. On the **Enable array pairs** screen, you will be presented with a list of discovered array pairs. Select the array pair corresponding to the protected and recovery sites and click on **Next** to continue:

10. On the **Ready to complete** screen, review the summary of the selected settings and click on **Finish** to create the array manager pair:

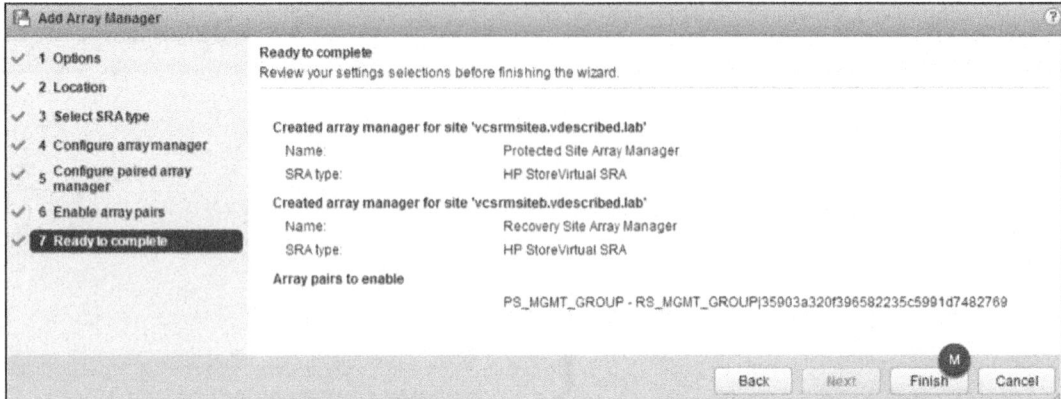

The information prompted on the **Configure array manager** screen (at step 8 and step 9) differs from array to array and from vendor to vendor. It is purely dependent on the SRA being used.

I have used an HP StoreVirtual (left-hand) SRA and have entered the **Virtual IP (VIP)** of the cluster the **Node Storage Module (NSM)** is part of. If none of the NSMs in the cluster are involved in the replication for SRM, then I could supply the IP addresses of the involved NSMs separated by a comma.

If the array managers are successfully added, then they will be listed with a **Status OK** under the **Object** tab:

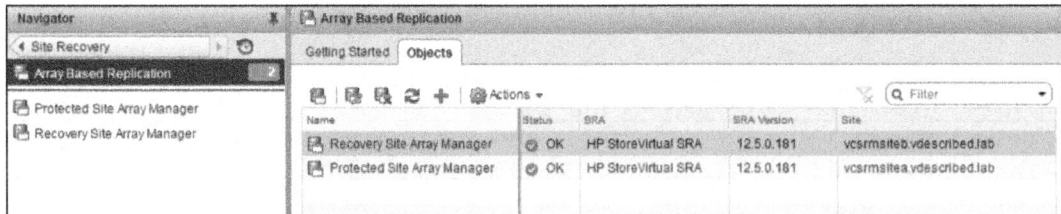

Now, you can select either of the array managers and navigate to **Manage |
Array Pair** to view a list of replicated devices and its direction of replication,
which will be **Outgoing Replication** for the **Protected Site Array Manager**
and **Incoming Replication** for the **Recovery Site Array Manager**:

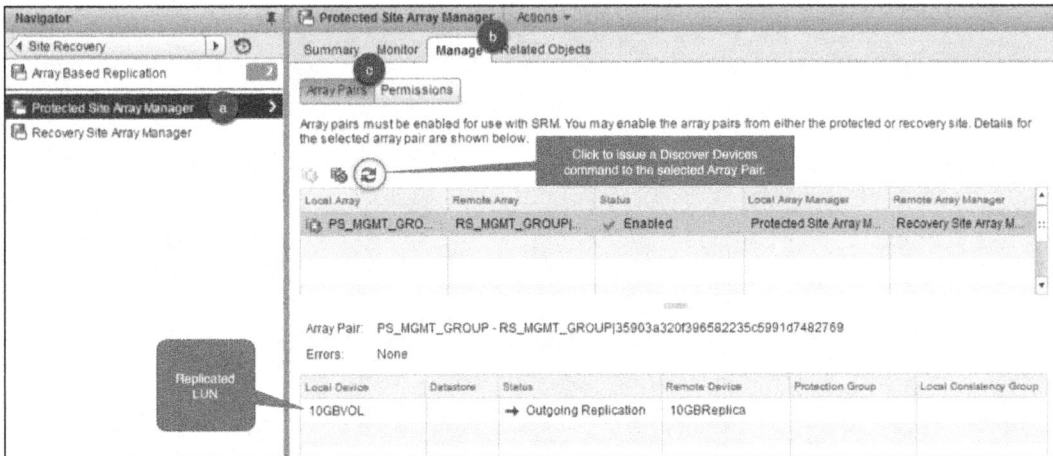

Also, to discover and list new replication-enabled LUN devices that are
presented to hosts, click on the ⮂ icon to run a **Discover Devices** operation
for the selected array pair.

The **Array Pairs** tab shows the replication relationship between two arrays.
Before you enable the array pair, you need SRA installed and the array
manager added at both the sites. For the array manager to detect an array
pair, there should be a replication schedule already created between the
arrays. Refer to the vendor documentation to understand what a replication
schedule would mean for the vendor's array and the procedure to create it.
When an array pair is enabled, it tries to discover the LUN devices for which
a replication schedule is enabled at the array. However, not all devices with
a replication schedule are displayed as a device for the array pair. Only the
devices that are presented to a host at the protected site are displayed.

If the replicated LUN devices are not presented to the hosts at the replication source (protected site), then it will complain about this:

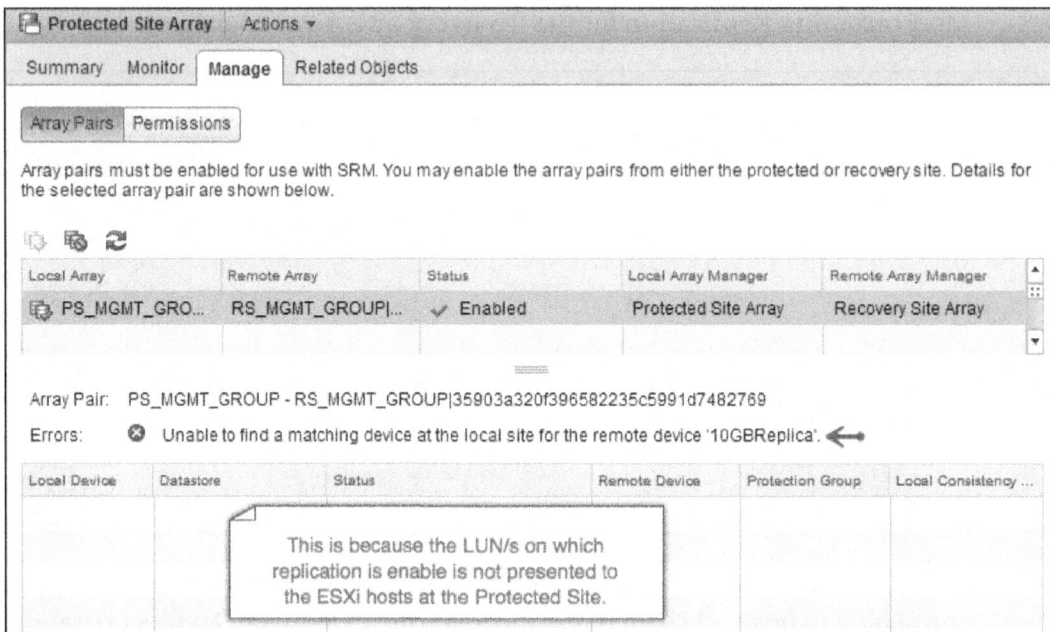

Configuring placeholder datastores

For every virtual machine that becomes part of a protection group, SRM creates a shadow virtual machine. A placeholder datastore is used to store files for the shadow virtual machines. The datastore used for this purpose should be accessible to all the hosts in the data center/cluster serving the role of a recovery host. We will learn more about protection groups and shadow virtual machines in the next chapter. For now, understand that configuring placeholder datastores is an essential step in configuring an SRM environment.

Assuming that each of these paired sites are geographically separated, each site will have its own placeholder datastore. The following figure shows the relationship between the site and placeholder datastore:

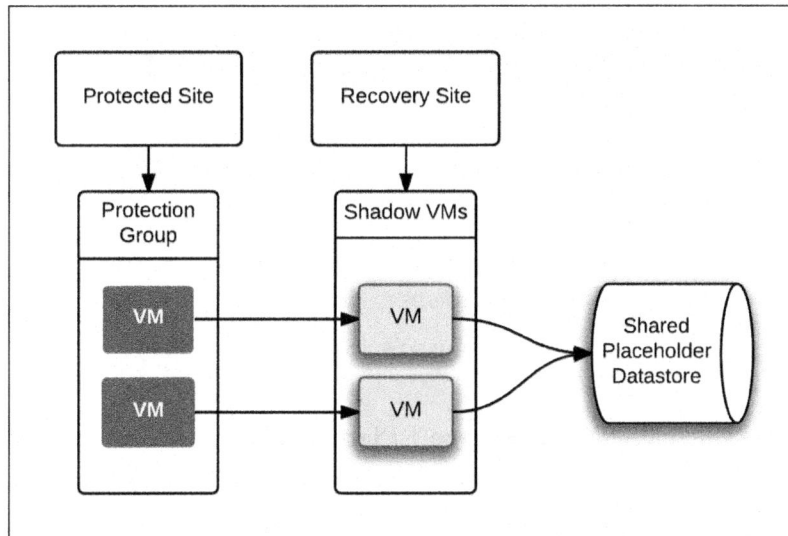

Here is how you can configure placeholder datastores:

1. Navigate to **Home | Site Recovery**:

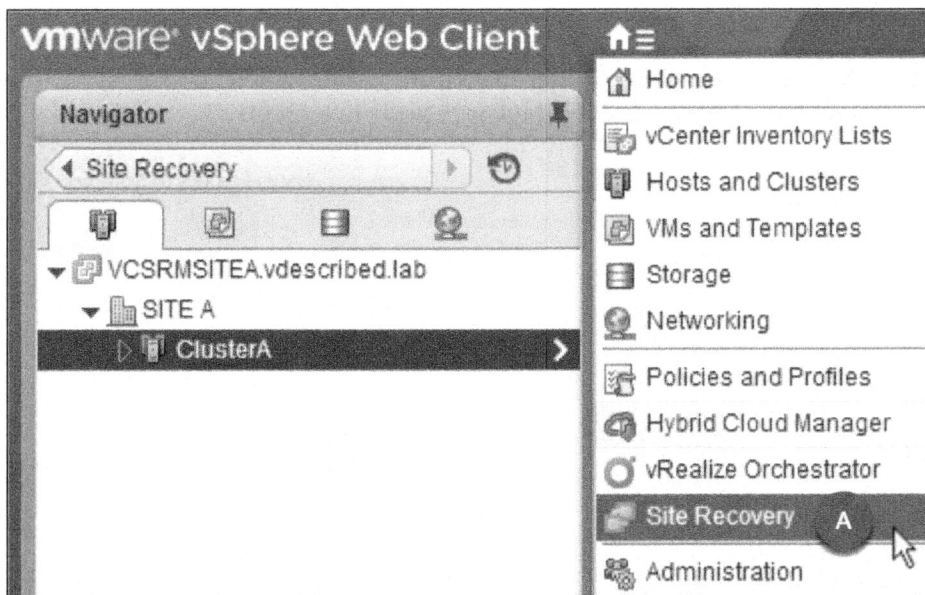

2. Click on **Sites** in the left pane to view the **Sites** page:

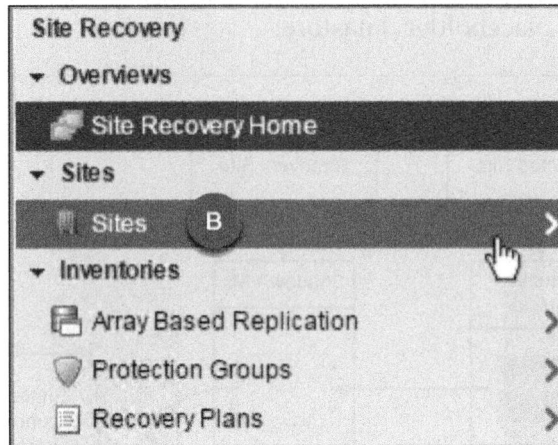

3. Select a site, navigate to **Manage | Placeholder Datastores**, and click on the icon to bring up the **Configure Placeholder Datastore** window:

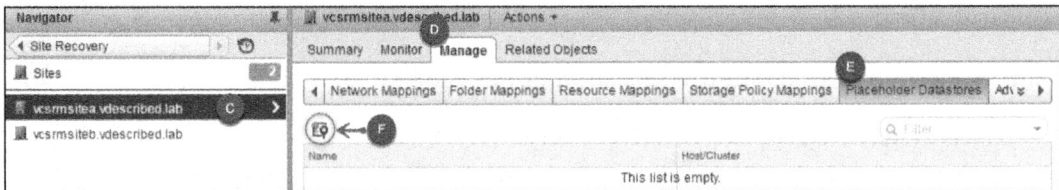

4. On the **Configure Placeholder Datastore** window, select a datastore to be designated as a placeholder datastore and click on **OK**:

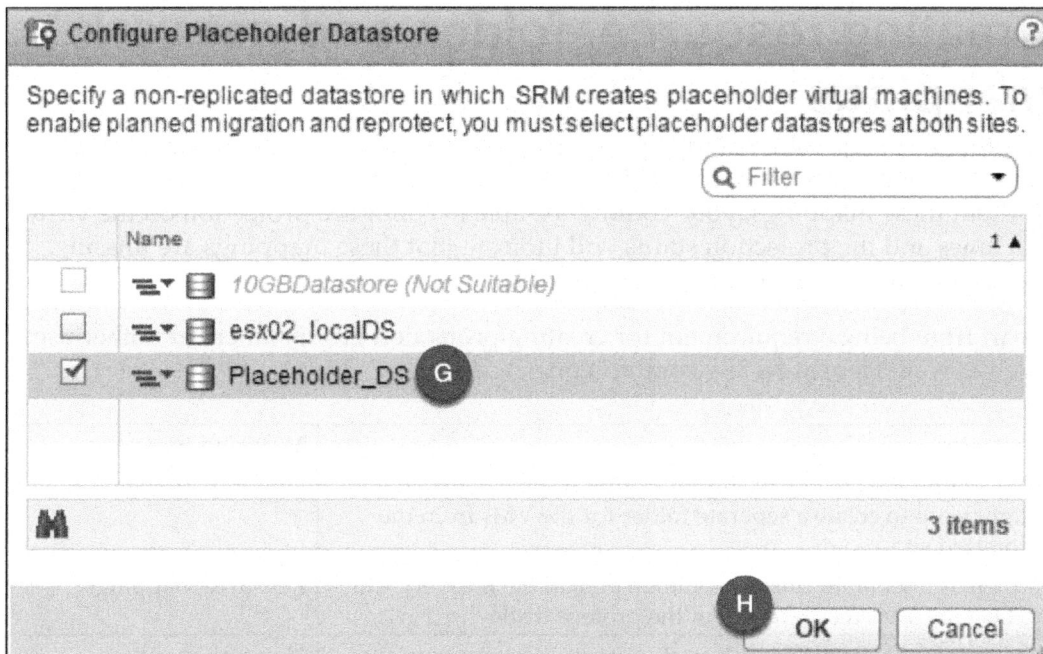

5. If successfully designated, it should be listed under the **Placeholder Datastores** tab:

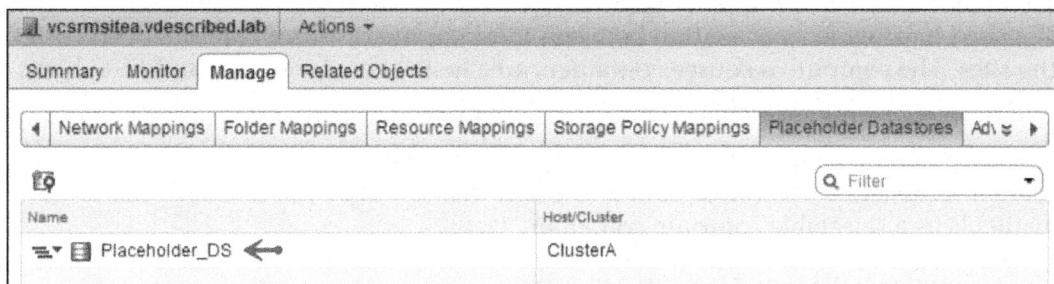

6. You should repeat the procedure at the secondary (recovery) site if you plan to failback.

Creating resource, folder, and network mappings

Creating resource, folder, and network mappings facilitates further orchestration of the recovery plan that will be executed for either a planned migration or a failover. Without these mappings, you wouldn't be able to configure protection on the virtual machines and the protection status will indicate that these mappings are missing. We will learn more about protection groups in the next chapter.

Apart from being a requirement for creating protection groups, there are other use cases as well. Here are a few common ones:

Use cases	Mapping to use
If the designated recovery site runs other workloads, then you might want to create a separate folder for the VMs from the protected site	Folder mappings
If there is a separate cluster/resource pool at the recovery site to host the VMs recovered from the protected site	Resource mappings
If there are vSwitch/DSwitch port groups at the recovery site for the recovered VMs	Network mappings

Resource mappings

We need to provide a correlation between the compute resource containers on both the sites. The compute resource containers are cluster, resource pool, and ESXi host. This is achieved with the help of resource mappings.

Resource mappings respects the presence of these containers. This means that, if there is a cluster or a resource pool at the site, then the ESXi hosts are not made available as a selectable compute container.

Here is how you configure resource mapping:

1. Navigate to **Home | Site Recovery** and click on **Sites** to list the paired sites.

2. Select the protected site, navigate to its **Manage | Resource Mappings** tab, and click on the 🐚 icon to bring up the **Create Resource Mapping** wizard:

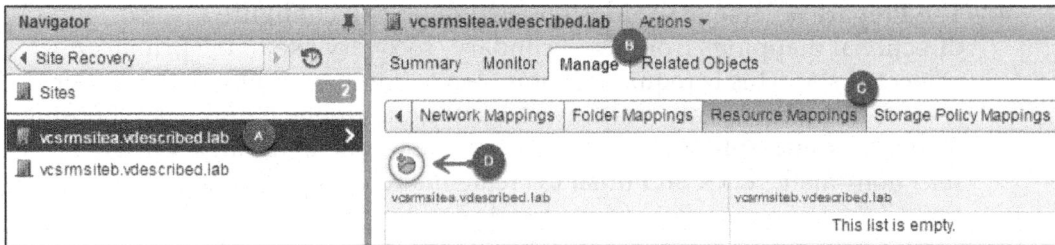

3. The **Create Resource Mapping** screen displays the vCenter inventory of the Protected Site on the left pane and the recovery site on the right pane:

   ° Expand the Protected Site's vCenter inventory tree to select the resource container (cluster/resource pool/ESXi host) that you want to map.

   ° Expand the recovery site's vCenter inventory tree to select the destination resource container. Once you have made the selections, click on **Add Mappings**.

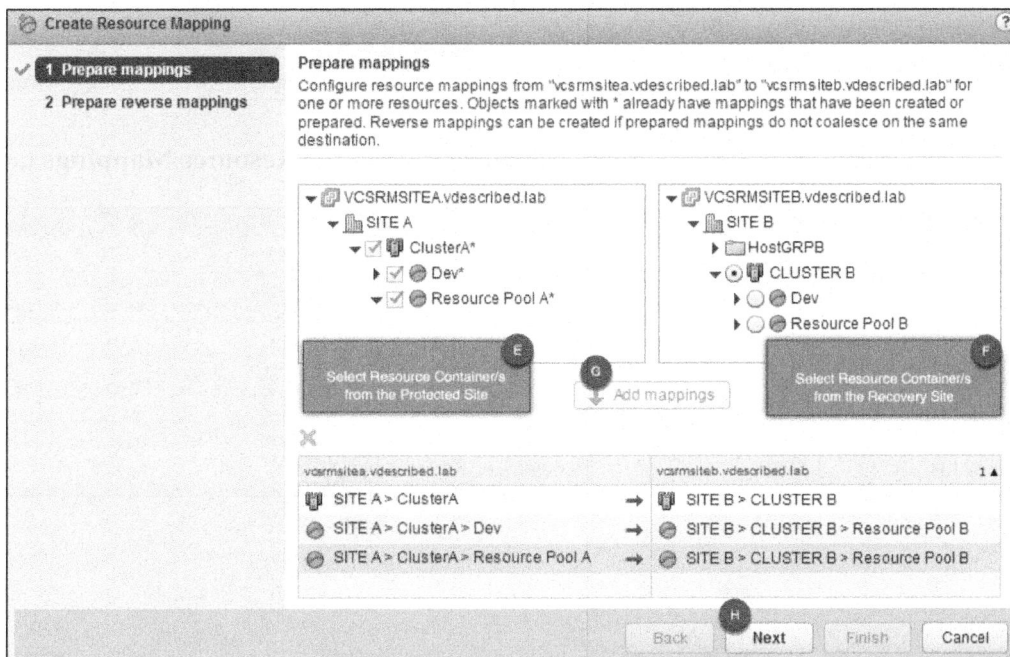

The mapping can be one-to-one or many-to-one. Click on **Next** to continue.

4. The **Prepare reverse mappings** screen will let you configure reverse-directional mappings from the secondary/recovery site to the primary/protected site. This is required if you plan to configure failback. However, reverse mapping is only made available for one-to-one mappings. Choosing **Select all applicable** will only select the one-to-one mappings. With the selections made, click on **Finish** to create the resource mapping:

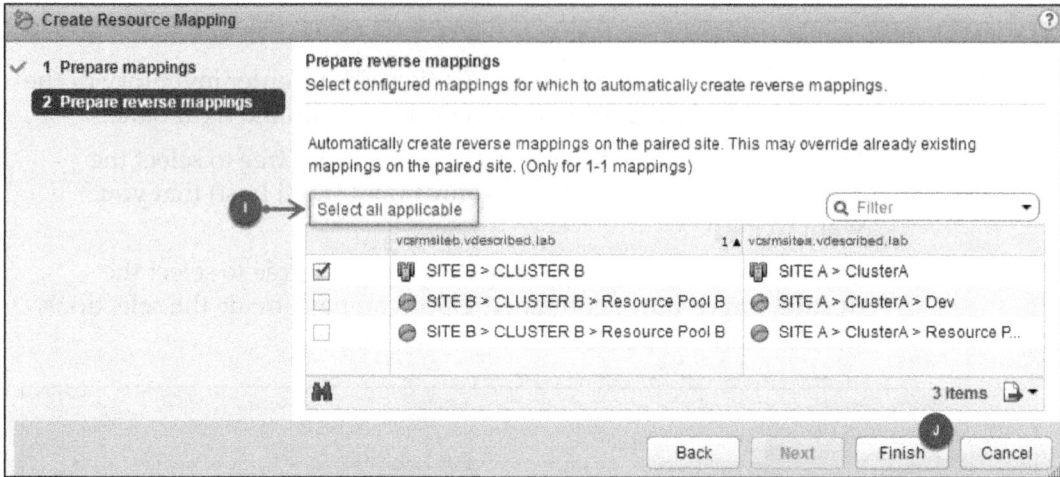

5. Once configured, the mappings are listed under the **Resource Mappings** tab:

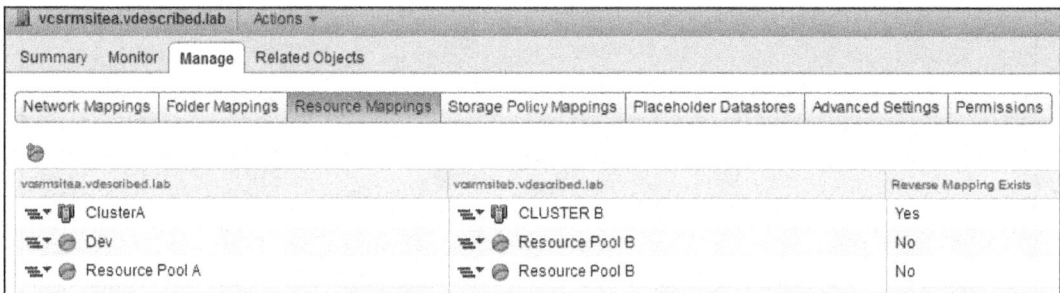

Folder mappings

Folders are inventory containers that can only be created using vCenter Server. They are used to group inventory objects of the same type/purpose for easier management.

There are different types of folders. This is determined by the inventory hierarchy level they are created at. The folder names are as follows:

- Data center folder
- Hosts and clusters folder
- Virtual machine and template folder
- Networks folder
- Storage folder

The vSphere Web Client provides UI menu options to create a folder of the following types, without needing to navigate to an appropriate inventory hierarchy level to create them:

- Hosts and clusters folder
- Networks folder
- Storage folder
- Virtual machine and templates folder

In the case of SRM folder mappings, we will be dealing only with virtual machine folders and their parent data center. You will not be able to configure mapping for any of the other folder types.

Here is how you configure Folder Mappings:

1. Navigate to **Site Recovery Manager Home** and click on **Sites** to list the paired sites.

2. Select the protected site, navigate to its **Manage | Folder Mappings** tab, and click on the 📁 icon to bring up the **Create Folder Mapping** wizard:

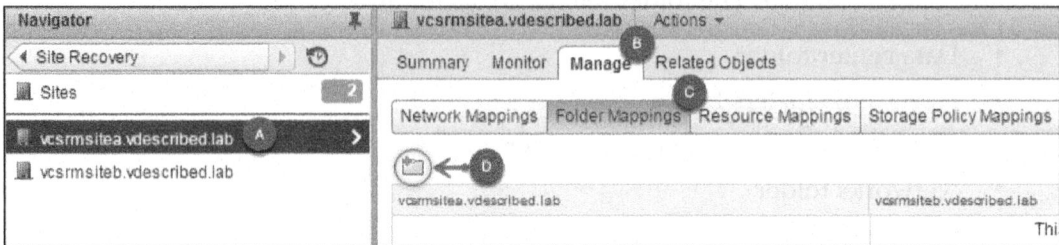

3. The **Select creation mode** screen presents you with two folder mapping methods—automatic and manual:

    ○   The **Automatically prepare mappings for networks with matching names** option is used to auto create one-to-one mapping between identically named Folders at the Protected and Recovery sites. This is generally the preferred option when you have a lot of folders to map and if they were identically named.

    ○   The **Prepare mappings manually** option is used to create both many-to-one and one-to-one mappings. This option should be used when you do not have identically named virtual machine folders at the secondary site.

    Choose the intended option and click on **Next** to continue:

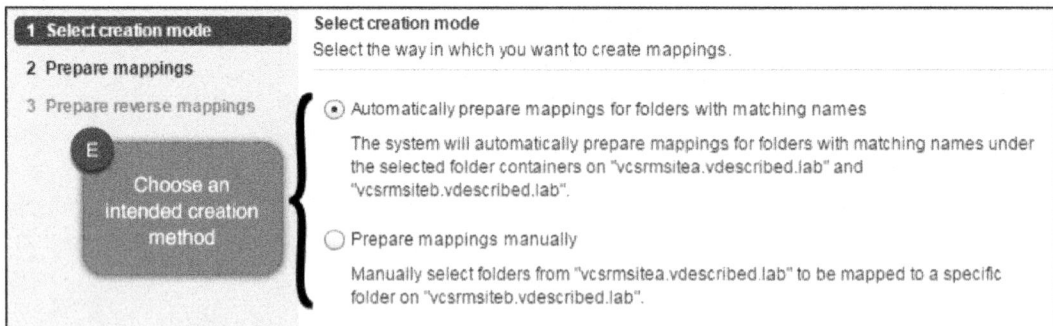

4. With both the options, once you have made the necessary selections on the **Prepare mappings** screen, click on the **Add mappings** button to confirm the selection. Click on **Next** to continue:

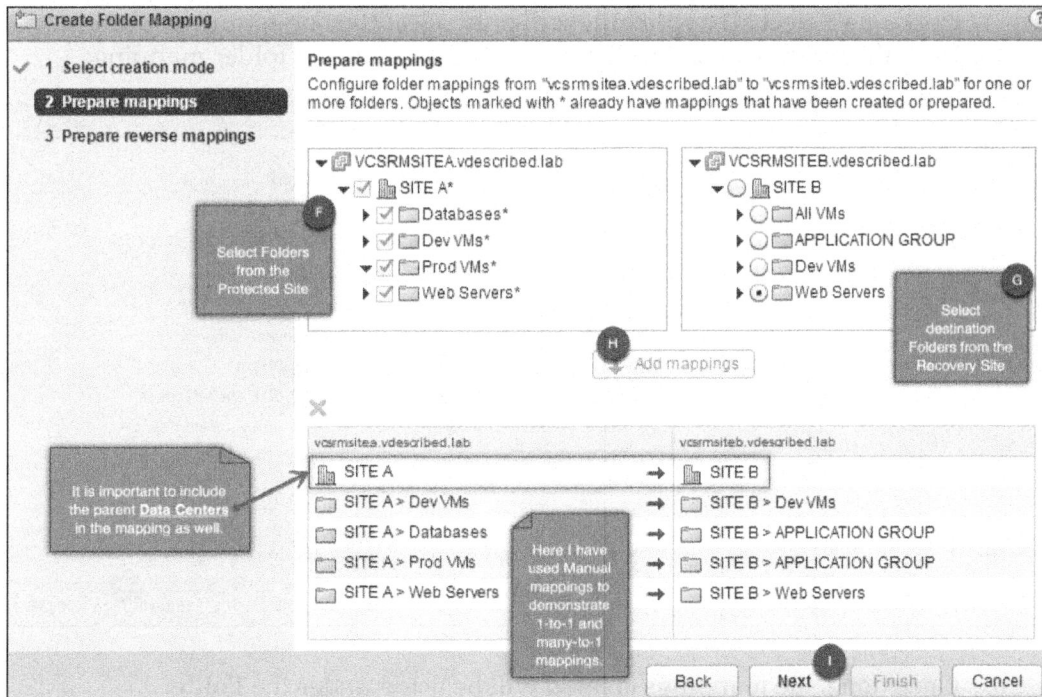

5. The **Prepare reverse mappings** screen will let you configure mapping reverse-directional folder mappings from the Secondary/Recovery site to the Primary/Protected site. This is required if you plan to configure failback. However, reverse mapping is only made available for one-to-one mappings. Choosing **Select all applicable** will only select the one-to-one mappings. With the selections made, click on **Finish** to create the folder mapping:

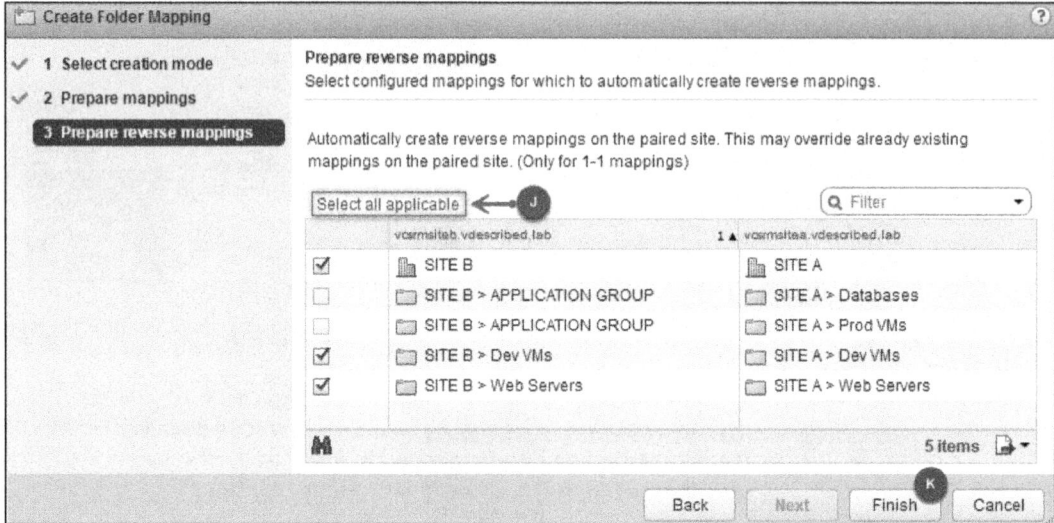

	Create Folder Mapping	⑦

Prepare reverse mappings

✓ 1 Select creation mode	Select configured mappings for which to automatically create reverse mappings.
✓ 2 Prepare mappings	
3 Prepare reverse mappings	

Automatically create reverse mappings on the paired site. This may override already existing mappings on the paired site. (Only for 1-1 mappings)

Select all applicable ← J   🔍 Filter ▼

	vcsrmsiteb.vdescribed.lab	1 ▲	vcsrmsitea.vdescribed.lab
☑	SITE B		SITE A
☐	SITE B > APPLICATION GROUP		SITE A > Databases
☐	SITE B > APPLICATION GROUP		SITE A > Prod VMs
☑	SITE B > Dev VMs		SITE A > Dev VMs
☑	SITE B > Web Servers		SITE A > Web Servers

🔍   5 items 📤 ▼

Back   Next   Finish ⓚ   Cancel

6. Once done, the mappings created will be listed under the **Folder Mappings** tab:

📄 vcsrmsitea.vdescribed.lab	Actions ▼

Summary   Monitor   **Manage**   Related Objects

Network Mappings	Folder Mappings	Resource Mappings	Storage Policy Mappings	Placeholder Datastores	Advanced Settings	Permissions

📁

vcsrmsitea.vdescribed.lab	vcsrmsiteb.vdescribed.lab	Reverse Mapping Exists
⇶▼ 📁 Databases	⇶▼ 📁 APPLICATION GROUP	No
⇶▼ 📁 Dev VMs	⇶▼ 📁 Dev VMs	Yes
⇶▼ 📁 Prod VMs	⇶▼ 📁 APPLICATION GROUP	No
⇶▼ 📑 SITE A	⇶▼ 📑 SITE B	Yes
⇶▼ 📁 Web Servers	⇶▼ 📁 Web Servers	Yes

Network mappings

Network configuration at the protected and recovery sites need not be identical. Network mappings provide a method to form a correlation between the port groups (standard or distributed) of the protected and recovery sites.

Let's say we have a port group with the name VM Network at the protected site and it is mapped to a port group with the name Recovery Network at the recovery site. In this case, a virtual machine that is connected to VM Network, when failed over, will be reconfigured to use the Recovery Network.

Here is how you configure Network Mappings:

1. Navigate to **Site Recovery Manager Home** and click on **Sites** to list the paired sites.

2. Select the Protected Site, navigate to its **Manage | Network Mappings** tab, and click on the 🌐 icon to bring up the **Create Network Mapping** wizard:

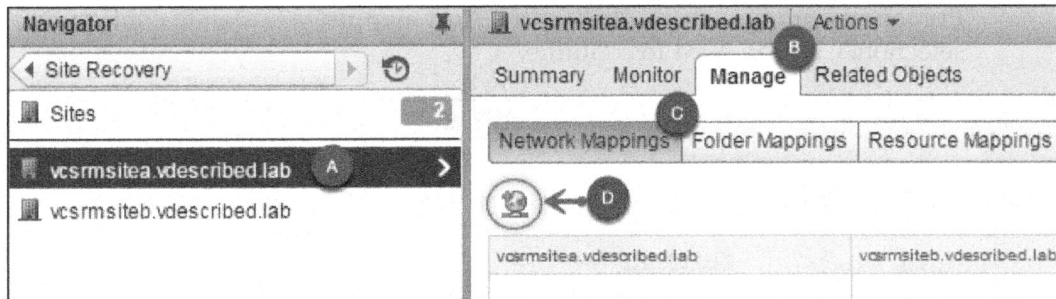

3. As with the folder mapping options, the **Select creation mode** screen presents you with two network mapping methods as well—automatic and manual mapping. Choose the intended option and click on **Next** to continue:

   ° The **Automatically prepare mappings for networks with matching names** option is used to auto create one-to-one mapping between identically named virtual machine port groups at the protected and recovery sites. This is generally the preferred option when you have a lot of port groups to map and if there were identically named.

     °   The **Prepare mappings manually** option is used to create both many-to-one and one-to-one mappings. This option should be used when you do not have identically named virtual machine port groups at the secondary site.

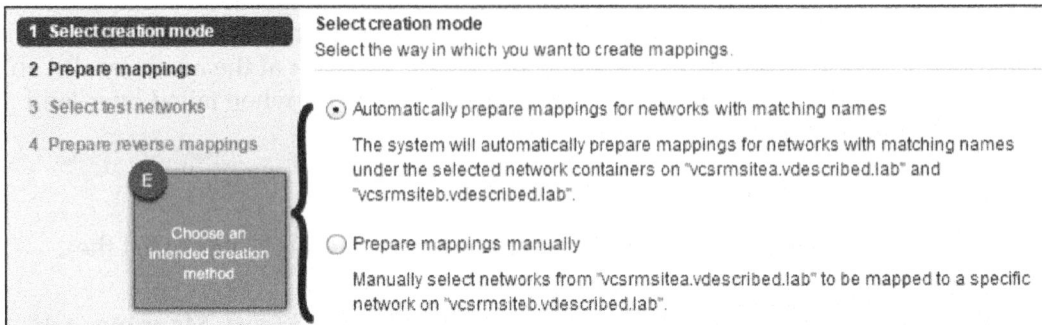

4.   With both these options, once you have made the necessary selections on the **Prepare mappings** screen, click on the **Add mappings** button to confirm the selection. Click on **Next** to continue:

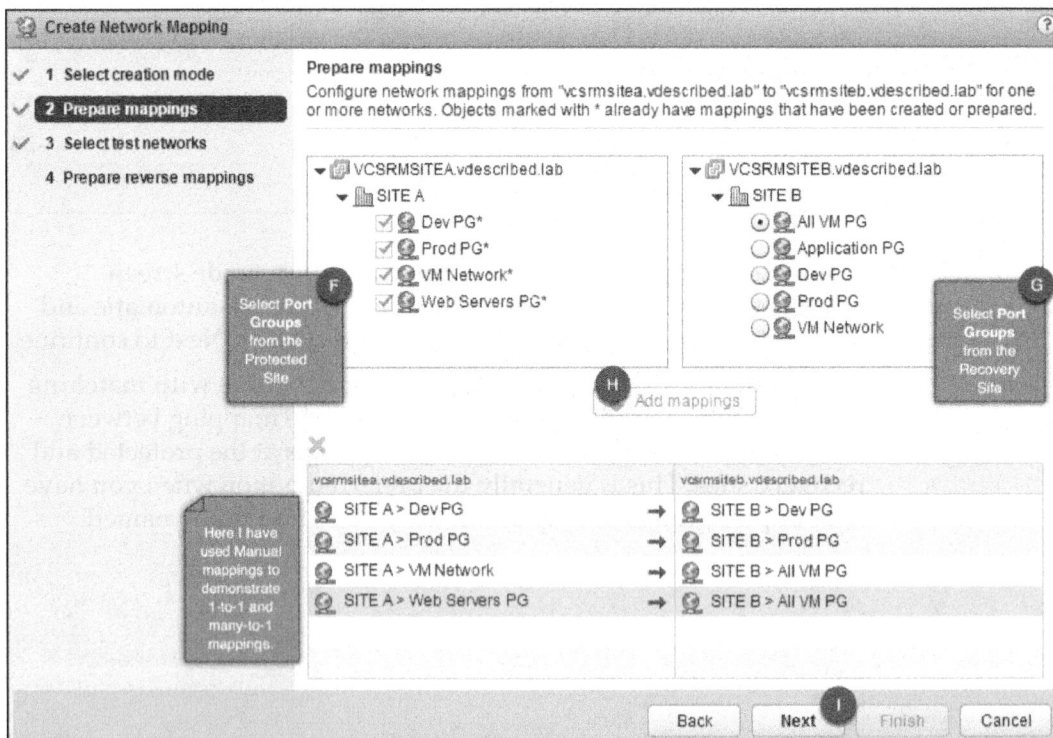

5. On the **Select test networks** screen, you can set a test network for all the recovery site port groups that were selected in the previous mapping screen. By default, the test network is an isolated network (a VM port group with no uplinks). These are used only while testing a recovery LAN. We will learn about recovery plans and their testing in a later chapter. You don't necessarily have to make any changes on this screen. Click on **Next** to continue:

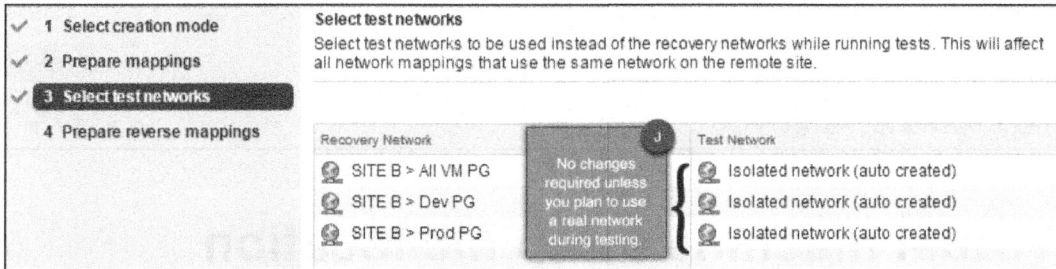

6. The **Prepare reverse mappings** screen will let you configure mapping reverse-directional port group mappings from the Secondary/Recovery site to the Primary/Protected site. This is required if you plan to configure failback. However, reverse mapping is only made available for one-to-one mappings. Choosing **Select all applicable** will only select the one-to-one mappings. With the selections made, click on **Finish** to create the network mapping:

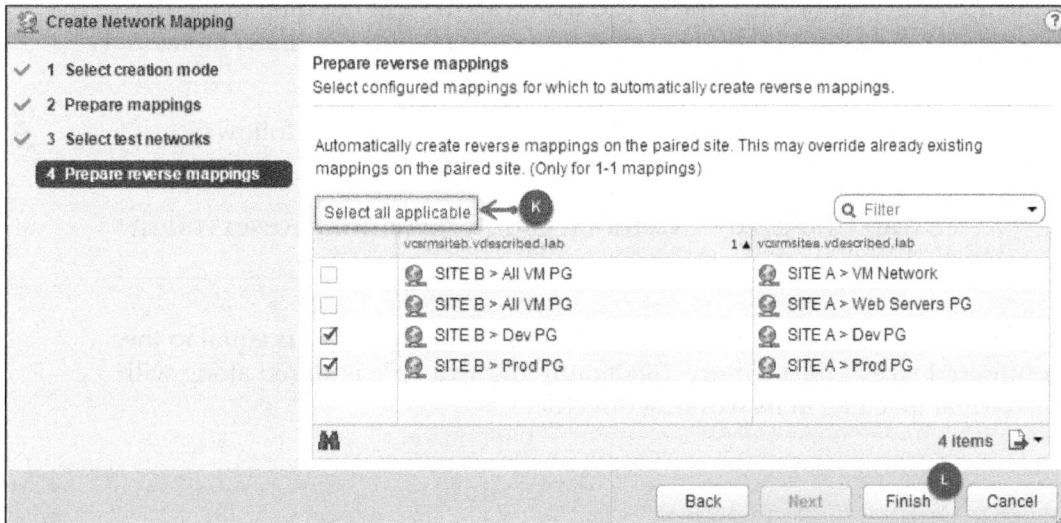

7. Once done, all the mappings created will be listed under the **Network Mappings** tab:

vcsrmsitea.vdescribed.lab	Actions ▾						
Summary	Monitor	**Manage**	Related Objects				

Network Mappings	Folder Mappings	Resource Mappings	Storage Policy Mappings	Placeholder Datastores	Advanced Settings	Permissions

vcsrmsitea.vdescribed.lab	vcsrmsiteb.vdescribed.lab - Recovery Network	Reverse Mapping Exists	vcsrmsiteb.vdescribed.lab - Test Network	IP Customization Rule
Dev PG	Dev PG	Yes		No
Prod PG	Prod PG	Yes		No
VM Network	All VM PG	No		No
Web Servers PG	All VM PG	Yes		No

Virtual machine swap file location

With SRM implementations, there is a common argument about the placement of the virtual machine swap files. Some would suggest maintaining a separate datastore for the virtual machine swap files, whereas some are against it. Before we try to understand the rationale behind these design choices, it is important to know what a virtual machine swap file is.

Every virtual machine will have a swap file (.vswp). This swap file is created every time a virtual machine is powered on. The size of the swap file is equal to the size of the memory assigned to the virtual machine, unless there is a reservation. If there is a memory reservation, then the size of the swap file will be equal to the size of the unreserved memory. Although rare, some environments use limits on memory as well.

So, the ideal formula to calculate the size of the swap file is as follows:

$$\text{Swap File Size} = \text{Memory Limit} - \text{Memory Reservation}$$

The default memory reservation is 0 MB and the default limit is equal to the configured size of the memory. By default, the swap file is stored along with the virtual machine in its working directory.

Design choice 1: Separate datastore for the swap files

Rationale: The swap file is created every time a virtual machine is powered-on. Since the VM will be powered on at the recovery site, and the swap file will be created at that time, there is no need to replicate the swap files.

The following table illustrates the pros and cons of this:

Pros	Cons
Swap file replication, if avoided, can reduce the bandwidth utilization for storage replication.	Single point of failure.
Reduces the need for the storage space at the recovery site, which otherwise would be needed for the swap files.	The swap location should be chosen at a per host level. This would require a lot of manual work in a large environment.
	Need to accommodate a separate large LUN. This could affect the available spare capacity of the array.

Design choice 2: Store the swap files in the VM's working directory

Rationale: Apart from the reduced replication bandwidth usage, there is no real advantage of maintaining a separate datastore for the swap files, and most SRM implementations would have already made sure that there would be more than enough bandwidth to make storage replication feasible. Also, not all virtual machines frequently use swap the files unless the vSphere environment is oversubscribed and the virtual machines are frequently contending for memory resources. In most cases, the swap files will be replicated during the initial sync. Subsequent synchronizations will include swap files created consequent to power-off and power-on operations. Keep in mind that a Guest OS reboot will not trigger the recreation of the swap files.

Pros	Cons
No administrative overhead, which would otherwise be needed to configure a swap datastore per host	Bandwidth wastage, due to the replication of the swap files
No single point of failure	Wasted storage capacity at the recovery site, which could be otherwise avoided if the swap files are not duplicated on the replica LUNs

> The design choices and the rationales behind them can vary depending on the environment you are dealing with. The rationales are only guidelines.

Summary

In this chapter, we learned what VMware vCenter Site Recovery Manager is and how it can be installed and configured to lay the groundwork for any SRM environment. In the next chapter, we will learn how to enable protection of the virtual machine workload by creating protection groups and recovery plans.

2
Creating Protection Groups and Recovery Plans

In the previous chapter, you learned how to install SRM, configure it, and lay the foundation for an SRM protected environment. You learned how to create resource, folder, and network mappings, as well as configure placeholder datastores and array managers. In this chapter, you will learn how to create protection groups and recovery plans.

In this chapter, we will cover the following topics:

- Understanding datastore groups
- Understanding protection groups
- Understanding recovery plans

Once you have done the groundwork required to form an SRM protected environment, the next step is to enable protection on the **virtual machines** (**VMs**). Before we delve into the procedural steps involved in protecting VMs, it is very important to understand a couple of basic concepts, such as the datastore and protection groups.

Understanding datastore groups

A datastore group is a container that aggregates one or more replication-enabled datastores. The datastore groups are created by SRM and cannot be manually altered. A replication-enabled datastore is one whose LUN has a replication schedule enabled at the array.

The following diagram shows the multi-datastore datastore and single-datastore datastore groups:

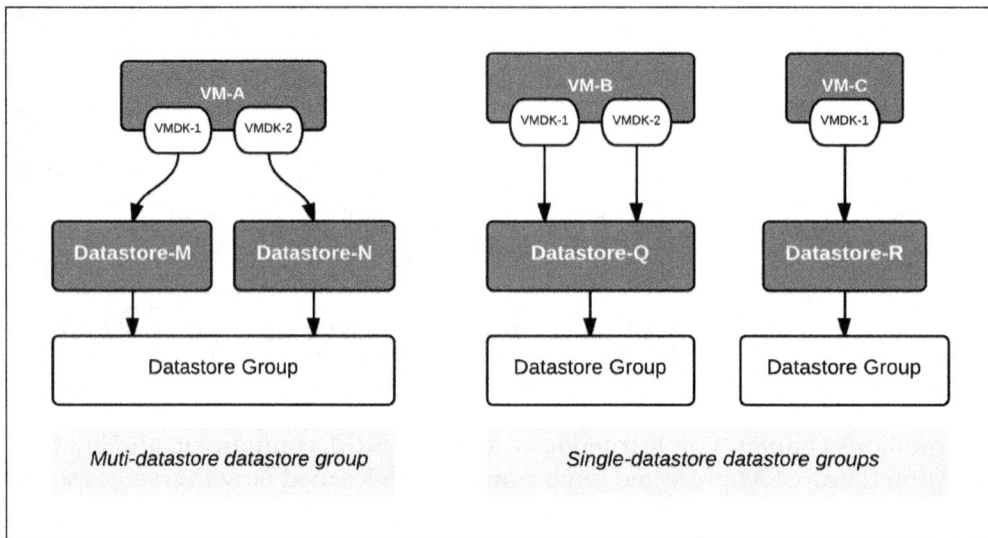

A datastore group will contain only a single datastore if that datastore doesn't store files of VMs from other datastores. See the single datastore group conceptual diagram.

A datastore group can also contain more than one datastore. SRM aggregates multiple datastores into a single group if they have VMs whose files are distributed onto these datastores. For example, if VM-A has two VMDKs, each placed on Datastore-A and Datastore-B, then both these datastores become part of the same datastore group.

These datastore groups further aid in the creation of protection groups.

Understanding protection groups

Unlike vSphere Replication, SRM cannot enable protection on individual VMs. All the VMs that are hosted on the datastores in a datastore group are protected. The protection is enabled at the datastore group level because with array-based replication, the LUNs backing the datastores are replicated. The array doesn't know which VMs are hosted on the datastore. It just replicates the LUN block by block. So, at the SRM layer, the protection is enabled at the datastore level. In a way, a protection group is nothing but a software construct to which datastore groups are added, which in turn includes all the VMs stored on them in the protection group.

When creating a protection group, you will have to choose the datastore groups that will be included. Keep in mind that you cannot individually select the datastores in a datastore group. If it were ever allowed, then you will have VMs with not all of their files protected. Let's assume that you have a virtual machine, VM-A, with two disks (vmdk-1 and vmdk-2) placed on two different datastores. Let's also say vmdk-1 is on datastore-X and vmdk-2 is on datastore-Y. When creating a protection group, if you were allowed to select the individual datastores, and if you chose only one of them, then you would leave one of the VM's disks unprotected. Hence, SRM doesn't allow selecting individual datastores from a datastore group as a measure to prevent such a scenario.

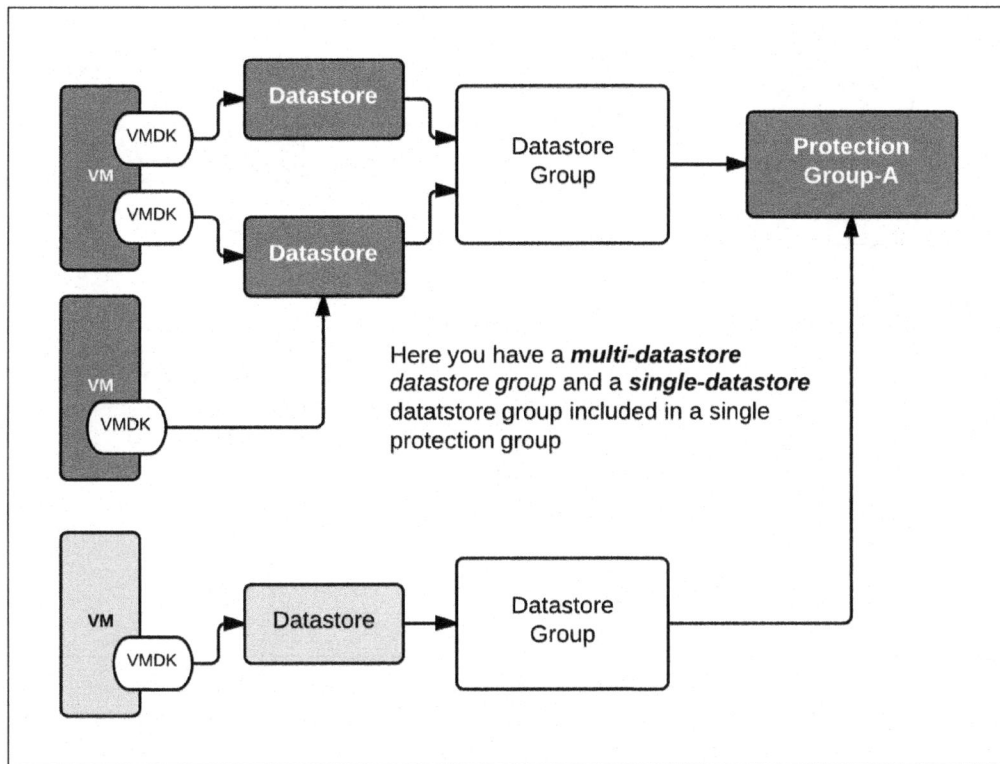

Here you have a **multi-datastore** *datastore group* and a **single-datastore** datatstore group included in a single protection group

Here, even though we have both the datastore groups included in the same protection group, **Protection Group-A**, it is possible to form separate protection groups for each of the datastore groups.

> A datastore group cannot be part of two protection groups at the same time.

Storage policy-based protection groups

Starting with SRM 6.1, you can create protection groups based on the virtual machine storage polices that exist in a vSphere environment. Storage polices enable the placement of virtual machine disk files on datastores that satisfy the workload characteristics of the virtual machine. They are created at the vCenter managing the environment and are based on storage capabilities learned via a VASA provider, or based on metadata tags manually created at the vCenter, or a combination of both.

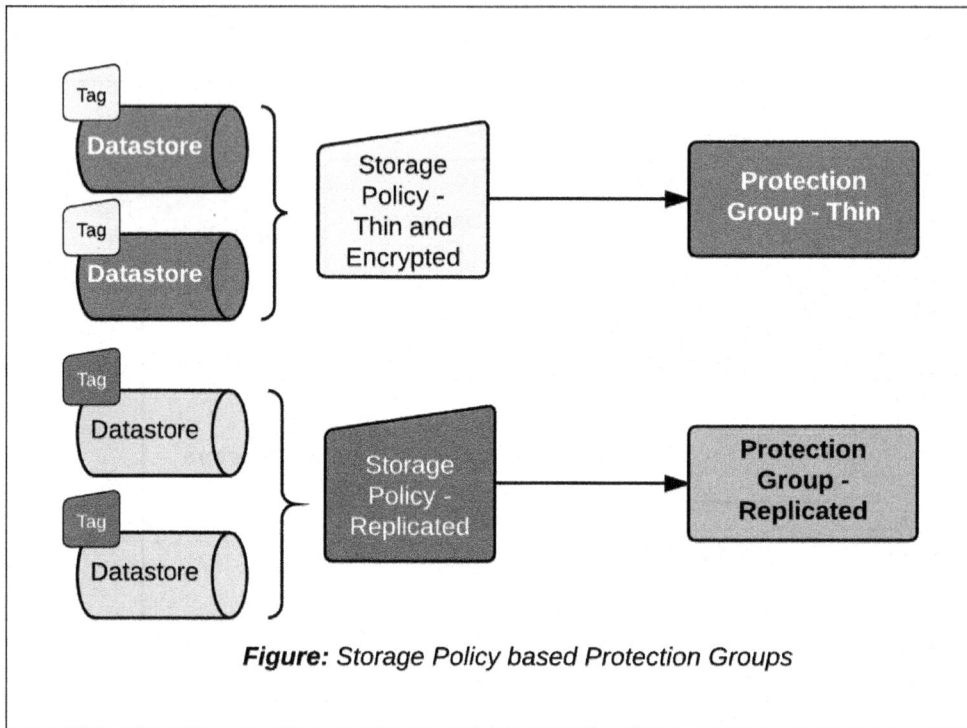

Figure: Storage Policy based Protection Groups

Refer to step 5 in the *Creating a protection group* section to understand how to create protection groups based on VM storage policies.

Creating a protection group

A protection group is created at the SRM UI, at the protected site. The following procedure will guide you through the steps required to create a protection group:

1. Navigate to the vCenter Server's inventory home and click on **Site Recovery**.

2. Click on **Protection Groups** in the left pane under the **Inventories** category:

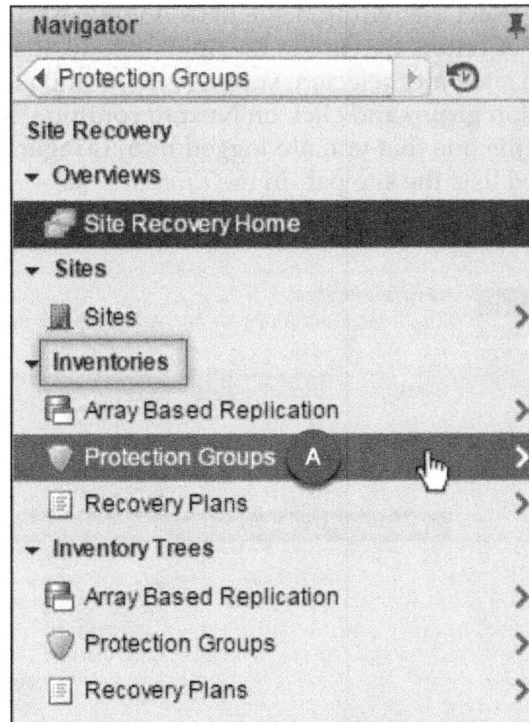

3. Click on the 🛡 icon to bring up the **Create Protection Group** wizard:

4. In the wizard, select the required site pair. If you have formed more than one site pair using vCenters that are in the linked mode, they would be listed for selection. With site pairs selected, supply a name and an optional description for the protection group and click on **Next** to continue. Keep in mind that the local vCenter (the one that you are logged into) is regarded as the protected site. The wizard lists the site pair in the *Protected Site – Recovery Site* format:

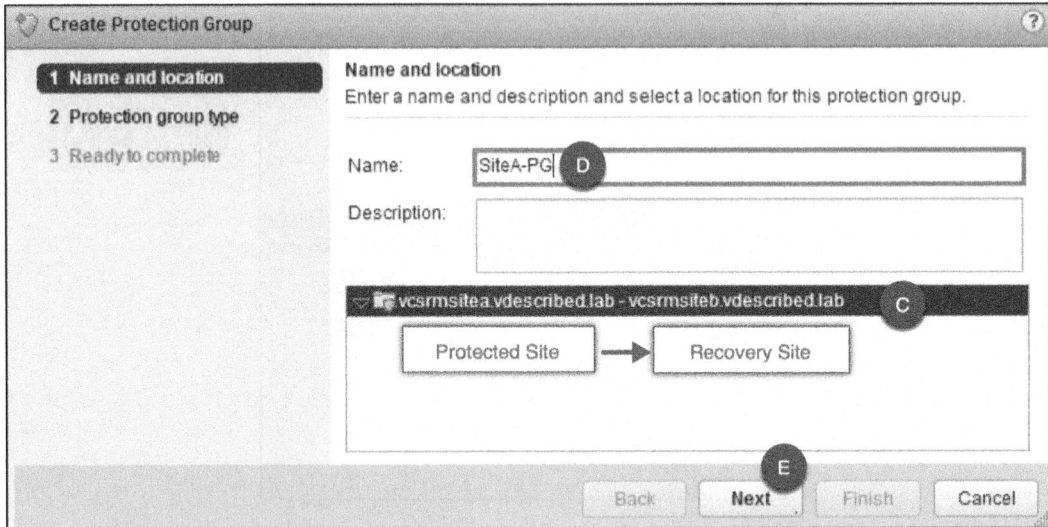

5. In the **Protection group type** screen, you will need to choose the **Direction of protection** and a **Protection group type**. Click on **Next** to continue:

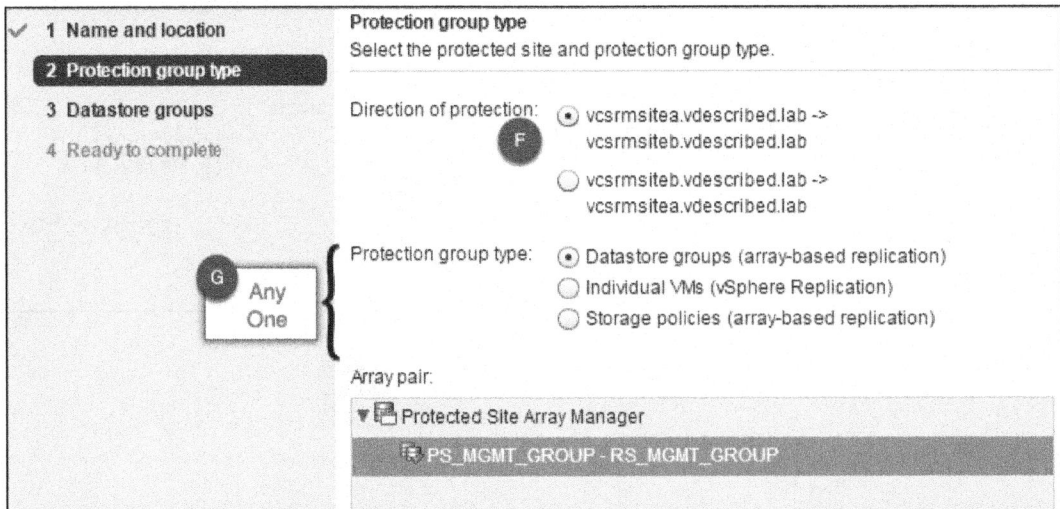

By selecting the direction of protection, you are basically identifying the protected and recovery sites. Keep in mind that the local site (the one that you're logged in to) is always selected as the protected site. In case you are using the SRM UI from the recovery site, it is important to make sure that you select the correct direction of protection.

There are three types of protection group types:

- **Datastore groups**: These can only be used with array-based replication. Selecting this option will list all the array pairs from which replication scheduled LUNs are presented to the ESXi hosts. If the wizard shows more than one array pair, make sure you select the correct one before proceeding.

- **Individual VMs**: These are used with vSphere Replication. You will learn about vSphere Replication later in this book.

○ **Storage policies**: These are used with array-based replication. They are used to protect virtual machines hosted on datastores tagged with a specific storage policy. vCenter lets you create storage policies to categorize datastores based on the capabilities of the LUNs backing them. The capabilities are learned either via a **VMware Storage API's for Storage Awareness (VASA)** provider or can be manually created using vCenter tags. If you select **Storage policies** as your protection type, then on the next screen you will be presented with a list of storage policies created at the protected site's vCenter, as shown here:

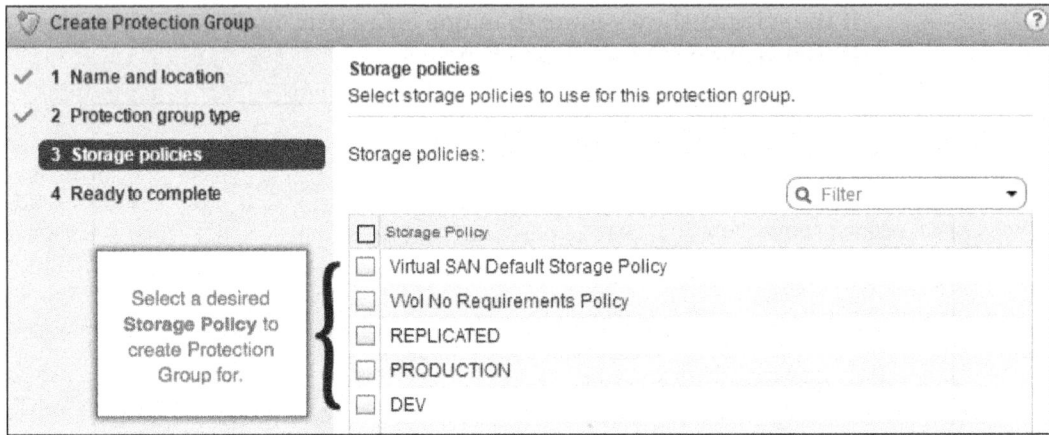

This is followed by the **Ready to complete** wizard screen, wherein you can review the options selected and click on **Finish** to create a storage policies-based protection group.

6. If you choose **Datastore groups** as the protection group type, then on the next screen, you will be presented with a list of datastore groups. As you learned before, a datastore group is a container that aggregates one of the more replication-enabled datastores:

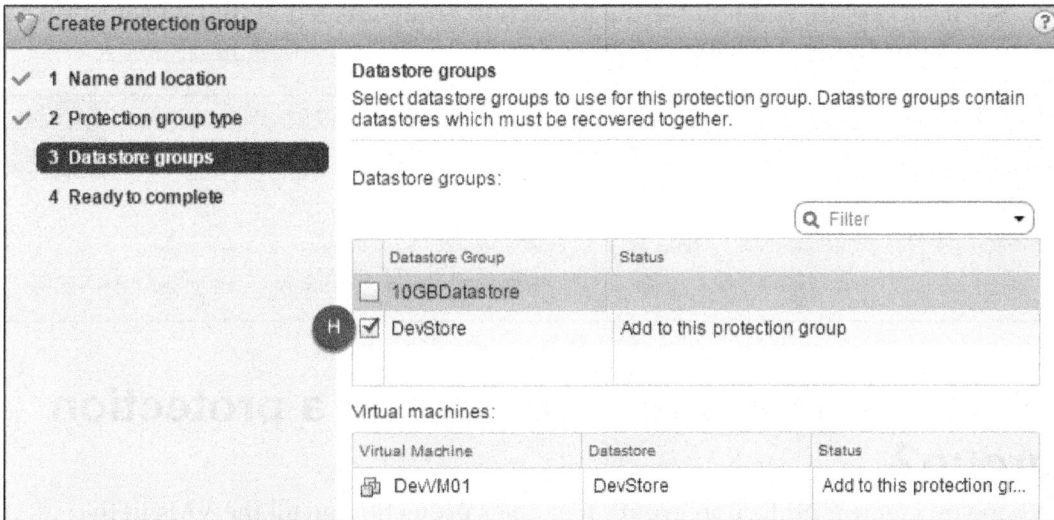

Although I have selected a single datastore group, we can select multiple datastore groups to become part of the protection group. Click on **Next** to continue.

7. On the **Ready to complete** screen, review the settings and click on **Finish** to create the protection group:

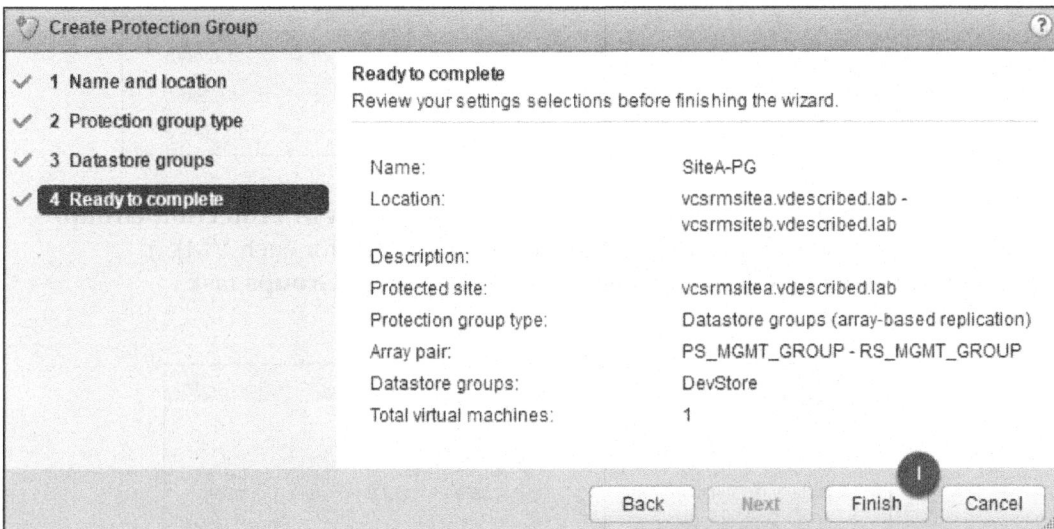

8. If successful, you will see the protection group created with the **Protection Status OK** and **Recovery Status Ready**:

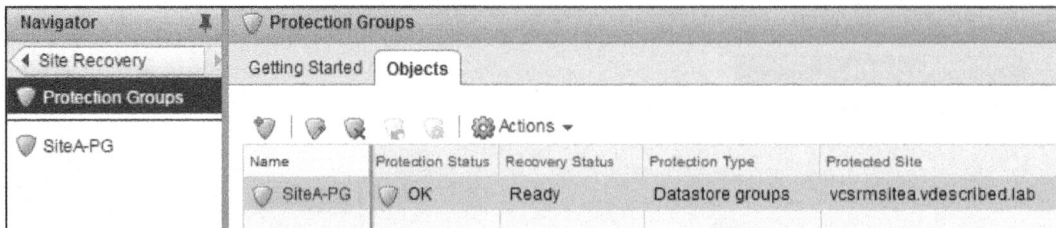

Navigator	Protection Groups				
◀ Site Recovery ▶	Getting Started	Objects			
▼ Protection Groups					
	🛡 Actions ▾				
▽ SiteA-PG	Name	Protection Status	Recovery Status	Protection Type	Protected Site
	▽ SiteA-PG	▽ OK	Ready	Datastore groups	vcsrmsitea.vdescribed.lab

What happens when you create a protection group?

When you create a protection group, it enables protection on all the VMs in the chosen datastore group and creates shadow VMs at the recovery site. In detail, this means that at the protected site vCenter Server, you should see a **Create VM Protection Group** task completed and subsequently a **Protect VM** task completed successfully for each of the VMs in the protection group:

📋 Task Console		
▸▬ ▾☰		
Task Name	Target	Status
Create VM Protection Group	📠 VCSRMSITEA.vdes...	✔ Completed
VirtualMachine.setCustomValue.label	🗄 DevVM01	✔ Completed
Protect VM	🗄 DevVM01	✔ Completed

At the recovery site vCenter Server, you will see a **Create VM Protection Group**, **Protect VM** (for each VM), a **Create virtual machine** (one for each VM), a **Recompute Device Groups**, and a **Recompute Datastore Groups** task completed successfully:

📋 Task Console		
▸▬ ▾☰		
Task Name	Target	Status
Create VM Protection Group	📠 VCSRMSITEB.vdes...	✔ Completed
Create virtual machine	🏢 SITE B	✔ Completed
Protect VM	📠 VCSRMSITEB.vdes...	✔ Completed
Recompute Device Groups	📠 VCSRMSITEB.vdes...	✔ Completed
Recompute Datastore Groups	📠 VCSRMSITEB.vdes...	✔ Completed

The shadow VMs appear in the vCenter Server's inventory at the recovery site:

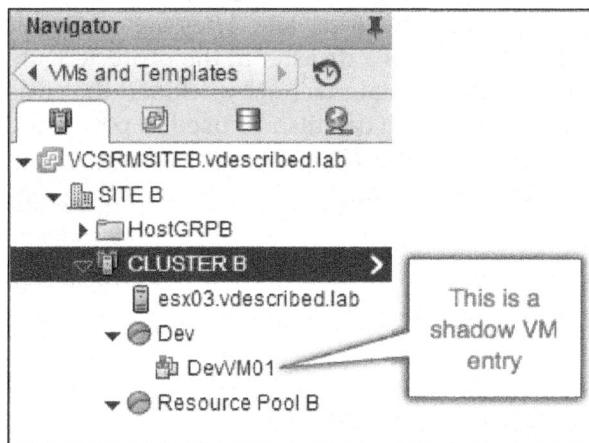

Since the shadow VMs are solely placeholders, you cannot perform any power operations on them. Other operations are possible, but are not recommended. Hence, a warning will be displayed, requesting confirmation:

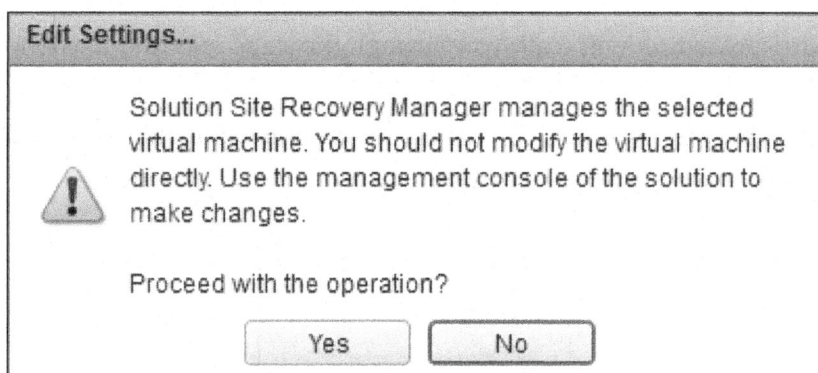

The placeholder datastores will only have the configuration file (.vmx) and a snapshot metadata file (.vmsd) for each VM:

Name	Size	Modified	Type
DevVM01.vmx	0.75 KB	26/03/2016 09:35	Virtual Machine
DevVM01.vmsd	0.00 KB	26/03/2016 09:35	File

These files will be automatically deleted when you delete the protection group.

Understanding recovery plans

Recovery plans are created at the recovery site. They are accessible and can be run from the recovery site when there is a disaster at the protected site. A recovery plan is executed to failover the virtual machine workload that was running at the protected site, to the recovery site. It can also be used to perform planned migrations. A recovery plan is a series of configuration steps that has to be performed to failover the protected VMs to the recovery site.

> A recovery plan should be associated with at least one protection group.

Creating a recovery plan

Once you have created protection groups, the next step would be to create a recovery plan for these protection groups. A recovery plan can be created either from the protected or the recovery sites. However, it is important to make sure that you select the direct recovery site while creating it. Since the sites are paired, a copy of the recovery plan will be created at the recovery site as well.

The following procedure will walk you through the steps required to create a recovery plan:

1. Navigate to the vCenter Server's inventory home and click on **Site Recovery**.

2. Click on **Recovery Plans** in the left pane under the **Inventories** category:

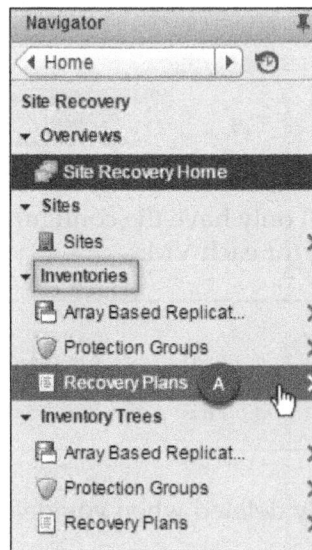

3. Click on the 📋 icon to bring up the **Create Recovery Plan** wizard:

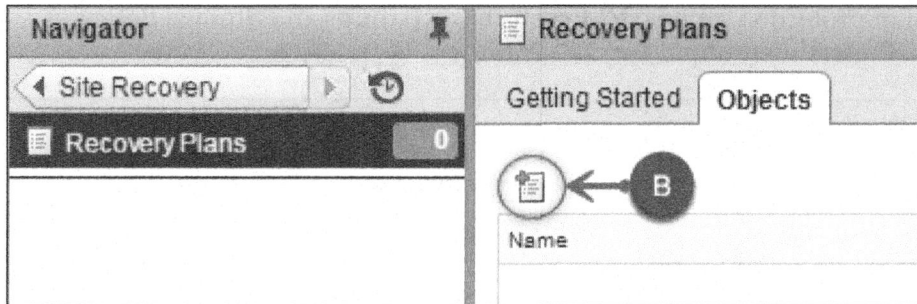

4. On the **Create Recovery Plan** wizard screen, select the intended site pair, then supply a name and an optional description and click on **Next** to continue:

5. On the next screen, select **Recovery Site** and click on **Next** to continue. If the recovery plan wizard is initiated at a site, then the wizard will select the other site in the site pair as the recovery site. For example, if you were to initiate the recovery plan wizard at SITE-A, then the wizard will autoselect the other site, SITE-B, as the recovery site, and vice versa.

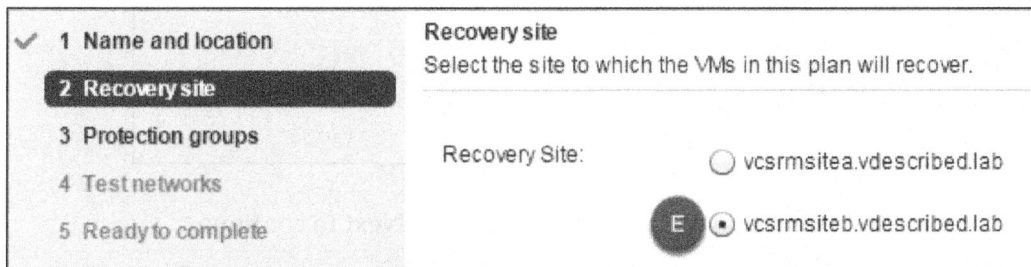

6. In the **Protection groups** screen, you will need to choose a protection group to associate with the recovery plan. The screen can list two types of protection groups: **VM protections Groups** and **Storage Policy Protection groups**:

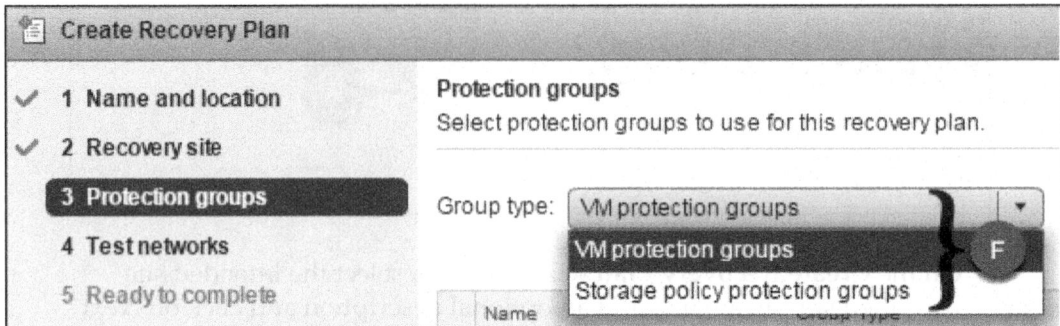

° If you select **VM protection groups**, then protection groups based on array-based replication (ABR) will be listed:

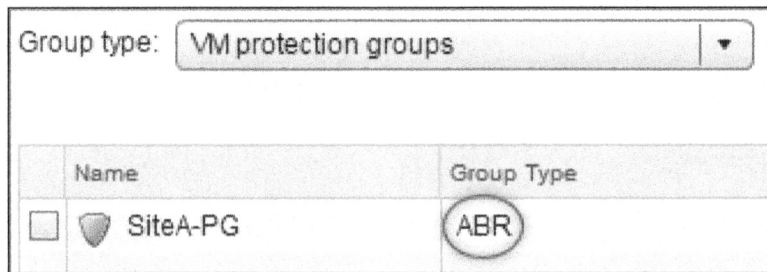

° If you select **Storage policy protection groups**, then protection groups based on storage policies (SP) will be listed:

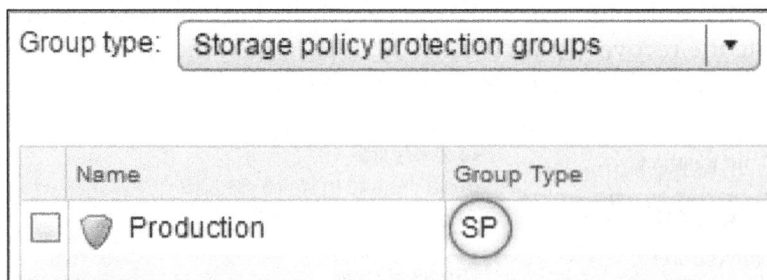

With the protection group selected, click on **Next** to continue.

7. In the next wizard screen, select **Test networks**. The test networks are set to **Auto*** by default. The auto networks are isolated bubble networks and don't connect to any physical network. They are used when testing a recovery plan. We will discuss testing a recovery plan and the use of bubble networks further in the next chapter. So, unless you have manually created an isolated test network port group at the recovery site, you can leave it at the auto setting. Click on **Next** to continue:

	Test networks
✓ 1 Name and location	Select the networks to use while running tests of this plan.
✓ 2 Recovery site	
✓ 3 Protection groups	Auto. Creates an isolated test network if the test network mapping at the site-level does not exist.
4 Test networks	
5 Ready to complete	

Recovery Network	Test Network	
SITE B > All VM PG	Auto*	
SITE B > Application PG	Auto*	The Auto* option will create an isolated bubble network when the recovery plan test is run.
SITE B > Dev PG	Auto*	
SITE B > Prod PG	Auto*	
SITE B > VM Network	Auto*	

8. In the **Ready to complete** screen, review the settings and click on **Finish** to create the recovery plan:

Create Recovery Plan

	Ready to complete
✓ 1 Name and location	Review your settings selections before finishing the wizard.
✓ 2 Recovery site	
✓ 3 Protection groups	
✓ 4 Test networks	
✓ 5 Ready to complete	

Name:	PLAN-SITEA
Location:	vcsrmsitea.vdescribed.lab - vcsrmsiteb.vdescribed.lab
Description:	
Protected site:	vcsrmsitea.vdescribed.lab
Recovery site:	vcsrmsiteb.vdescribed.lab
Protection groups:	SiteA-PG

9. Once done, you will see the plan listed with the status **Ready**:

Summary

In this chapter, you learned what datastore groups, protection groups, and recovery plans are. You learned how to create protection groups based on datastore groups and storage policies. You learned how to create a recovery plan using either VM protection groups or storage policy protection groups.

In the next chapter, you will learn how to test the recovery plans and execute a failover and a failback.

3
Testing and Performing a Failover and Failback

In the previous chapter, you learned how to create protection groups and recovery plans. Recovery plans are nothing but precreated workflows for the recovery of failed sites. In this chapter, you will learn how to test the recovery plans that are already created, and how to use them to perform a failover, planned migration, reprotect, and failback.

Here is a list of topics that will be covered in this chapter:

- Testing a recovery plan
- Performing a planned migration
- Performing a disaster recovery (failover)
- Performing a forced recovery
- Reprotecting an SRM site
- Performing a failback to an SRM protected site
- IPv4 customization rules
- Configuring VM recovery properties

Testing a recovery plan

A recovery plan should be tested for its readiness to make sure that it would work as expected in the event of a real disaster. Most organizations periodically review and update their recovery runbook to make sure that they have an optimized and working plan for a recovery. The same process can be applied here to periodically test the recovery plans created.

With Site Recovery Manager, the testing of a recovery plan can be automated. It is important to understand the workflow involved in testing a Recovery Plan before we delve into the details of what really happens in the background.

Test workflow

The testing of a Recovery Plan is done in a manner that doesn't affect the current operations, which include replication schedules, the actual replicas, or the protected VMs. In this section of the chapter, we will learn how this is achieved.

The following figure shows an overview of the steps involved during the testing of a recovery plan:

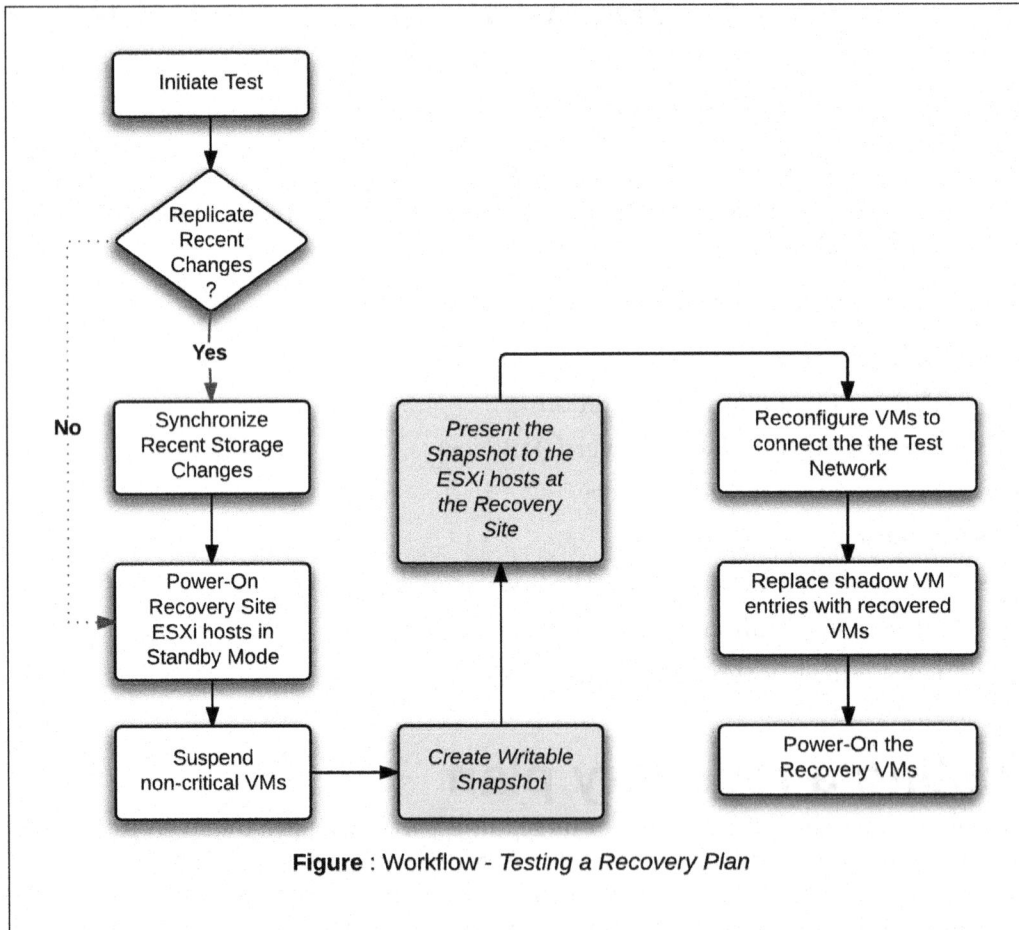

Figure : Workflow - *Testing a Recovery Plan*

Running the test

The test is initiated via SRM's vSphere Web Client interface. The following steps will guide you through the procedure for testing a recovery plan:

1. Navigate to the vCenter Server's inventory home and click on **Site Recovery** to bring up **Site Recovery Home**.

2. At **Site Recovery Home**, use the left pane to navigate to **Recovery Plans** under **Inventories**:

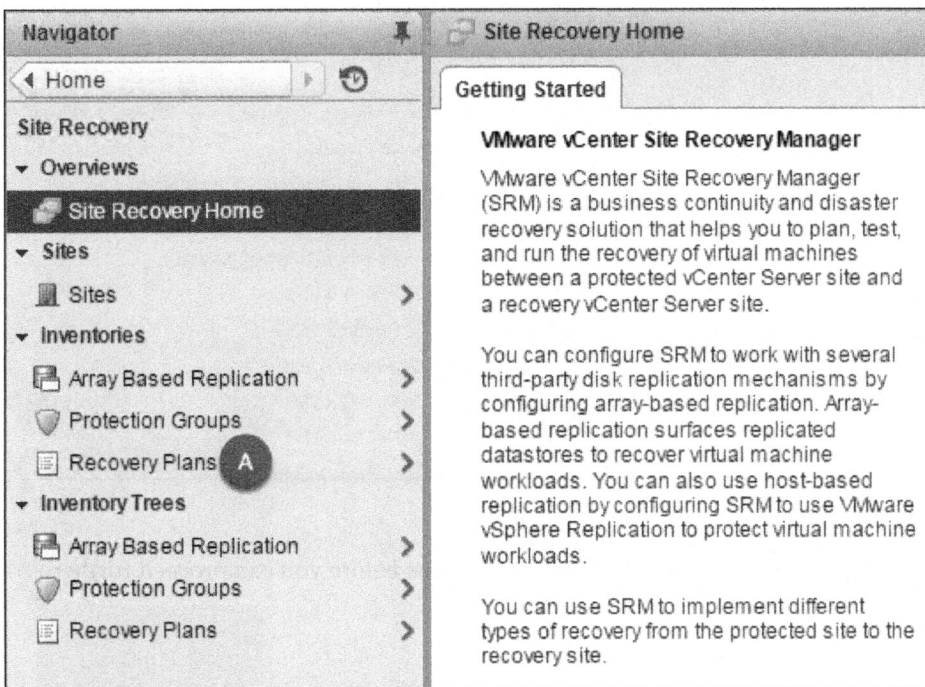

3. The **Recovery Plans** page will list all the available recovery plans. Click on the one that you intend to test:

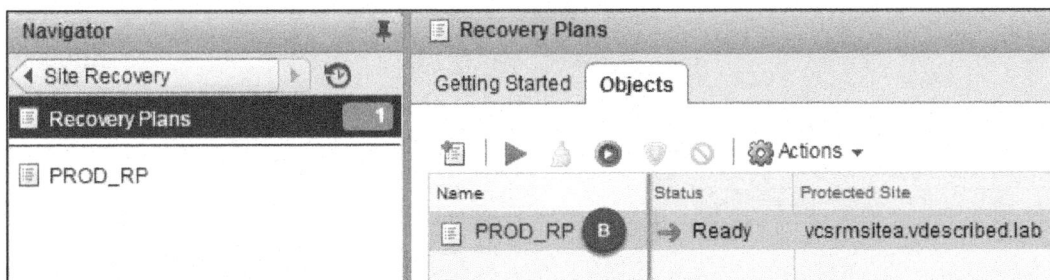

4. You will now be presented with the selected recovery plan's **Monitor |
    Recovery Steps** page. Click on the ▶ icon to bring up the test wizard:

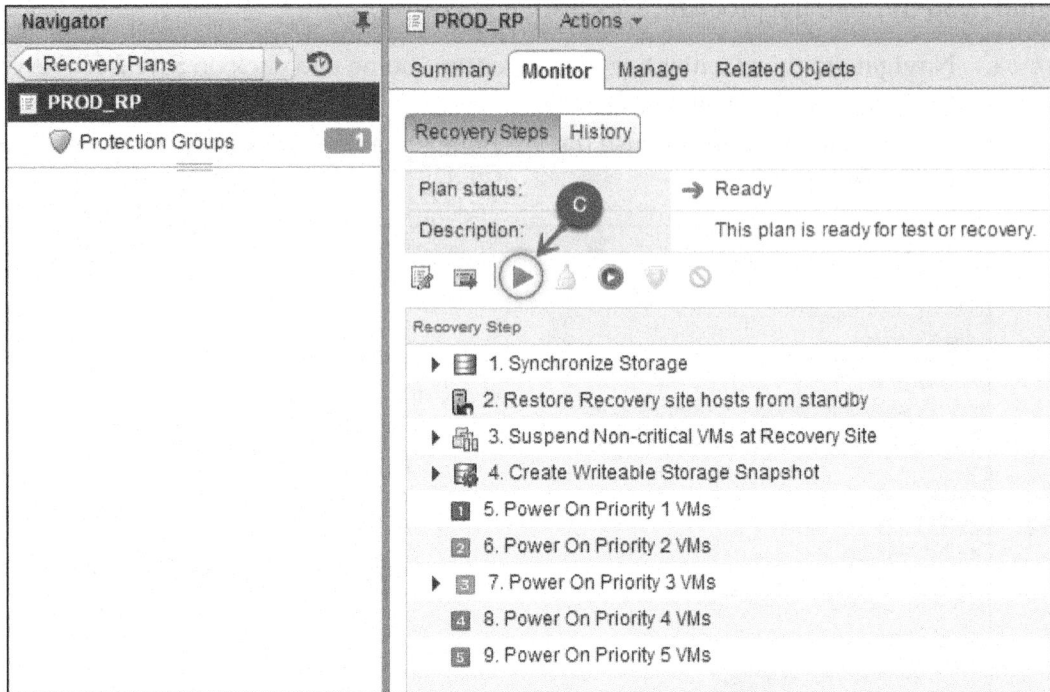

The plan should have a **Ready** status before you can proceed further.

5. The first screen of the wizard will indicate which of the sites have been designated as the protected and recovery sites, the site connection status, and the number of VMs protected:

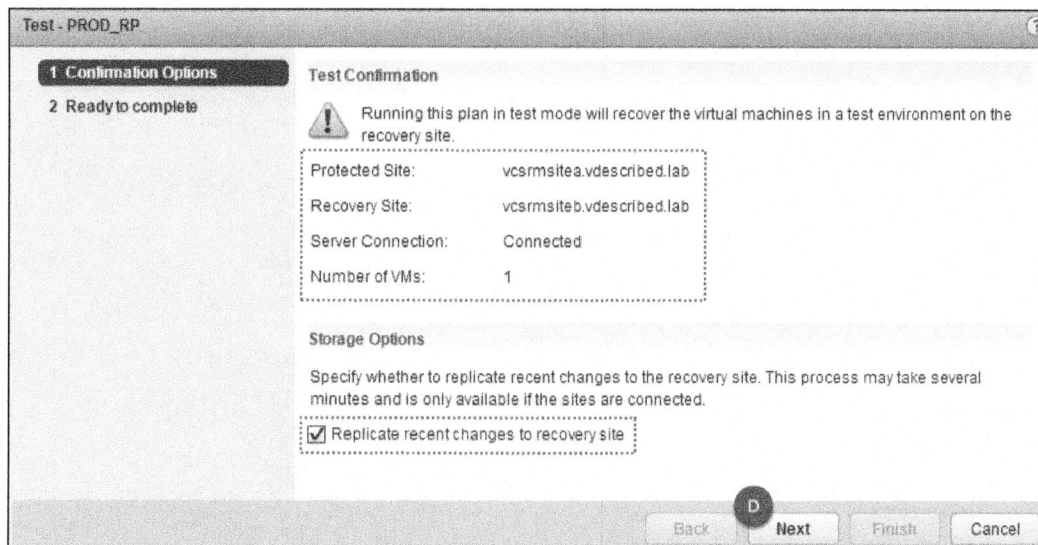

By default, the storage option **Replicate recent changes to the recovery site** is selected. I would recommend you don't deselect this option because we replicate the recent changes during a planned migration. So, it is an important ability of the array to respond to a nonscheduled replication request that is tested. However, we might not need to do this if the replication is synchronous. Click on **Next** to continue.

6. The **Ready to complete** screen will summarize the settings; review them and click on **Finish** to initiate the test.

7. You should now see a test recovery plan task in the **Recent Tasks** pane. Also, navigate to the **Recovery Steps** tab to watch the progress of the test:

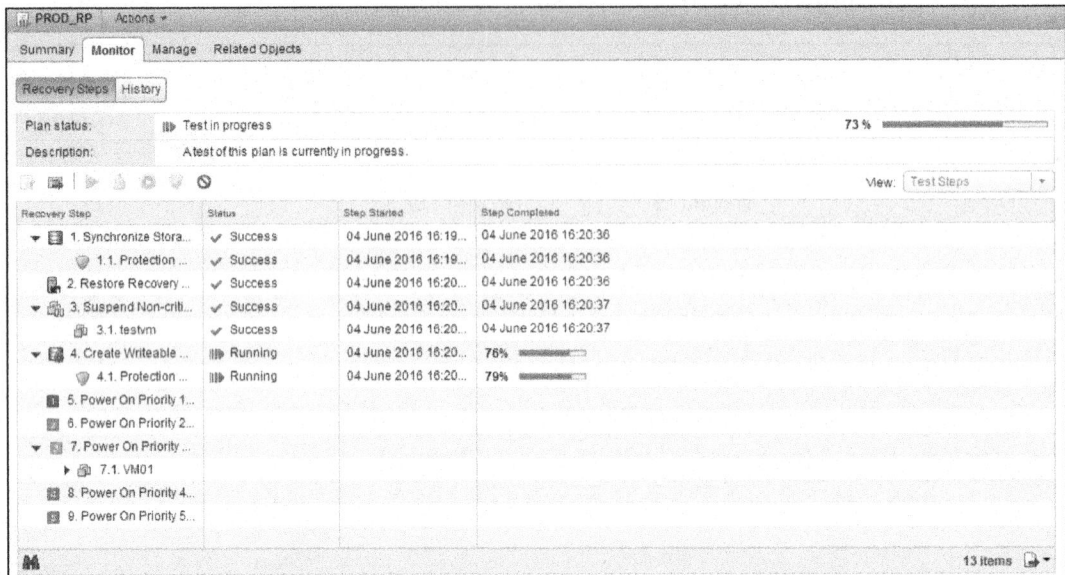

8. Once the test completes successfully, the **Plan status** changes from **Test in progress** to **Test Complete**:

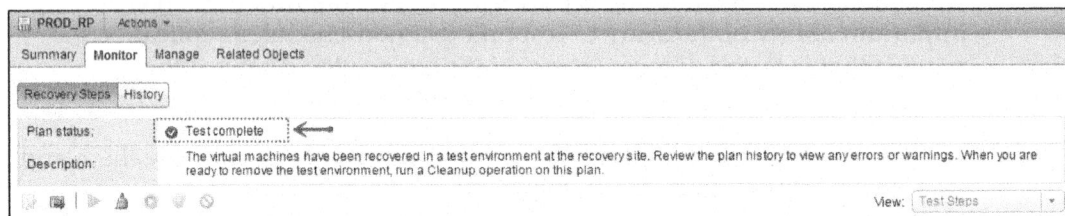

Testing a recovery plan – background

When you initiate a test, SRM instructs the Storage Replication Adapter to execute a replication cycle to replicate the latest changes to the replica LUN at the recovery site. This, however, will only happen if you have chosen to leave the default option to replicate recent changes checked. You wouldn't need to replicate the recent change when the replication is synchronous since the replica would already have the latest change. Refer to your replication vendor documentation for more information.

Once the replication is complete, it then needs to find a way to present the replica LUN's data to the recovery-ESXi hosts so that the VMs can be powered on. This is achieved differently by different storage arrays. The most common methodology is to create a writeable snapshot of the replica LUN and then present the snapshot to the recovery-ESXi hosts. The hosts will subsequently scan their HBAs to detect the VMFS volumes on the LUN.

Before the snapshot is presented to the ESXi hosts, SRM needs to make sure that there is enough room (compute capacity) at the recovery site to power on the recovered VMs. To make room for the VMs, SRM could power off the noncritical VMs (if included in the recovery plan) and also power up the ESXi hosts that were put into standby mode (if any) by **Distributed Power Management (DPM)**.

> The noncritical VMs that SRM chooses to suspend are those that were marked as noncritical for the recovery plan using the **Add NonCritical VM** option.

To power on the recovered VMs, they have to be registered to the recovery site's vCenter Server. This is achieved by replacing the shadow VM entries with the entries corresponding to the recovered VMs. Keep in mind that the shadow VMs are mere inventory objects and do not have any VMDKs mapped to them.

The VMs are then configured to connect to the test network. The test network can either be a port group that you precreated for the test, or an auto bubble network created on a new vSphere Standard Switch with no physical uplinks.

The following screenshot shows a vSphere Standard Switch and a port group that was automatically created during a test for the auto (bubble) network:

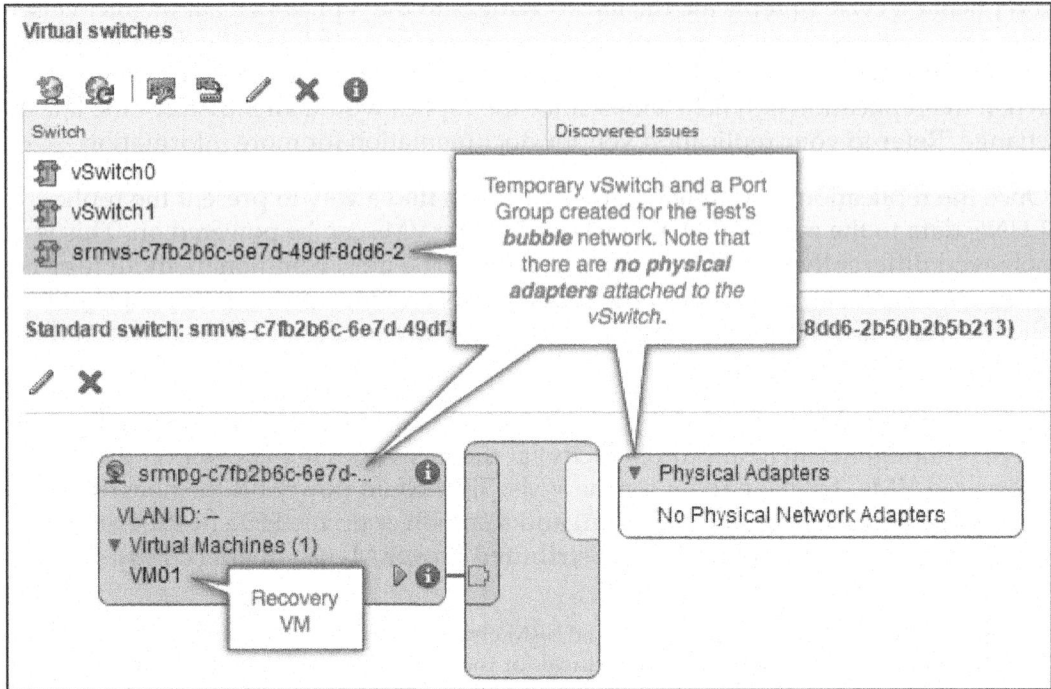

Once the VMs have been configured to connect to the test network, they are powered on. Keep in mind that the testing of a recovery plan does not affect the power state of the protected VMs at the protected site.

Performing the cleanup after a test

We know from the previous section that during the course of the testing of a recovery plan, SRM executes the creation of certain elements to enact a disaster recovery in a manner that wouldn't affect the running environment. Hence, the changes done and the objects created are temporary and have to be cleaned up after a successful test. Fortunately, this is not a manual process either. SRM provides an automated method for preforming a cleanup. Keep in mind that a cleanup can only be performed on a recovery plan that has been tested successfully.

The following will happen during a cleanup:

- Putting the ESXi hosts back into DPM standby mode
- Powering off the recovery VMs

- Powering on the suspended noncritical VMs
- Replacing the inventory entries of the recovery VMs with their corresponding shadow VM entries
- Unmounting the VMFS volume
- Detaching the LUN device
- Rescanning the storage initiators and refreshing the storage system
- Deleting the writable snapshot that was created
- Removing the port group and the vSwitch that were created for the bubble network

The following procedure will guide you through the steps required for the cleanup:

1. Navigate to the vCenter Server's inventory home and click on **Site Recovery** to bring up **Site Recovery Home**.

2. At **Site Recovery Home**, use the left pane to navigate to **Recovery Plans** under **Inventories**.

3. Select the recovery plan that was tested successfully, navigate to its **Monitor | Recovery Steps** tab, and click on the ![icon] icon to bring up the cleanup wizard:

Recovery Step	Status	Step Started	Step Completed
▶ 1. Synchronize Storage	✔ Success	04 June 2016 16:19:54	04 June 2016 16:20:36
2. Restore Recovery site hosts from standby	✔ Success	04 June 2016 16:20:36	04 June 2016 16:20:36
▶ 3. Suspend Non-critical VMs at Recovery Site	✔ Success	04 June 2016 16:20:36	04 June 2016 16:20:37
▶ 4. Create Writeable Storage Snapshot	✔ Success	04 June 2016 16:20:37	04 June 2016 16:21:03
5. Power On Priority 1 VMs			
6. Power On Priority 2 VMs			
▶ 7. Power On Priority 3 VMs	✔ Success	04 June 2016 16:21:04	04 June 2016 16:22:59
8. Power On Priority 4 VMs			
9. Power On Priority 5 VMs			

4. In the **Cleanup** wizard, the details regarding the current protected and recovery sites, their connection status, and the number of protected VMs are displayed. Note that the **Force Cleanup** option is greyed out. It will only be available if the cleanup operation had failed during the previous attempt. Click on **Next** to continue:

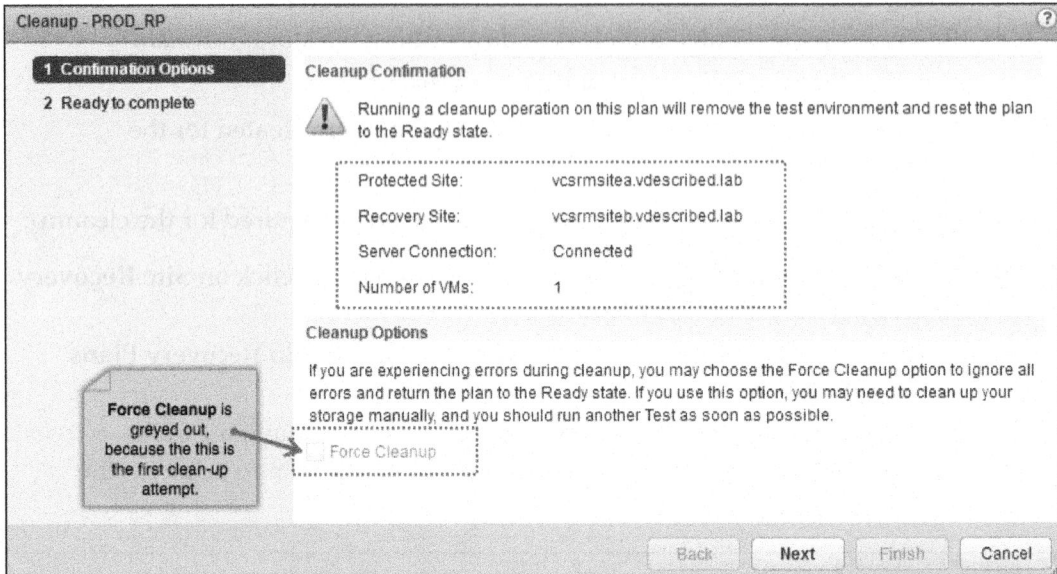

5. The **Ready to complete** screen will summarize the cleanup options selected. Click on **Finish** to initiate the cleanup.

6. The **Recovery Steps** page shows the cleanup steps are in progress:

Recovery Step	Status	Step Started	Step Completed
1. Restore Recovery site hosts from standby	✔ Success	04 June 2016 18:45:13	04 June 2016 18:45:13
2. Power Off Test VMs at Recovery Site	✔ Success	04 June 2016 18:45:13	04 June 2016 18:45:18
2.1. VM01	✔ Success	04 June 2016 18:45:13	04 June 2016 18:45:18
3. Resume Non-critical VMs at Recovery Site	✔ Success	04 June 2016 18:45:14	04 June 2016 18:45:17
3.1. testvm	✔ Success	04 June 2016 18:45:14	04 June 2016 18:45:17
4. Discard Test Data and Reset Storage	▶ Running	04 June 2016 18:45:17	55%
4.1. Protection Group PROD_PG	▶ Running	04 June 2016 18:45:17	55%

7. On successful completion of the cleanup, the **Plan status** will change to **Ready**:

Performing a planned migration

VMware SRM can be used to migrate your workload from one site to another. A planned migration is done when the protected site is available and running the virtual machine workload.

There are many use cases, of which the following two are prominent:

- When migrating your infrastructure to new hardware
- When migrating your virtual machine storage from one array to another

> A planned migration will replicate the most recent changes with the help of storage replication. This is not optional.

The following procedure will guide you through the steps required in performing a planned migration:

1. Navigate to the vCenter Server's inventory home and click on **Site Recovery** to bring up **Site Recovery Home**.

2. At **Site Recovery Home**, use the left pane to navigate to **Recovery Plans** under **Inventories**.

3. Select the recovery plan, navigate to its **Monitor | Recovery Steps** tab, and click on the ⊙ icon to bring up the **Recovery** wizard:

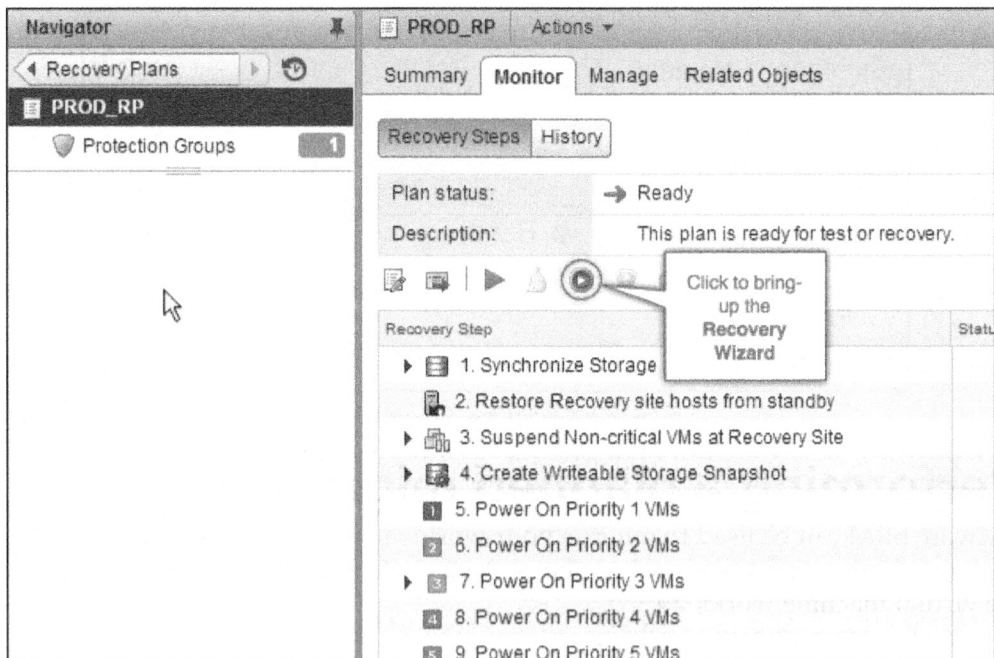

4. The first screen will seek a **Recovery Confirmation**. The **Recovery Type** will be preselected as **Planned Migration**. You should acknowledge the recovery confirmation to proceed further. Click on **Next** to continue:

5. The **Ready to complete** screen will summarize the wizard options that were selected. Click on **Finish** to initiate the migration.

6. The **Recovery Steps** tab will show the progress of the planned migration:

7. Once completed successfully, the **Plan status** will change to **Recovery Complete**:

The planned migration will not proceed further if any of the recovery steps fail.

However, when you reattempt the planned migration, it would resume the operation from the step at which it failed. This enables you to fix the problem and resume from where it failed, saving a considerable amount of time.

The following flowchart shows the logical sequence of events that would occur during the course of a planned migration:

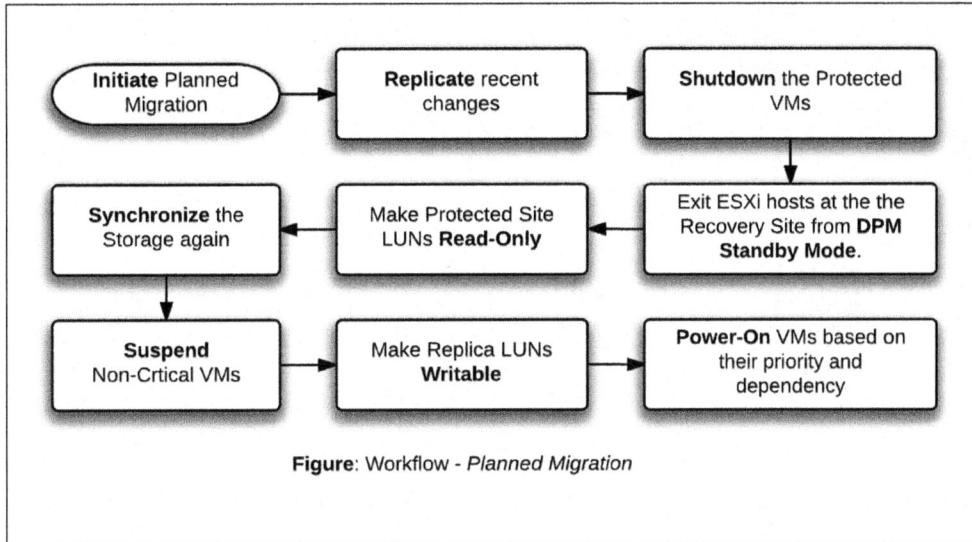

Figure: Workflow - *Planned Migration*

Performing a disaster recovery (failover)

A failover is performed when the protected site becomes fully or partially unavailable. We use a recovery plan that is already created and tested, to perform the failover. Keep in mind that SRM does not auto-determine the occurrence of a disaster at the protected site, hence a recovery is always manually initiated.

Here is how you perform a failover:

1. Navigate to the vCenter Server's inventory home and click on **Site Recovery** to bring up **Site Recovery Home**.

2. At **Site Recovery Home**, use the left pane to navigate to **Recovery Plans** under **Inventories**.

3. Select the recovery plan that was created for disaster recovery, navigate to its **Monitor | Recovery Steps** tab, and click on the ⊙ icon to bring up the **Recovery** wizard.

In the **Recovery** wizard, agree to the **Recovery Confirmation**, set the **Recovery Type** as **Disaster Recovery**, and click on **Next** to continue:

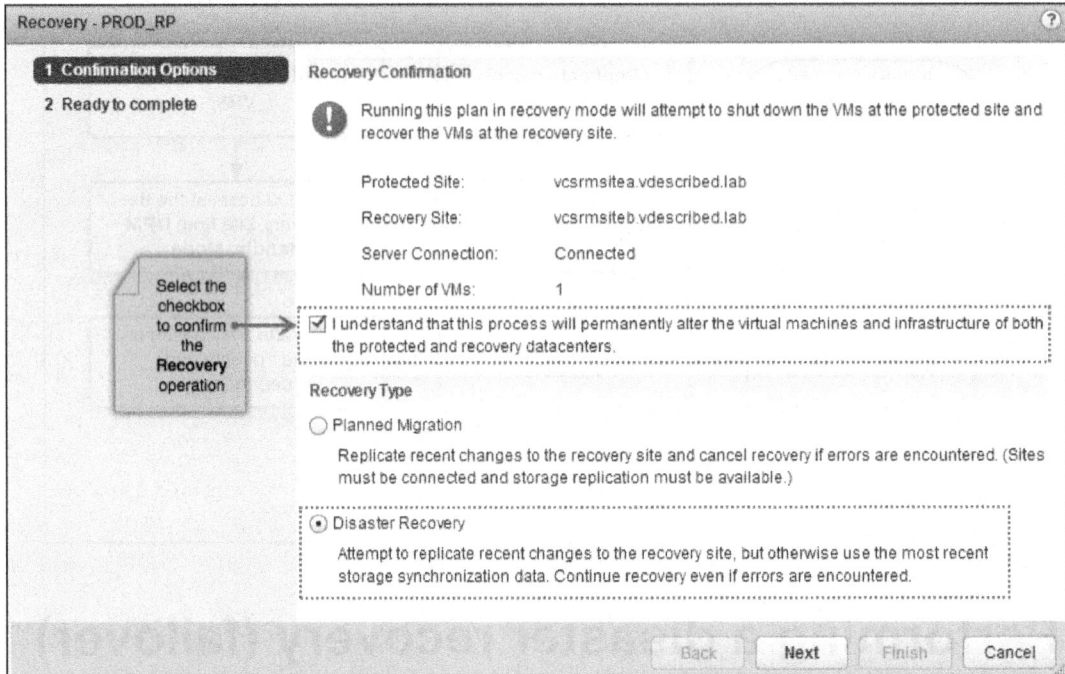

4. The **Ready to complete** screen will summarize the options selected. Review and click on **Finish** to initiate the recovery operation.

5. The **Recovery Steps** tab of the **Recovery Plan** will show the progress of each of the steps involved:

Recovery Step	Status	Step Started	Step Completed
▼ ☰ 1. Pre-synchronize Storage	✓ Success	05 June 2016 00:56:...	05 June 2016 01:01:27
🛡 1.1. Protection Group PROD_PG	✓ Success	05 June 2016 00:56:...	05 June 2016 01:01:27
▶ 🖥 2. Shutdown VMs at Protected Site	✓ Success	05 June 2016 01:01:...	05 June 2016 01:01:40
🖥 3. Resume VMs Suspended by Previous Re...			
🖥 4. Restore Recovery site hosts from standby	✓ Success	05 June 2016 01:01:...	05 June 2016 01:01:40
🖥 5. Restore Protected site hosts from standby			
▼ 🖥 6. Prepare Protected Site VMs for Migration	✓ Success	05 June 2016 01:01:...	05 June 2016 01:01:59
▶ 🛡 6.1. Protection Group PROD_PG	✓ Success	05 June 2016 01:01:...	05 June 2016 01:01:59
▼ ☰ 7. Synchronize Storage	▐▐▶ Running	05 June 2016 01:01...	23% ▬▬▬
🛡 7.1. Protection Group PROD_PG	▐▐▶ Running	05 June 2016 01:01:...	23% ▬▬▬
▶ 🖥 8. Suspend Non-critical VMs at Recovery Site			
▼ 🖥 9. Change Recovery Site Storage to Writeable			
🛡 9.1. Protection Group PROD_PG			
🔲 10. Power On Priority 1 VMs			
🔲 11. Power On Priority 2 VMs			
▶ 🔲 12. Power On Priority 3 VMs			
🔲 13. Power On Priority 4 VMs			
🔲 14. Power On Priority 5 VMs			

6. Once the failover is complete, the status of the recovery plan should read **Recovery Complete**.

The recovery steps involved in a disaster recovery (failover) are the same as in those of a planned migration, except for the fact that SRM ignores any unsuccessful attempts to presynchronize the storage or the shutting down of the protected VMs.

Performing a forced recovery

Forced recovery is used when the protected site is no longer operational enough to allow SRM to perform its tasks at the protected site before the failover. It is enabled at the recovery site, thereby letting the recovery site to failover machines from the protected site by skipping the protected site operations.

For instance, if there is an unexpected power outage at the protected site, not only the ESXi hosts but also the storage array become unavailable. In this scenario, SRM cannot perform any of its tasks at the protected site, such as shutting down the protected VMs or replicating the most recent storage changes (if the replication is asynchronous).

Enabling forced recovery for a site

Forced recovery is not enabled by default, but it can be enabled at the site's **Advanced Settings**. It is enabled at the recovery site and not the protected site.

Here is how it is done:

1. Navigate to the vCenter Server's inventory home and click on **Site Recovery** to bring up **Site Recovery Home**.

2. Click on **Sites** on the left pane to navigate to the **Sites** page.

3. On the **Sites** page, select the recovery site from the left pane and navigate to **Manage | Advanced Settings | Recovery**. With **Recovery** selected, click on **Edit** to bring up the **Edit Advanced Settings** window:

4. In the **Edit Advanced Settings** window, select the **Enabled** listed against the **recovery.forceRecovery** setting, and click on **OK** to enable forced recovery:

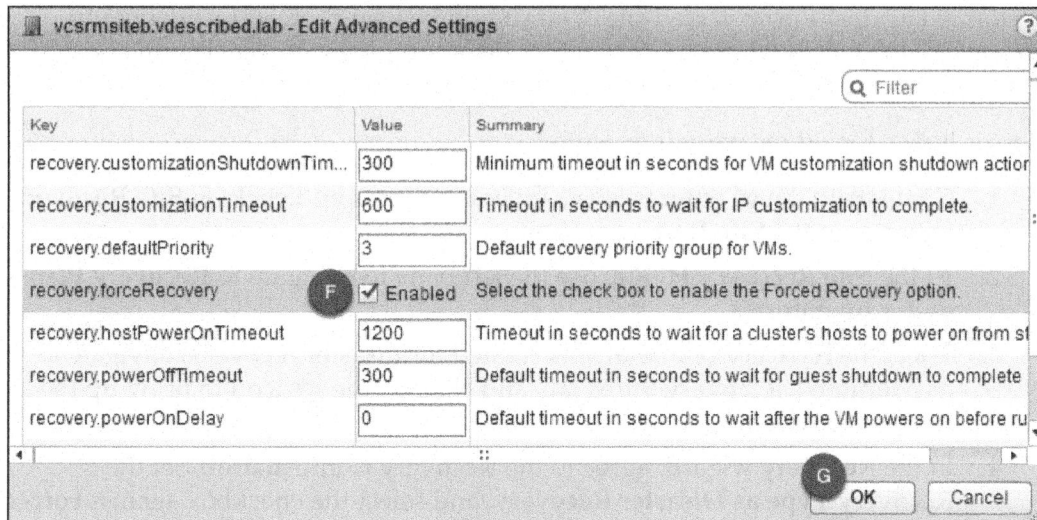

5. If enabled, then the **recovery.forceRecovery** setting will have a value of **true** configured:

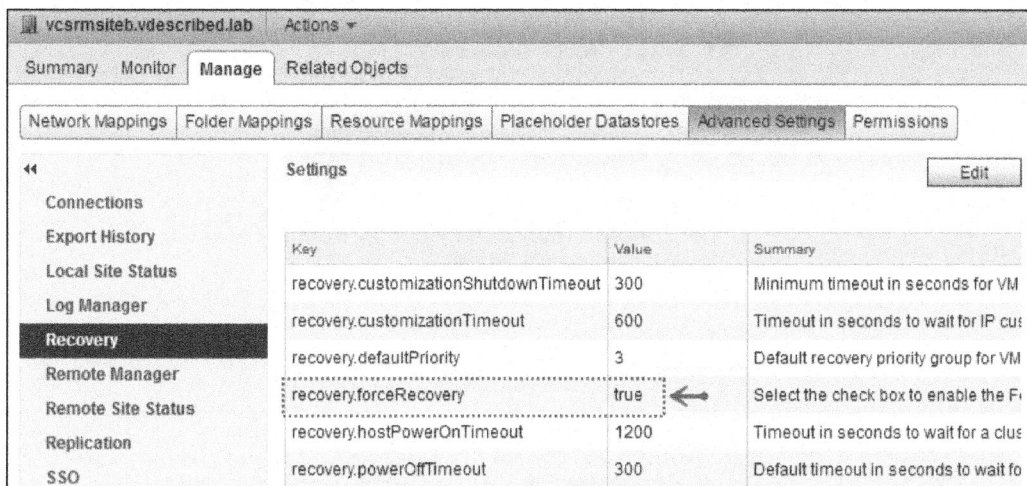

Running a forced recovery

Running a forced recovery will skip all the steps that otherwise should have been performed against the protected site. You should be using forced recovery only during circumstances where the protected site is completely down, leaving no connectivity to either the ESXi hosts or the storage array.

Here is how a forced recovery is executed:

1. Navigate to the vCenter Server's inventory home and click on **Site Recovery** to bring up the **Site Recovery Home**.

2. At the **Site Recovery Home,** use the left pane to navigate to **Recovery Plans** under **Inventories**.

3. Select the recovery plan that was created for disaster recovery, navigate to its **Monitor | Recovery Steps** tab, and click on the ⊙ icon to bring up the **Recovery** wizard.

4. In the **Recovery** wizard, agree to the **Recovery Confirmation**, set the **Recovery Type** as **Disaster Recovery**, and select the checkbox against **Forced Recovery – recovery site operations only**. Click on **Next** to continue:

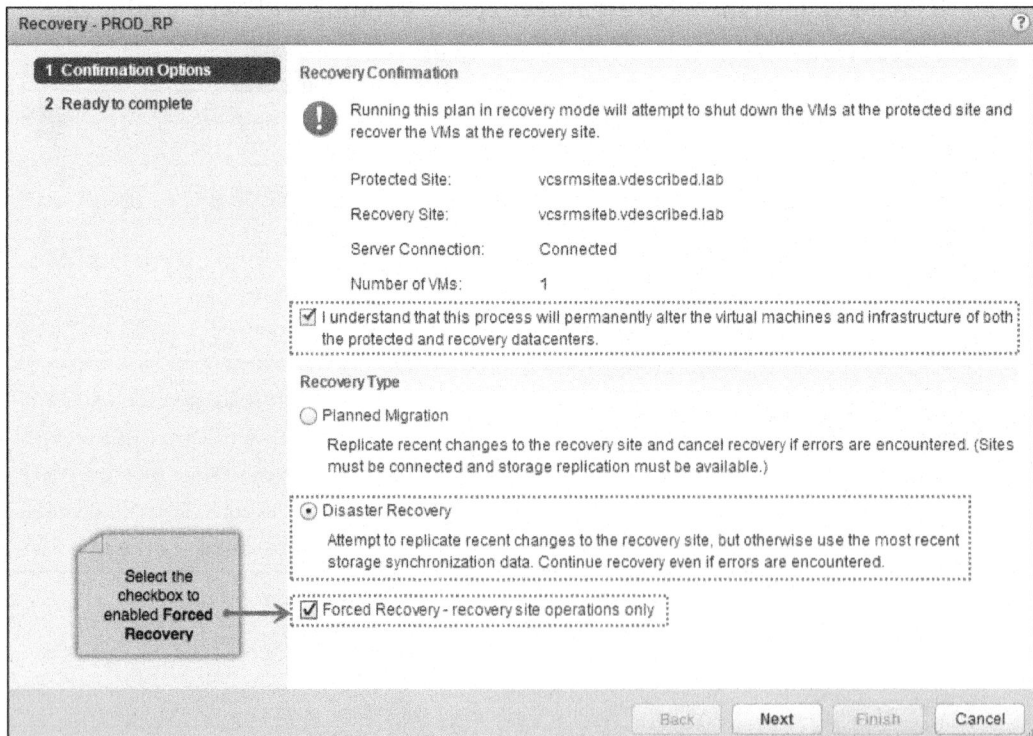

5. On the **Ready to complete** screen, review the settings and click on **Finish** to initiate a forced recovery.

> If a forced recovery is executed while the protected site is still online and available, then it would leave the VMs running at both the protected and recovery sites, causing a split-brain condition for SRM. Furthermore, if the array-based replication was asynchronous, then the chance is that the VMs that were started at the recovery site are running from old data compared to the ones that protected the site. So, it is very important that you are cautious when you plan to execute a forced recovery.

Reprotecting an SRM site

After you failover the workload from a protected site to the recovery site, the recovery site has no protection enabled for the new workload that it has begun hosting. SRM provides a method to enable protection of the recovery site. This method is called **reprotect**.

A reprotect operation will reverse the direction of the replication, hence the recovery site is designated as the new protected site. The reprotect operation can only be done on a recovery plan with the **Recovery complete** status. Also, keep in mind that a reprotect operation can only be executed when you have repaired the failed site and made it available to become a recovery site.

For instance, let's assume that site-A and site-B are the protected and recovery sites, respectively. If workload at site-A were failed over to site-B, then to reprotect site-B, site-A should be made accessible. This would mean fixing the problems that caused the failure at site-A.

Here is how you perform the reprotect operation:

1. Navigate to the vCenter Server's inventory home and click on **Site Recovery** to bring up the **Site Recovery Home**.
2. At the **Site Recovery Home**, use the left pane to navigate to **Recovery Plans** under **Inventories**.

3. Select the recovery plan with **Plan status Recovery complete**, navigate to its **Monitor | Recovery Steps** tab, and click on the 🛡 icon to bring up the **Reprotect** wizard:

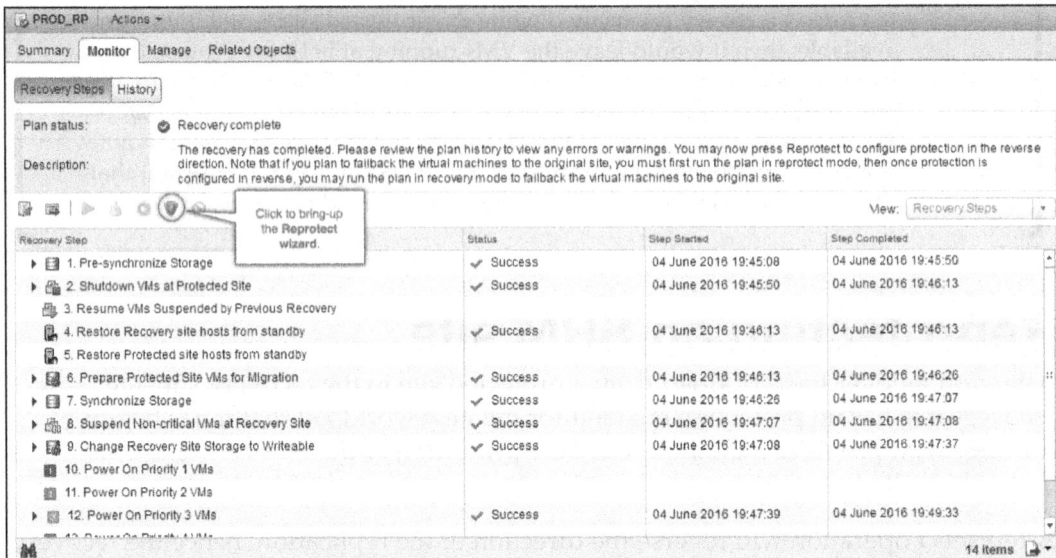

4. In the reprotect wizard screen, agree to the **Reprotect Confirmation** and click on **Next** to continue:

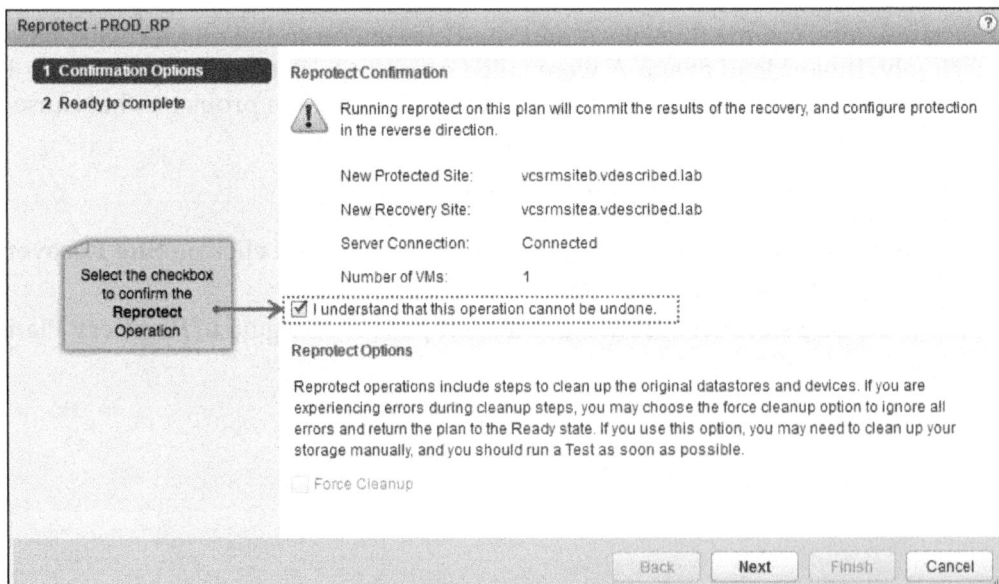

5. In the **Ready to complete** screen, click on **Finish** to begin the reprotect operation.

6. The **Recovery Steps** tab will show the progress of every step involved in the reprotect operation:

7. The status of the recovery plan after a successful reprotect operation should be **Ready**.

8. Navigate to the **Summary** tab of the recovery plan to verify that the direction of protection is now reversed. In this case, site-B will now be designated as the protected site and site-A as the recovery site:

Performing a failback to an SRM protected site

In a scenario wherein, after a failover the original protected site is fixed and is made available to host the virtual machine workload, you can use SRM to automate a failback.

The failback, although automated, is a two-step process:

- Step 1 will be to perform a reprotect. Read the *Reprotecting an SRM site* section in this chapter, to learn how to perform a reprotect operation.

- Step 2 will be to perform a failover. Read the *Performing a disaster recovery (failover)* section in this chapter to learn how to perform a failover.

IPv4 customization rules

Post a successful planned migration or disaster recovery operation, it becomes important to make sure that the VMs recovered are able to connect to the IP network at the recovery site.

An administrator can always log on to each of the virtual machines and change the IP settings, but that could become a time-consuming ordeal when you have a lot of VMs to work with. VMware SRM allows you to create IP customization rules that enable SRM to reconfigure the recovered virtual machines with IP configuration required for it to be network-alive at the recovery site.

The customization rules are created for a network mapping (a mapping between port groups of protected and recovery sites). Since they are created for port group mappings, they are called subnet-level IP mapping rules.

> To learn how to create network mappings, refer to the topic *Creating resource, folder, and network mappings* in *Chapter 1, Installing and Configuring vCenter Site Recovery Manager (SRM) 6.1*.

Since the customization involves modifying the IP configuration of the guest operating systems, it is important to be aware which of the guest operating systems are supported for customization. SRM 6.1 supports the customization of all guest operating systems that vSphere 6.0 update 1 supports customizing.

Here is the URL to the latest guest OS customization support matrix:

```
http://partnerweb.vmware.com/programs/guestOS/guest-os-customization-matrix.pdf
```

Creating an IPv4 customization rule

Let's figure out how to create an IP rule first, and then later on we will delve deeper into how it is used by SRM. The following procedure will help you create an IP customization rule:

1. Navigate to **Site Recovery Manager Home** and click on **Sites** to list the paired sites.

2. Select the recovery site and navigate to its **Manage | Network Mappings** tab to view all the configured network mappings. Choose the network mapping (port group mapping) that you would like to create a customization rule for and click on the **Add IP Customization Rule** button to bring up the **IP Customization rule** window:

3. In the **IP Customization rule** window, supply a rule name, subnet mapping, optional gateway, and DNS and WINS settings. Click on **OK** to confirm the settings:

Add IP Customization Rule

IP Customization rule
This rule will be used for IP customization of the eligible virtual machines.

Rule name: ProdRule F

Specify subnet IP ranges to be mapped on the protected and recovery sites.

Site: vcsrmsiteb.vdescribed.lab   vcsrmsitea.vdescribed.lab

Network: Prod PG   Prod PG

Subnet: G 192 . 168 . 40 . 0 / 24   H 192 . 168 . 80 . 0 / 24

Subnet mask: 255.255.255.0   255.255.255.0

Range: 192.168.40.0 - 192.168.40.255   192.168.80.0 - 192.168.80.255

Enter network settings to be applied to the recovery site network.

Gateway: 192 . 168 . 80 . 1

DNS addresses: 192.168.80.3

DNS suffixes: vdescribed.lab

These are optional settings. SRM can auto generate these if the rule does not specify I

Primary WINS server:

Secondary WINS server:

J OK   Cancel

4. Once done, the network mapping will now show an IP customization rule with its configuration:

How does SRM use IP customization rules?

During a test/failover, SRM uses IP customization rules, if present, to find the static IP configuration of the virtual machine vNICs that matches the protected site subnet specified in the rule, and replace it with a static IP from the recovery site's subnet. When doing so, it will retain the host bits of the new IP and replace the network bits to match the recovery site's network subnet. For instance, if the VM's static IP is 192.168.40.33, then SRM will replace this with 192.168.80.33.

IP customization does not affect virtual machine vNICs with **Dynamic Host Configuration Protocol** (**DHCP**) enabled on them.

If the destination default gateway was not configured in the rule, then SRM will retain the host bit in the gateway address and replace the network bits to match the recovery site's network subnet. For instance, if the default gateway of the VM is 192.168.40.1, then SRM will replace it with 192.168.80.1.

> DNS/WINS settings will not be modified by SRM if they are not specified in the rule.

SRM uses IP customization rules for test, planned migration, and disaster recovery operations. There is a one-to-one mapping between an IP customization rule and a network mapping. Once used, the same IP customization rule cannot be used for another network mapping.

> As of version 6.1, VMware SRM does not support IPv6 customization rules yet.

IP customization rules, once created, are by default applied to the virtual machines during a failover (planned/test/DR) of a recovery plan. However, the behavior can be changed at a per-VM level. This is done via the recovery properties of a VM. We will cover more about this in the *Configuring VM recovery properties* section of this chapter.

Configuring VM recovery properties

The VM recovery properties help in further customizing the recovery procedure at a per-VM level. Although, these properties are only available via a recovery plan, the changes made to these properties are retained for the VM, regardless of the recovery plan they would be included in.

Here are the properties that can be set on a protected virtual machine:

- IP customization mode
- Recovery properties
- Priority group
- VM dependencies
- Shutdown action

- Startup action
- Pre-power on steps
- Post-power on steps

Before we learn what each of these properties are, let's figure out how to get to the recovery properties of a protected virtual machine in a recovery plan. Here is how you do it:

1. Navigate to the vCenter Server's inventory home, and click on **Site Recovery** to bring up **Site Recovery Home**.

2. At **Site Recovery Home**, use the left pane to navigate to **Recovery Plans** under **Inventories**.

3. Select the recovery plan, navigate to its **Related Objects | Virtual Machines** tab, and click on the 🐘 icon to bring-up the **VM Recovery Properties** window:

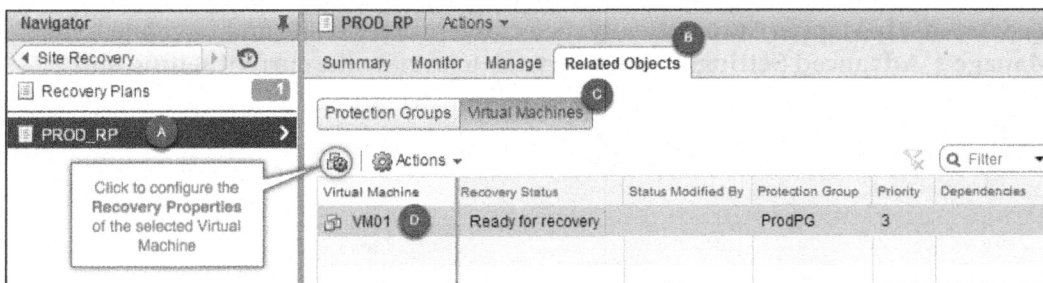

4. In the **VM Recovery Properties** window, you will be presented with two tabs: **Recovery Properties** and **IP Customization**. We will cover each of these in separate sub-sections of this topic.

IP customization

The **IP Customization** tab provides you with a drop-down list to choose the IP customization mode for the selected virtual machine. The mode is set to **Auto** by default, which is SRM's site-level global default for every protected virtual machine of that site:

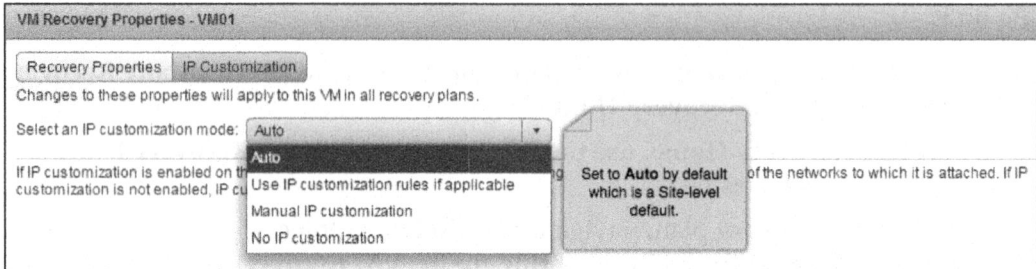

VM Recovery Properties - VM01

Recovery Properties	IP Customization

Changes to these properties will apply to this VM in all recovery plans.

Select an IP customization mode: Auto ▾

Auto
Use IP customization rules if applicable
Manual IP customization
No IP customization

If IP customization is enabled on th... ...g **Set to Auto by default** of the networks to which it is attached. If IP customization is not enabled, IP cu... **which is a Site-level default.**

This behavior can be changed by disabling the protected site's advanced setting **recovery.useIpMapperAutomatically**. Select the protected site and navigate to its **Manage | Advanced Settings | Recovery** tab to review the current setting and modify it:

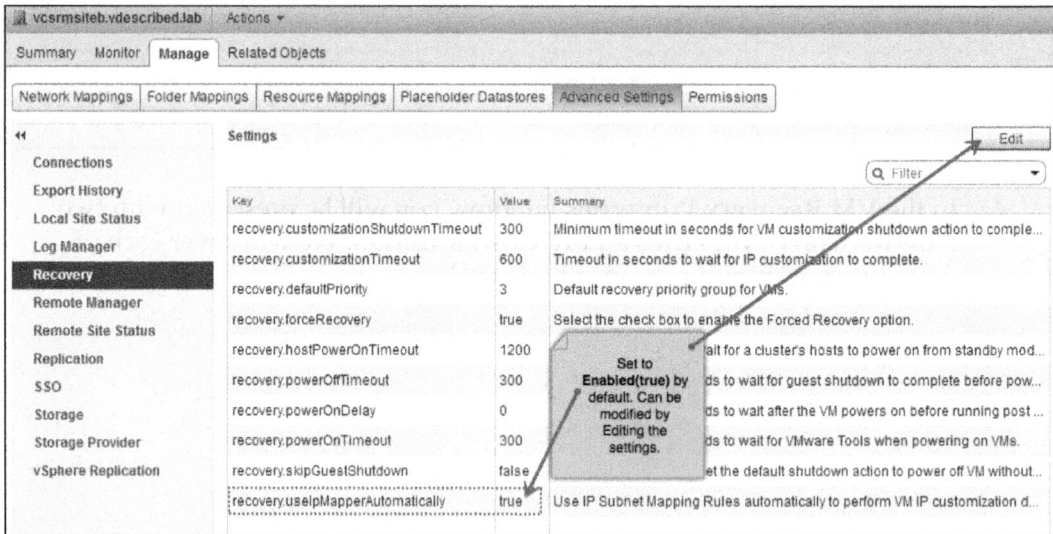

vcsrmsiteb.vdescribed.lab	Actions ▾

Summary	Monitor	Manage	Related Objects

Network Mappings	Folder Mappings	Resource Mappings	Placeholder Datastores	Advanced Settings	Permissions

Settings — Edit — Q Filter ▾

Key	Value	Summary
recovery.customizationShutdownTimeout	300	Minimum timeout in seconds for VM customization shutdown action to comple...
recovery.customizationTimeout	600	Timeout in seconds to wait for IP customization to complete.
recovery.defaultPriority	3	Default recovery priority group for VMs.
recovery.forceRecovery	true	Select the check box to enable the Forced Recovery option.
recovery.hostPowerOnTimeout	1200	...ait for a cluster's hosts to power on from standby mod...
recovery.powerOffTimeout	300	...ds to wait for guest shutdown to complete before pow...
recovery.powerOnDelay	0	...ds to wait after the VM powers on before running post ...
recovery.powerOnTimeout	300	...ds to wait for VMware Tools when powering on VMs.
recovery.skipGuestShutdown	false	...et the default shutdown action to power off VM without...
recovery.useIpMapperAutomatically	true	Use IP Subnet Mapping Rules automatically to perform VM IP customization d...

Connections
Export History
Local Site Status
Log Manager
Recovery
Remote Manager
Remote Site Status
Replication
SSO
Storage
Storage Provider
vSphere Replication

Set to Enabled(true) by default. Can be modified by Editing the settings.

We can change the IP customization mode from **Auto** to **No IP customization**, **Manual IP customization**, and **Use IP customization rules if applicable**.

- **Auto**: It is the site-level global default mode controlled by the advanced parameter **recovery.useIpMapperAutomatically**. It will perform IP customization on the virtual machine's network interfaces if there is an IP customization rule associated with the network mapping the VM connects to.

- **No IP Customization**: It is used to disable IP customization for the selected VM.

- **Use IP customization rules if applicable**: It is used when the site-level global default to automatically use IP customization (**recovery.useIpMapperAutomatically**) is disabled.

- **Manual IP customization**: It is used to manually supply the static IP configuration for both protected and recovery sites. This method will require you to modify the settings of each vNIC of the selected virtual machine. The main difference that stands out when compared with using the IP customization rules is that you can modify the IPv6 settings when doing the manual IP customization, if necessary. As mentioned earlier in this topic, SRM currently does not support the use of IP customization rules for IPv6 addresses.

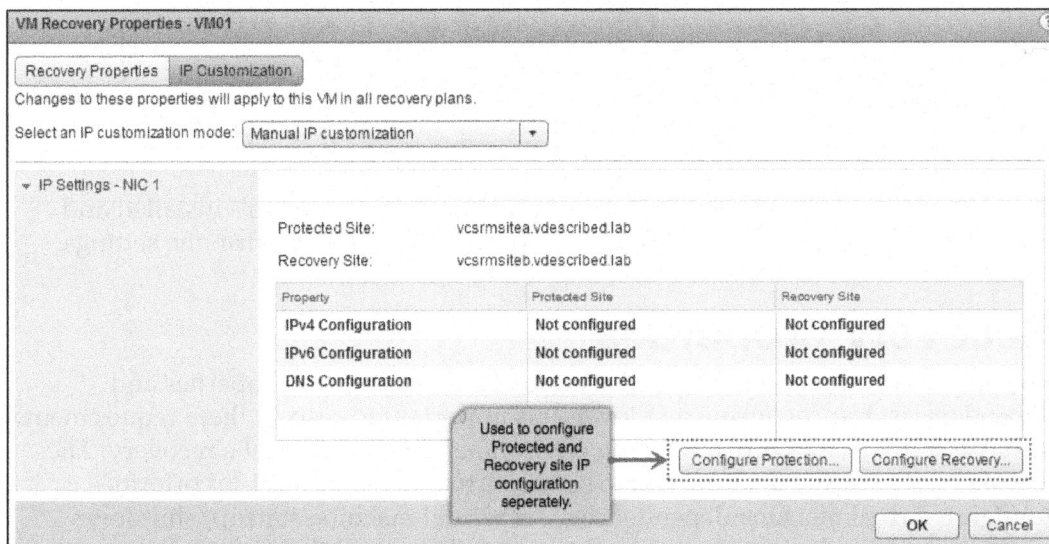

- Here, the **Configure Protection...** and **Configure Recovery...** buttons can be used to supply the vNIC's IP configuration for protected and recovery sites. This will be used when you failover and failback between both the sites.

- When you click on either **Configure Protection...** or **Configure Recovery...**, a new IP setting window is shown. You can choose to use either DHCP, IPv4, or IPv6. It also has options to supply the DNS server details. You could also choose to fetch the current IP configuration of the VM using the **Retrieve** button:

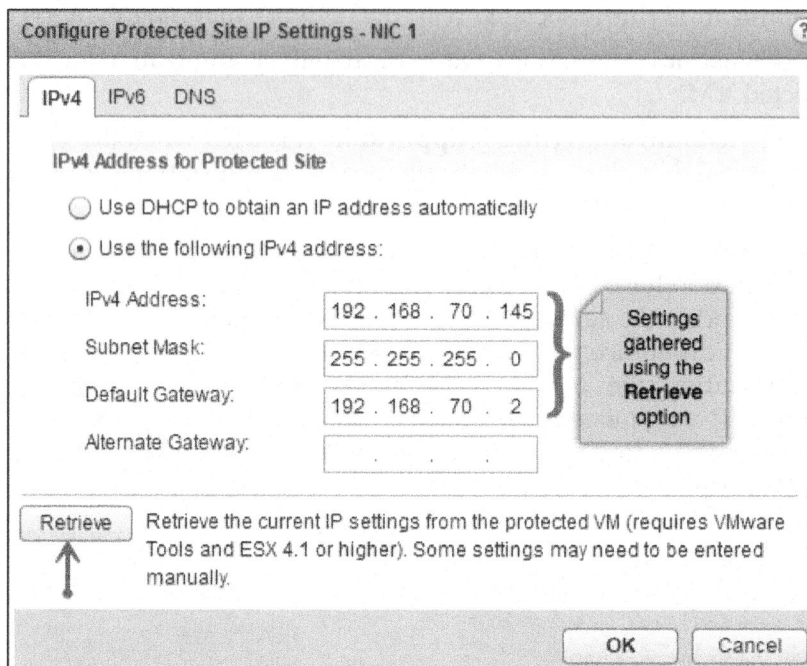

- For the retrieve operation to work, you need VMware tools installed and running in the VM. Once configured, click on **OK** to confirm the settings.

Recovery properties

In a modern day datacenter, hosted workloads have different properties and dependencies. Hence, during a failover, it is important to respect these requirements to successfully reconfigure a working environment in the event of a recovery. The recovery properties will allow you to set up virtual machine start-up priorities, configure virtual machine dependencies, set virtual machine startup/shutdown methods, and much more. In this section, we will cover all the recovery properties available for a protected virtual machine.

Priority group

Priority groups are used to set the start up order of the VMs. VMware SRM uses five priority groups numbered 1 through 5.

The VMs of the lowest numbered priority group are started first.

Priority Group	Priority	Startup Order
Priority Group 1	Highest	First
Priority Group 2	Higher than Group 3	Before Group 3
Priority Group 3	Higher then Group 4	Before Group 4
Priority Group 4	Higher that Group 5	Before Group 5
Priority Group 5	Lower	Last

Table : Priority Groups and their Startup Order

By default, every virtual machine is in **Priority Group** 3. During a failover, SRM will wait for all the VMs in a **Priority Group** to failover successfully, or fail to failover, before it attempts to power on VMs from a group with lower priority. For instance, SRM will wait for all the VMs in **Priority Group 2** to failover before it attempts the failover of the VMs in **Priority Group 3**. This is because **Priority Group 2** has a higher priority than **Priority Group 3**.

VM dependencies

So, what happens if all the VMs running the services of a three-tier application are in the same priority group? Can we configure a startup order within a priority group? The answer is **Yes**. This is where VM dependencies come in handy.

Let's consider a three-tier application that has a database, a server component, and the user interface component hosted on three different VMs. Now in this case, the server component is dependent on the availability of the database, and the user interface component is dependent on the server component. This means the database VM should start first, then the VM hosting the service component, and finally the VM hosting the user interface component. Such a startup order can be achieved using the VM dependencies recovery property.

Here is how a VM dependency startup order is created:

1. Open the **Recovery Properties** of the virtual machine.
2. Select the **VM Dependencies** property from the left pane and click on **Configure** to bring up the **Configure VM Dependencies** window:

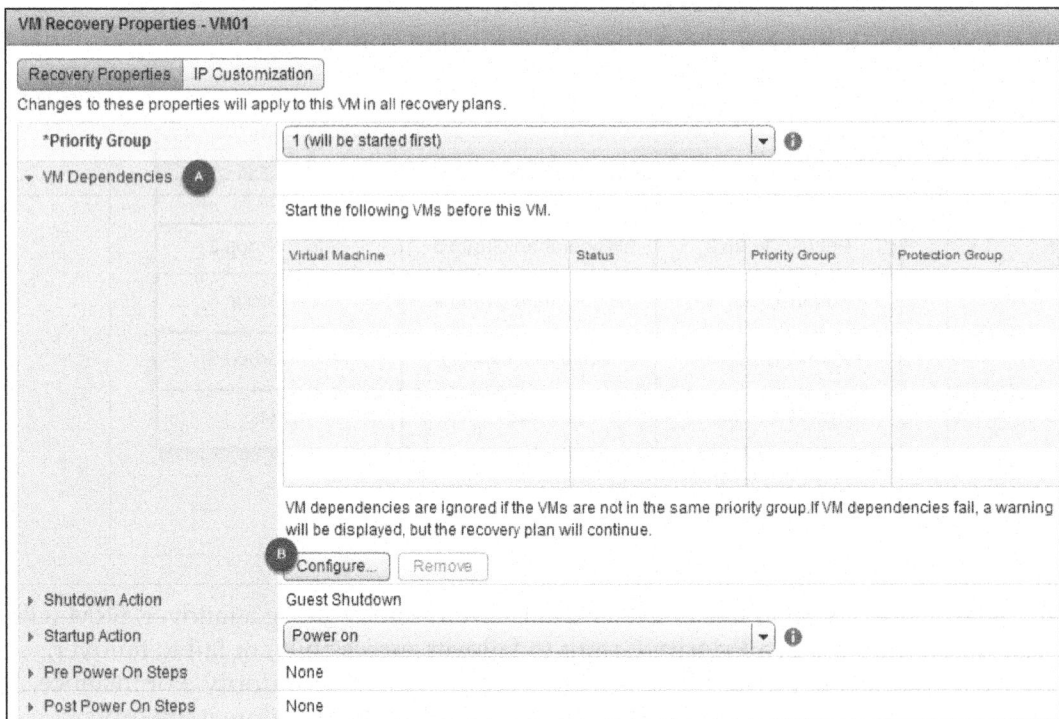

3. In the **Configure VM Dependencies** window, select the virtual machines that have to be started before the current VM and click on **OK** to close the VM dependencies window:

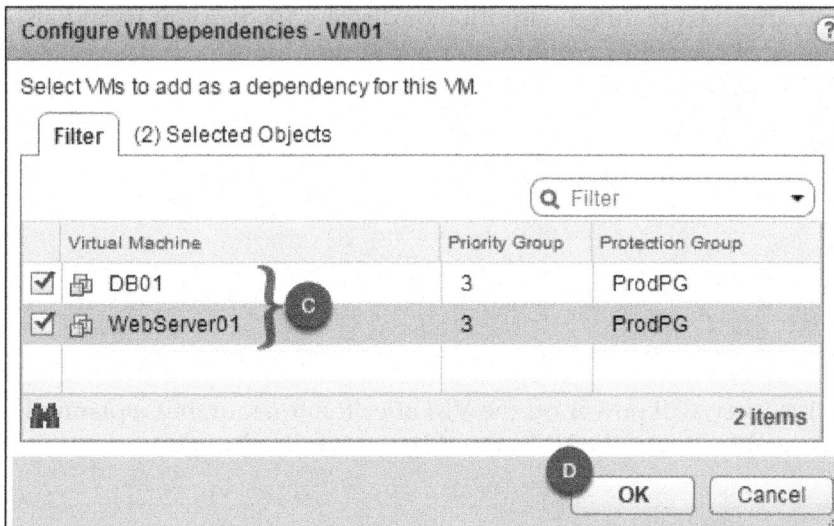

4. Click on **OK** in the **VM Recovery Properties** window to save the settings.

Keep in mind that the VMs are started in the order of their appearance in the list. So make sure that you plan to add the VMs in the order in which you want them to start. You can also remove a VM from the list by hitting the **Remove** button.

> The dependencies between VMs of different priority groups are ignored by SRM. Also, the dependencies are not mandatory rules, hence they wouldn't stop the recovery plan from continuing. In case a VM dependency fails, it throws a warning and proceeds with the execution of the recovery plan.

Shutdown action

The shutdown action VM recovery property will let you choose whether a virtual machine at the protected site will be attempted to gracefully shut down or be powered off, during a planned migration or disaster recovery. It would also let you set the amount of time SRM would wait on VMware tools to shutdown the virtual machine before it issues a power off. The default timeout value is **5** minutes:

> ▼ Shutdown Action
>
> Shutdown actions are used to power off VMs at the protected site during a Recovery. Shutdown actions are not used for Test or Cleanup.
>
> ⦿ Shutdown guest OS before power off (requires VMware Tools)
>
> Timeout: 5 ▲▼ minutes 0 ▲▼ seconds
>
> In Disaster Recovery mode, the VM will be powered off if Shutdown guest OS fails.
>
> ○ Power off

A disaster recovery will power off the VM after the timeout, but a planned migration will not proceed further if the VM cannot be gracefully shut down.

Startup action

The startup action property will let you choose whether or not to power on a virtual machine at the recovery site during a test or a recovery operation. By default, after a virtual machine is powered on at the recovery site, SRM waits for 5 minutes to determine whether the virtual machine tools have started. If it sees no response from VMware tools, it marks a failure of that task and proceeds further with the recovery. But the recovery operation will have an **Incomplete Recovery** status. You can also add a further delay before any of the dependent VMs are started, or before the execution of any post-power on steps. This is commonly used to give the service running inside of the VM some additional time to start:

> ▼ Startup Action   Power on   ▼ ⓘ
>
> VMware Tools   ☑ Wait for VMware tools
>
>   Timeout: 5 ▲▼ minutes 0 ▲▼ seconds
>
> Additional Delay   ☑ Additional delay before running Post Power On steps and starting dependent VMs.
>
>   Delay: 0 ▲▼ minutes 0 ▲▼ seconds

Pre-power on and post-power on steps

The pre-power on and post-power on steps are VM recovery properties that let you insert additional steps into the recovery plan.

With the pre-power on steps property, you can create the following types of step:

- A Windows `batch` command on the SRM server
- A message prompt, which the user/administration should dismiss before the recovery plan can begin its execution

With the post-power on steps property, you can create the following types of step:

- A command on the recovered virtual machine
- A Windows `batch` command on the SRM server

Creating a message prompt is straightforward. Here is how it is done:

1. Select the pre-/post-power on steps property from the left plane and click on the ✚ icon to bring up the **Add Pre/Post Power On** Step window.

2. In the **Add Pre/Post Power On Step** window, select the **Type** as **Prompt (requires a user to dismiss before the plan will continue)**.

3. Supply a **Name** and the **Message content**, and click on **OK** to save the settings.

Here is how to create a Windows batch command on the SRM Server:

1. Select the **Pre/Post power on steps** property from the left plane and click on the ✚ icon to bring up the **Add Pre/Post Power On Step** window.

2. In the **Add Pre/Post Power On Step** window, select the Type as **Command on SRM Server** or **Command on Recovered VM**.

Add Pre Power On Step   ⑦

Type: ⦿ Command on SRM Server

                ◯ Prompt (requires a user to acknowledge the prompt before the plan
                  continues)

Name: BatchCM01

Content: c:\windows\system32\cmd.exe /c d:\demoscipt.bat

Timeout: 5 ⬍ minutes 0 ⬍ seconds

                                              OK   Cancel

---

3. Supply a name for the script and the command script in the content section, and type the actual command. For instance, to run a batch script in D:\demoscript.bat, include the following command:

    ```
    "c:\windows\system32\cmd.exe /c d:\demoscript.bat"
    ```

> For cmd.exe, always mention the absolute path
> c:\windows\system32\cmd.exe.

The default timeout for a batch command is 5 minutes. If the batch file doesn't finish executing within 5 minutes, then the execution of the recovery plan will stop with an error indicating this.

Summary

This chapter detailed the workflows involved in testing recovery plans, running planned migrations, and performing disaster recovery failovers. You learned how to perform a forced recovery in the event of the protected site being nonfunctional. You then learned how to reprotect a site after a successful failover. You also learned how to failback to the original protected site.

Details regarding how the failed over virtual machines can be reconfigured with the new IP configuration using the SRM IP customization rules were also covered. Finally, we covered the recovery properties available for protected virtual machines and their use cases.

4

Deploying vSphere Replication

In this chapter, you will learn the following:

- New features in vSphere Replication 6.1
- Understanding the vSphere Replication architecture
- Downloading the vSphere Replication bundle
- Deploying the vSphere Replication Appliance
- Setting the VRA hostname and a VRM site name for the VRA
- Configuring a SQL database for VRMS
- Deploying a vSphere Replication server
- Registering vSphere Replication servers

Introduction

Most organizations will have a DR plan in place, regardless of whether it is a large enterprise or a small or medium business. VMware Site Recovery Manager leveraging an array-based replication is a very effective DR solution. However, an array-based replication can be a costly solution for some businesses, especially the small and medium businesses. VMware's proprietary replication engine called vSphere Replication offers a very cost-effective DR solution without the need for investments on storage replication technologies.

One of the advantages for businesses using vSphere Replication is the fact that the replication can be managed without the need for an SRM license. The vSphere Web Client GUI provides an interface to configure and manage replication on virtual machines.

In this chapter, we learn what vSphere Replication actually is, its architecture, and how it can be deployed in your vSphere environment.

vSphere Replication is a replication engine that can be leveraged to configure replication on individual VMs. It can replicate a virtual machine and its disks from one location to another without the need to incorporate expensive array-based replication. What it really does is to provide a mechanism to replicate a virtual machine using the existing Ethernet infrastructure and recover them when there is a need.

The concept of vSphere Replication was introduced with VMware Site Recovery Manager version 5.0. At that time, vSphere Replication was not a standalone product. With the release of vSphere 5.1, vSphere Replication has been released as a standalone product and it integrates directly into the vSphere platform, registering itself as a plugin to the vCenter server. All the replication and recovery operations are done using the vSphere Web Client.

It is included in Essential Plus and higher versions of vSphere.

It is storage agnostic, which means that a virtual machine or its disk files can be replicated to a datastore regardless of it being either a VMFS volume or an NFS mount. For instance, if the virtual machine that you want to protect by enabling replication is located on a VMFS volume, then the replica can be either on another VMFS volume or on a NFS mount. The reverse is also true.

> vSphere Replication can protect a maximum of 2000 VMs. Read VMware KB article 2102543 for more details regarding the operational limits of vSphere Replication.

VMware Site Recovery Manager can be configured to leverage the vSphere Replication engine to perform recovery tests, failovers, planned migration, failback, and so on.

New features in vSphere Replication 6.1

The first edition of this book covered version 5.5. However, since then, VMware has released several upgrades. We will briefly review what each of those version upgrades introduced:

- **vSphere Replication 5.5** Update 1 added full support for VMware VSAN.
- **vSphere Replication 5.6** introduced support for replicating virtual machines to vCHS (now known as vCloud Air).

- **vSphere Replication 5.8** added enhanced reporting and improved support for vCHS.

- **vSphere Replication 6.0** was the first major release since version 5.5. It introduced VR scalability and the following performance features:

  - VMware now allows the optional compression of the replication data prior to its transmission over the network reducing network bandwidth and replication time. Data compression, however, puts additional load on the source and destination ESXi hosts.

  - vSphere Replication management and Replication traffic can now be network-separated.

  - Improved replication engine with capabilities to compress replication data.

  - **vSphere Replication Management Server (VRMS)** now supports up to 2,000 simultaneous active replications, up from 500 replications in the previous version.

  - Support for the the quiescing of Linux guest operating systems enabling filesystem-level crash consistency.

  - Storage DRS is now fully supported. If storage DRS moves a replica VM or its disks to another datastore at the recovery site, vSphere Replication can now detect this change and seamlessly update the replication schedule accordingly. Previously, storage DRS was supported only at the protected site.

- **vSphere Replication 6.1** introduced several UI enhancements and now has added support for NFSv4.1 datastores. It now also enables an RPO as low as 5 minutes for workloads on VSAN datastores.

Understanding the vSphere Replication architecture

vSphere Replication is VMware's hypervisor-based replication solution. Unlike array-based replication, the data is replicated over the network, using the VMware **Network File Copy (NFC)** protocol. VMware NFC is a proprietary VMware protocol, which is used to transfer disk (VMDK) blocks between ESXi hosts.

A vSphere Replication Appliance is a Linux virtual machine running SUSE Linux Enterprise Server 11 SP3 for VMware. The machine runs VRMS, a vSphere Replication Server, and an embedded database.

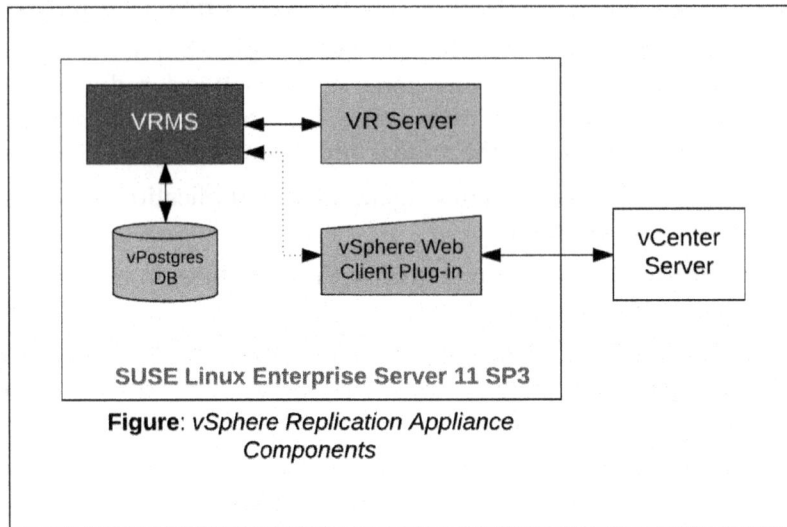

Figure: *vSphere Replication Appliance Components*

The vSphere Replication architecture comprises of the following components:

- One or more instances of vCenter servers managing the protected and the recovery sites
- A vSphere Replication Server deployed at the protected site
- A vSphere Replication Server deployed at the recovery site
- The VRM plugin for the vSphere Web Client
- The vSphere Replication agent that runs on every ESXi host

For vSphere Replication to work, you will need a VRMS at the protected site and a VR server at the target recovery site, be it local or remote. However, there can be only one VRMS per vCenter server.

Figure: *vSphere Replication with SRM*

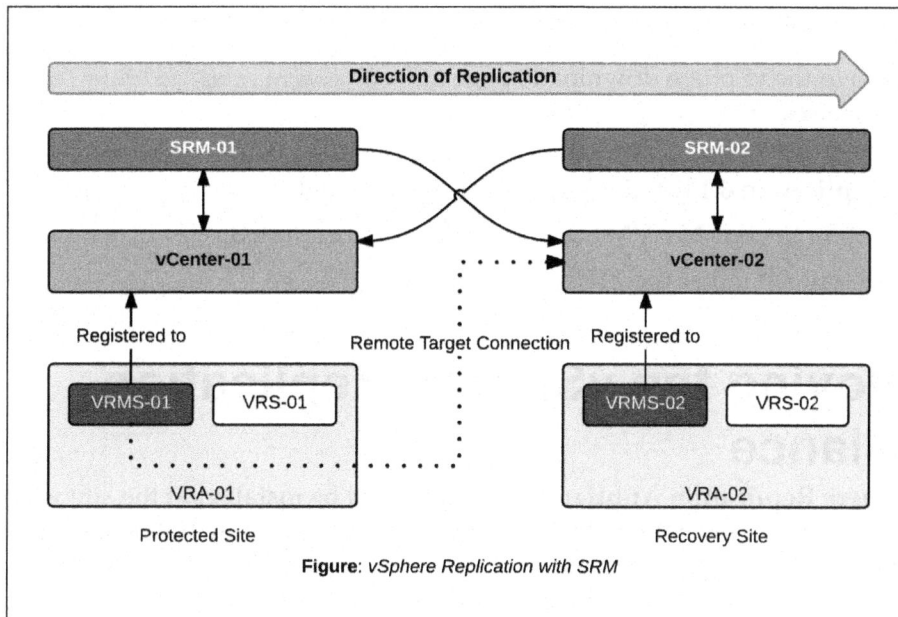

The recovery site is the site at which you plan to maintain the replicas of the VMs from the protected site. It is the site to which you will be sending the replication traffic. The vSphere Replication appliances provide a replication management interface via the vSphere Web Client. It registers itself as a plugin for the Web Client.

> Every ESXi host, starting with version 5.1, has the vSphere Replication agent already built into the VMkernel, thereby removing the dependency on Site Recovery Manager and installing additional packages into each ESXi host.

Downloading the vSphere Replication bundle

The vSphere Replication Server appliance is available for download as an ISO data file or a compressed ZIP package, both of which contain separate OVFs for the vSphere Replication Appliance and Add-On servers.

The following steps help you to download the ISO or ZIP bundle:

1. Go to the vSphere downloads page at `www.vmware.com/go/download-vsphere`.

2. Click on the **Go to Downloads** hyperlink corresponding to **vSphere Replication 6.1** listed under your license model.

3. Log in to your **My VMware** account when prompted.

4. Download either the ZIP or ISO package.

Deploying the vSphere Replication Appliance

The **vSphere Replication Appliance** (**VRA**) should be installed at the site where you have virtual machines that need to be protected. It may or may not be required to be installed on both the protected and recovery sites. You will need VRA to be deployed at the recovery site only if you intend to pair it with the protected site.

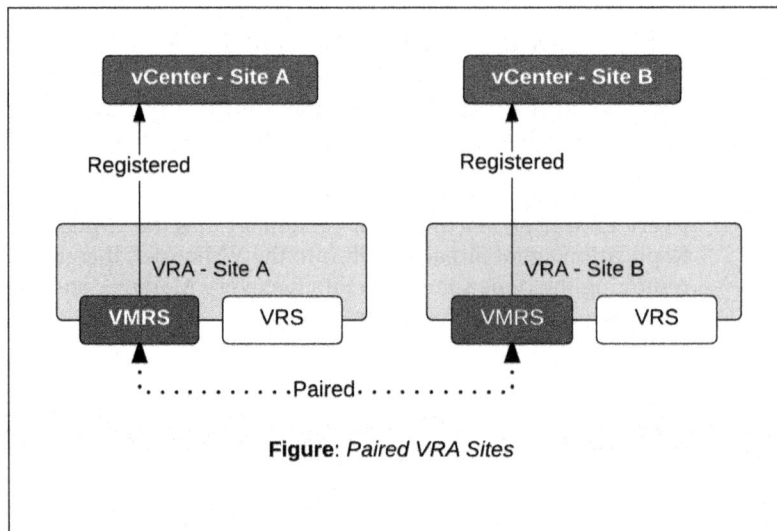

Figure: *Paired VRA Sites*

The pairing is done by adding the recovery site as a target site to the VRMS at the protected site. Read the *Adding a remote site as a target* section in *Chapter 5, Configuring and Using vSphere Replication 6.1*, for information on how to achieve this.

The total number of VMs that can be protected by vSphere Replication is 2,000 per site. The limit is imposed at a per VR server level. Each VR server can protect up to 200 VMs and there can only be a maximum of 10 VR server per VRMS. Since there can be only one VRMS registered to a site's vCenter, the 2,000 VM limit cannot be exceeded.

If the VRMSs are paired, then the cumulative limit of VMs from both the sites becomes 2,000 and not 4,000.

To deploy the VRA, you need the following components:

- A compatible version of vCenter server
- ESXi hosts compatible with the vCenter server
- Downloaded bundle for vSphere Replication 6.1

The appliance's OVF can be deployed using the **Deploy OVF Template** wizard. The wizard can be initiated from various levels (vCenter, Datacenter, or ESXi). We will do it at the vCenter level, although this is not a technical requirement:

1. Extract (unzip) the downloaded package, or in case you have downloaded the ISO bundle then mount the ISO to the vCenter server virtual machine or the machine that the vSphere client is being accessed from.

2. Right-click on the vCenter server and click on **Deploy OVF Template**:

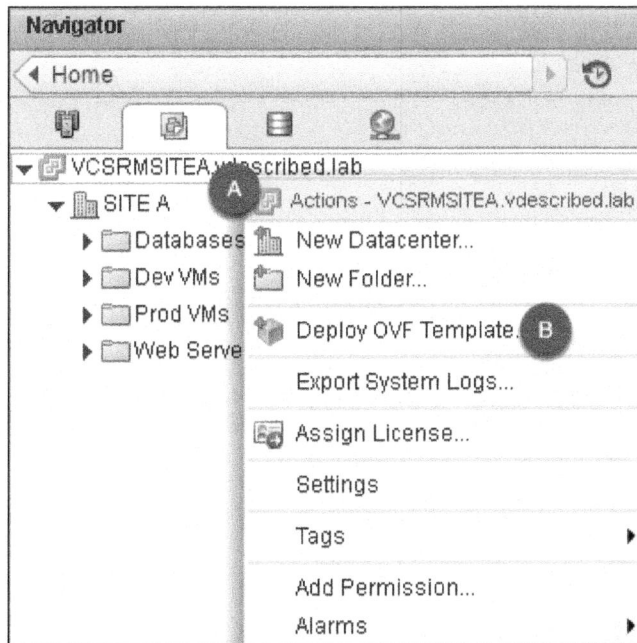

3. On the wizard screen, set the source as **Local file** and click on **Browse...**:

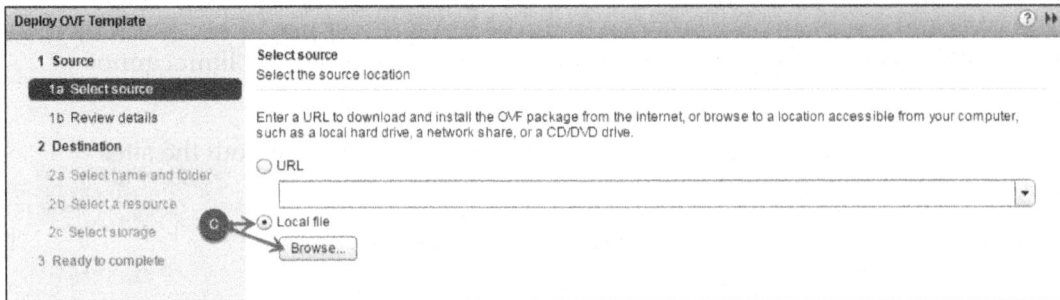

4. Navigate to the extracted bundle folder and then to the `bin` subfolder:

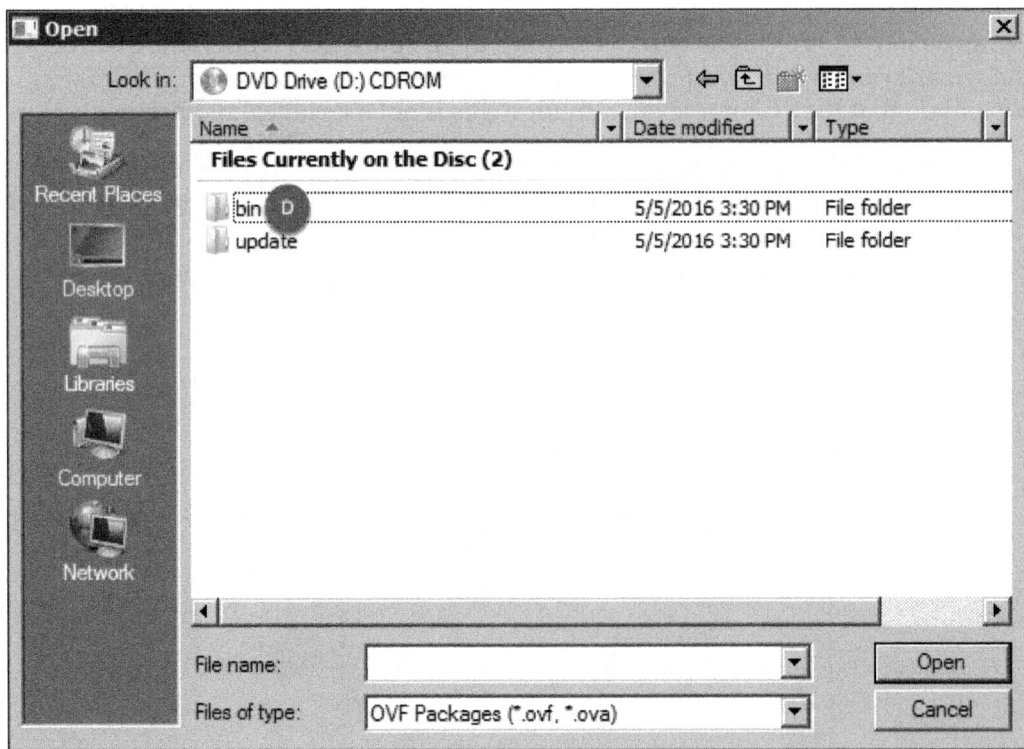

5. Select the `vSphere_Replication_OVF10.ovf` OVF file and click on **Open** to make the selection and return to the wizard:

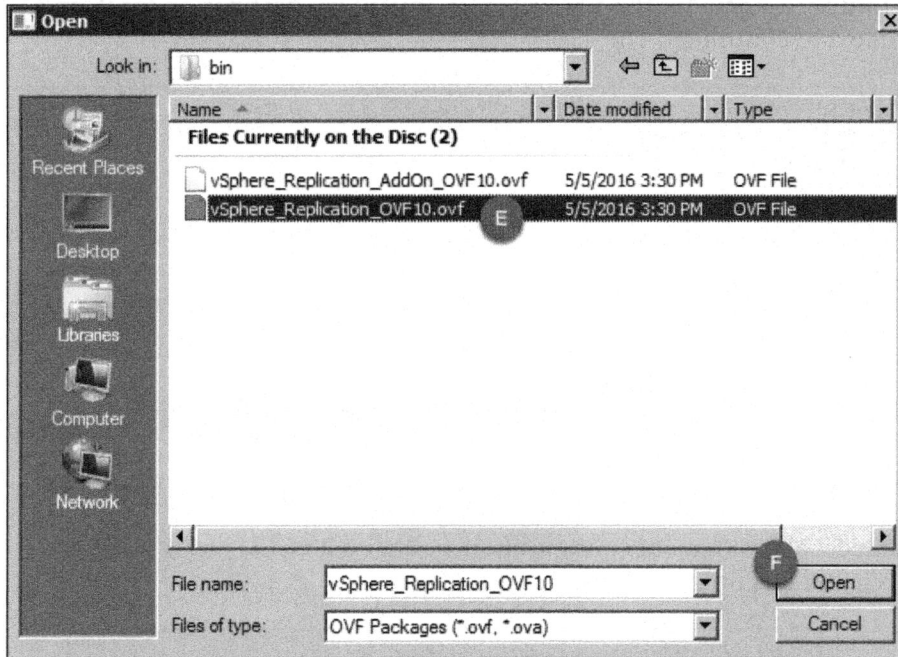

6. On the wizard screen, click on **Next** to continue.
7. The **Review details** screen summarizes the appliance's details. Click on **Next** to continue:

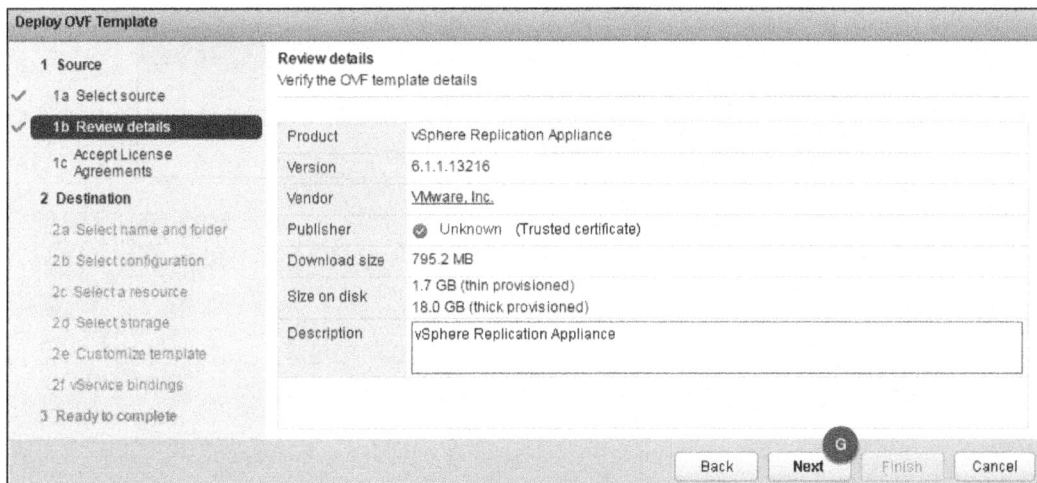

8. On the license agreement screen, accept the license and click on **Next** to continue.

9. Supply a name for the VM, select an inventory destination for it, and click on **Next** to continue:

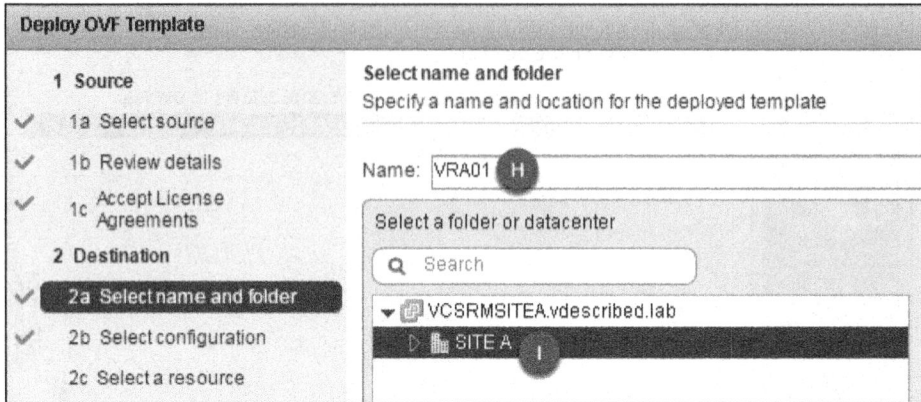

10. Select a deployment configuration—either a **2 vCPU** or a **4 vCPU** virtual machine:

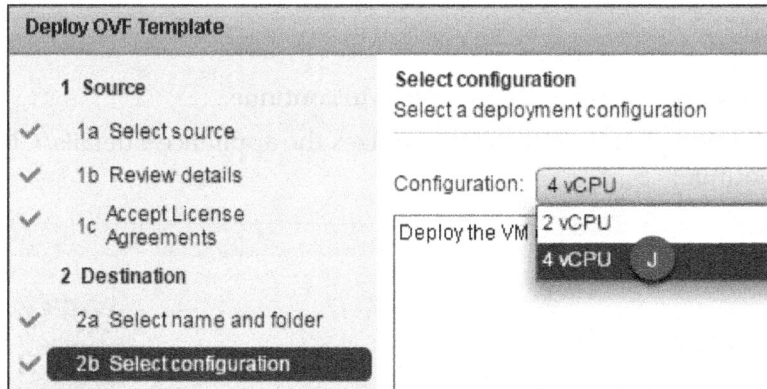

11. Select a compute location for the VM. The compute location could be an ESXi host or a cluster of ESXi hosts. Once a selection has been made, click on **Next** to continue:

12. Select the VMDK type and a datastore for the VM and click on **Next** to continue. The default disk format is **Thick Provision Lazy Zeroed**. However, this can be changed to either Thin Provision or Thick Provision Eager Zeroed. A VM Storage Policy can also be chosen to display appropriate datastores:

13. Select a network (port group) for the VM's vNIC, choose between **IPv4** and **IPv6**, and an IP allocation policy (DHCP/Static). We have selected **Static**, hence, we will have to manually specify the DNS Server, the subnet mask, and the gateway of the subnet the VM will be part of. Once done, click on **Next** to continue:

14. Set the password and the static IP for the appliance. Click on **Next** to continue:

15. The vService bindings screen will show the binding status of the vCenter extension registration. This is a method to allow the appliance VM to connect to the vCenter without requiring the user to enter the vCenter credentials. There is nothing to modify here, so click on **Next** to continue.

16. On the **Ready to complete** screen review the settings and click on **Finish** to deploy the appliance VM. You can select the **Power on after deployment** checkbox to start the VM if the deployment is successful.

How does it work

Once deployed, the appliance will be powered on and finish the initial configuration, which includes the configuration of the embedded database and the registration of VRMS to the vCenter server.

You can only have a single instance of VRMS registered to a vCenter server. This means you can't deploy multiple instances of VRA at a site. If you do so, then the appliance will detect that there is another appliance that is already registered to the vCenter server and will prompt for an override or a shutdown of the newly deployed appliance.

The following screenshot capture shows an appliance initialization detecting the presence of another VRA:

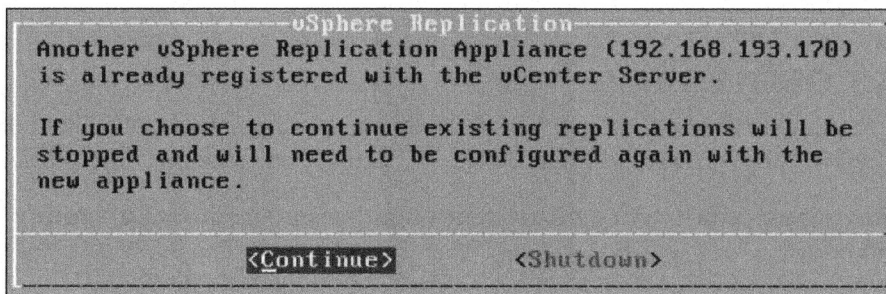

```
                    ──vSphere Replication──
Another vSphere Replication Appliance (192.168.193.170)
is already registered with the vCenter Server.

If you choose to continue existing replications will be
stopped and will need to be configured again with the
new appliance.

          <Continue>              <Shutdown>
```

> If you select **<Continue>** you should shut down the already registered VRA.

You can, however, deploy multiple instances of the vSphere Replication Server (Add-On) appliance which does not initialize the VRMS component. The Add-On server appliance is deployed using a different OVF.

As with any VMware appliance, the VRA also has a web-based management interface that can be accessed for appliance specific configuration tasks. This web interface is called **Virtual Appliance Management Interface (VAMI)**.

You can use the IP address of the appliance to connect to its management web interface using the URL format: `https://<IP address or FQDN>:5480`.

When you reach the login page for the appliance, log in using the **root** user and the password you set in the OVF deployment wizard. Once you are in, you will see a **Getting Started** tab, which is a sub tab under the **VR** tab. There is nothing much you could do at the **Getting Started** tab. The other sub tabs available under **VR** are **Configuration**, **Security**, and **Support**. We do not need to review or change the options under these sub tabs unless necessary.

The other main tabs available are **Network**, **Update**, and **System**. These will be covered in other sections of the chapter.

Setting the VRA hostname and a VRM site name for the VRA

Although not mandatory, you might need to set a hostname and a target name for the VRA that you have deployed.

VRA hostname

The hostname for the appliance can be set from the appliance's VAMI. The default hostname post deployment will be `localhost.localdom`. This can be modified.

The following procedure will guide you through the steps required to modify the hostname:

1. Connect to the VAMI of the appliance. The URL: is `https://<IP address or FQDN>:5480`.

2. Log in using the root user and the password that was supplied in the OVF deployment wizard.

3. Navigate to the **Network | Address** tab.

> Prior to supplying the hostname, it is important to create a new host (A) record at the DNS Server. Only then you will be able to connect to the appliance using its hostname.

4. Supply a hostname in the input box corresponding to it and click on
    Save Settings:

VRM site name

Every VRM server registered to a vCenter server will have a site name. By default,
during the initial configuration of the appliance, the address of the vCenter server to
which the VRMS gets registered to, is set as the VRM site name. The site name is only
a display name; hence, it is not mandatory that you change it. For instance, the VRM
site name of a VRMS registered to the protected site vCenter server can be just called
protected site.

The following procedure will guide you through the steps required to modify the
VRM site name:

1. Connect to the VAMI of the appliance using URL: `https://<IP address or
    FQDN>:5480`.

2. Log in using the root user and the password that was supplied in the OVF
    deployment wizard.

3. Navigate to the **VR | Configuration** tab.

4. Modify the **VRM Site Name** using the input box corresponding to it and restart the VRM service by clicking on **Save and Restart Service**:

[✎ The appliance can sometimes take a while to save the setting and restart the VRM service.]

Configuring a SQL database for VRMS

The VRA by default initializes the default embedded **vPostgres** database. All of the initial configuration data and the replication configuration data will be stored in the embedded database. Therefore, it is important that you plan the type of database before you configure replication for the VMs. This is because, if you were to reconfigure the VRMS component to use an external database then you will lose the existing replication configuration information. You will also need to reconfigure the replication on the VMs. Backup and restoration of an external database is easier because you will only have to back up the database files. If you were to plan a backup of the embedded database, then you have to back up the entire appliance.

To know which versions of SQL Server are supported, use the solution/database interoperability filter on the VMware product interoperability matrixes web portal.

The portal can be reached by going to the VMware compatibility guides URL, `http://www.vmware.com/in/guides.html`, and clicking on the hyperlink *Product Interoperability Matrixes*.

At the **VMware Product Interoperability Matrixes** web portal, select **Solution/ Database Interoperability**, select the VMware product as **VMware vSphere Replication** and the version as **6.1.1**. You can then choose a database from the list and verify its compatibility:

The following procedure will guide you through the steps required to configure a SQL database for the VRMS:

1. Log in to your database server and start **Microsoft SQL Server Management Studio**.

2. In **Object Explorer**, right-click on **Databases** and click on **New Database...**:

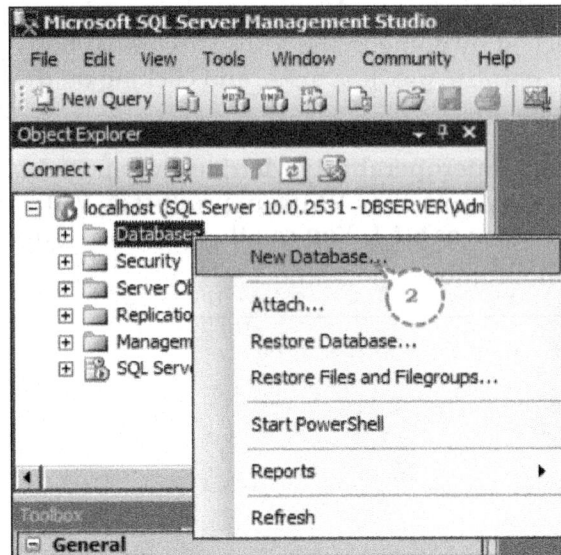

3. In the **New Database** window, supply a **Database name** and leave the rest of the attributes at their defaults for now, and click on **OK**:

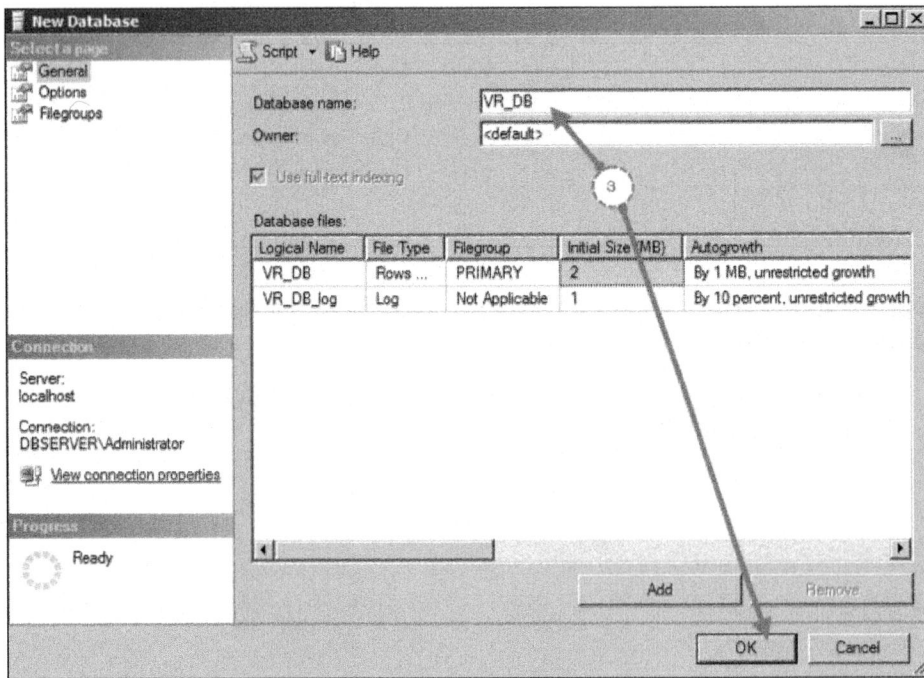

4. In **Object Explorer**, expand **Security**, right-click on **Logins,** and click on **New Login...**:

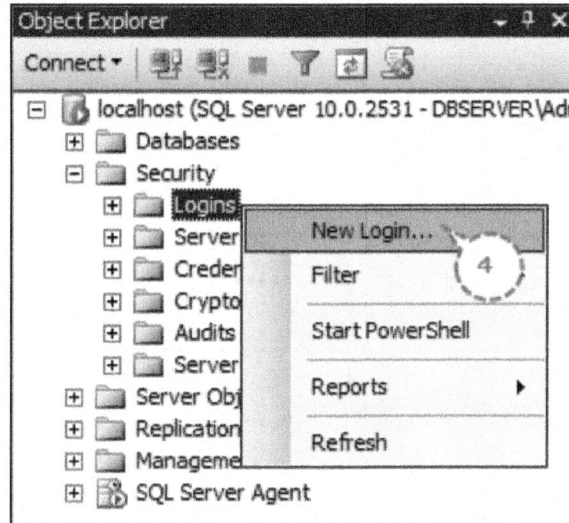

5. In the **New Login** window, select **SQL Server authentication** and supply a **Login name**, set the password, and deselect **Enforce password policy**, which will void the other two password policies (**User must change password at the next login** and **Enforce password expiration**) as well.

6. Set the **Default database** to the newly created DB for vSphere Replication, and click on **OK**.

> In this example, we created a DB named VR_DB, so we should change the default database to VR_DB.

7. In the **Object Explorer**, expand **Databases**, right-click on the new database
   (VR_DB) and click on **Properties**:

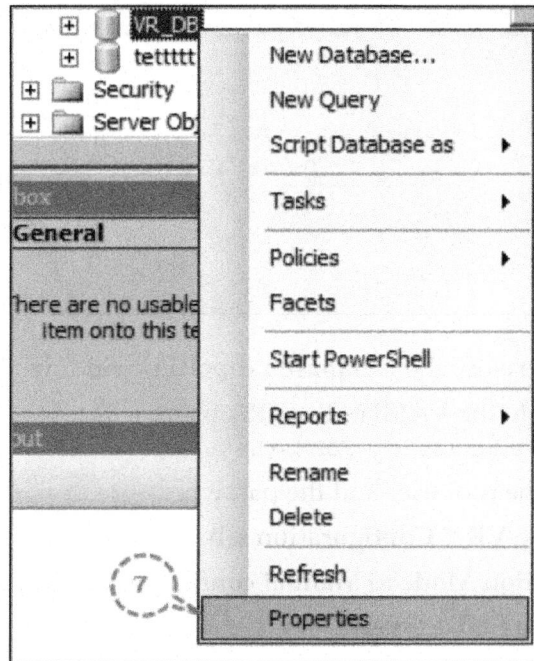

8. At the **Database Properties** window, select the **Files** page and change the
   database **Owner** to the login you created:

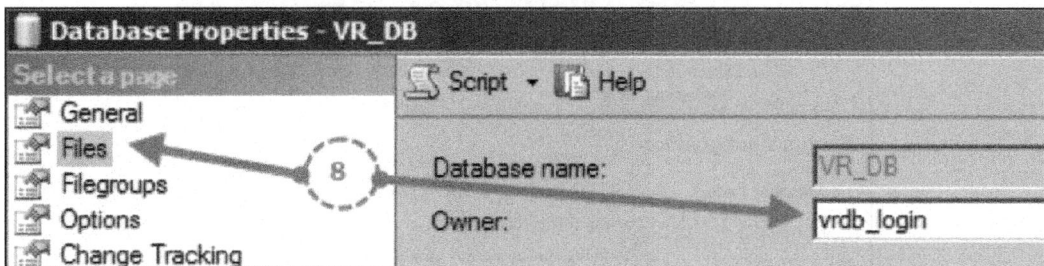

9. From the same window, select the **Options** page, and change the **Recovery model** to **Simple**:

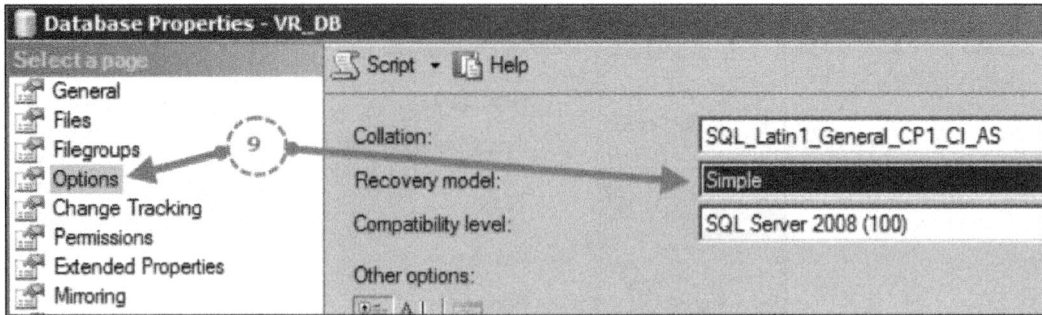

10. Click on **OK** to close the **Database Properties** window.

11. Now, connect to the VAMI of the VRA using URL:
    `https://<IP address or FQDN>:5480`.

12. Log in using the root user and the password.

13. Navigate to the **VR | Configuration** tab.

14. Set **Configuration Mode** to **Manual configuration**.

15. Set **DB Type** to **SQL Server**.

16. Supply the **DB Host**, which could be the address (FQDN/IP) of the DB server.

17. Specify the **DB Username**, **DB Password**, and **DB Name**:

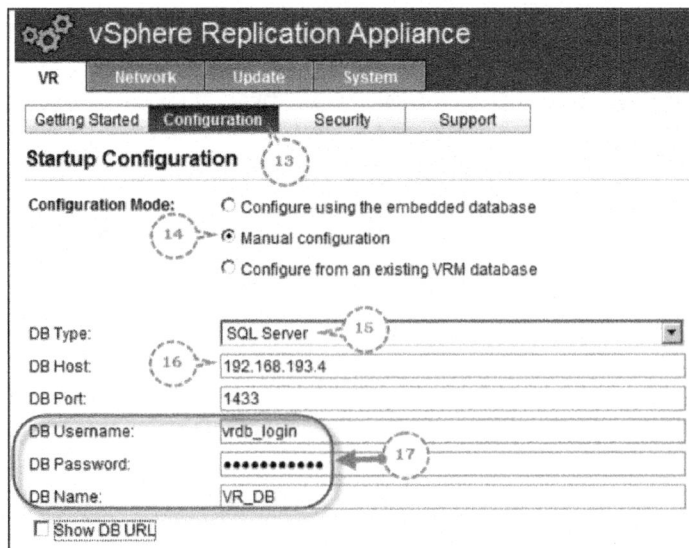

18. Click on **Save and Restart Service**. Clicking on **Save and Restart** will save the new settings and restart the vSphere Replication Management Service. It might take some time to finish, owing to the time it needs to prepare the database. Once done, you will have to reconfigure replications on the VM.

Deploying a vSphere Replication Server

Unlike the vSphere Replication Appliances, you can deploy additional vSphere Replication Servers using an Add-On appliance available in the vSphere Replication deployment bundle that was downloaded.

> You can deploy up to 10 VR server appliances per vCenter server instance.

There are several use cases for deploying additional VR servers. One of the prime reasons is manual load distribution. Each VR server with a default memory configuration of 716 MB can handle up to 200 replications. If there more than 200 VMs are replicated, then you could choose to either increase the memory of the appliance or deploy additional appliances and load balance by distributing the replication traffic to different appliances.

The following procedure will guide you through the steps required to deploy additional VR servers:

1. On the vSphere Web Client's **Home** page, click on **vSphere Replication** to bring up the vSphere Web Client's interface for vSphere Replication:

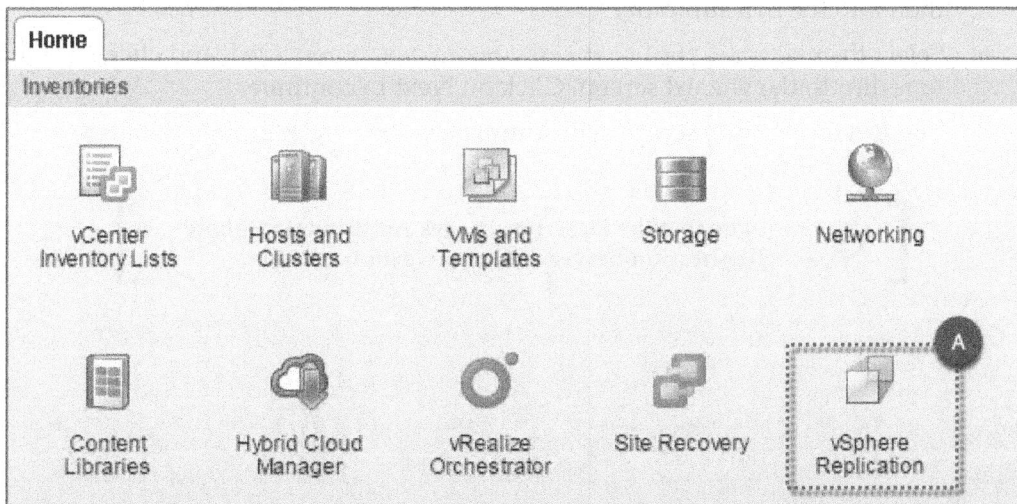

2. The vSphere Replication interface will list the vCenter the VRMS is registered to. Click on the toolbar item **Manage**, which should bring up the **Manage** tab for that vCenter server with the **vSphere Replication** sub tab selected:

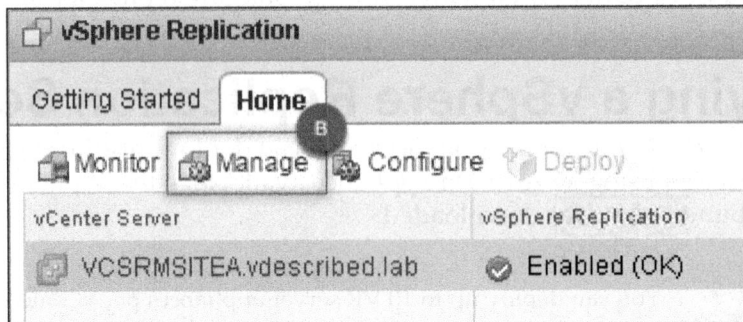

3. The **Replication Servers** view will show a list of registered VR servers. Click on the 🐚 icon to bring up the **Deploy OVF Template** wizard:

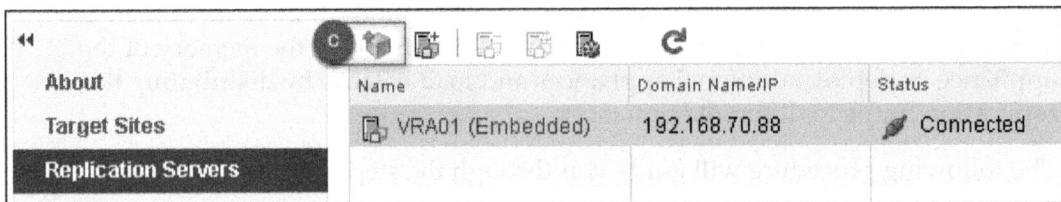

4. Set the source as **Local file** and click on **Browse...**.

5. Navigate to the vSphere replication bundle folder (or the ISO mounted) and then into the `bin` subfolder.

6. Select the `vSphere_Replication_AddOn_OVF10.ovf` OVF and click on **open** to return to the wizard screen. Click on **Next** to continue.

7. The **Review details** screen will summarize the OVF template details:

> Note that the **Description** says **Additional vSphere Replication Server**. Click on **Next** to continue.

Review details
Verify the OVF template details

Product	vSphere Replication Server
Version	6.1.1.13216
Vendor	VMware, Inc.
Publisher	⊘ Unknown (Trusted certificate)
Download size	795.2 MB
Size on disk	1.7 GB (thin provisioned) 18.0 GB (thick provisioned)
Description	Additional vSphere Replication Server

This confirms that you have chosen the correct OVF

8. Supply a name and inventory location of the appliance VM and click on **Next** to continue.

9. Select the compute resource for the VM and click on **Next** to continue. The compute resource could be a cluster or a single ESXi host.

10. On the **Select storage** screen, choose an intended disk format for the appliance's VMDKs and choose a datastore to store the VM files. The default option is **Thick Provisioned Lazy Zeroed**. Click on **Next** to continue.

11. Select a network (port group) for the VM's vNIC, choose between IPv4 and IPv6, and an IP allocation policy (DHCP/Static). You will have to manually specify the DNS server, the subnet mask and the gateway, if you choose the Static IP allocation method. Click on **Next** to continue.

12. Set the password, supply the static IP for the appliance, and NTP server IP addresses. Click on **Next** to continue.

13. On the **Ready to complete** screen, review the settings and click on **Finish** to deploy the appliance VM. You can select the **Power on after deployment** checkbox to start the VM if the deployment is successful.

14. Once the VRS is deployed, you will have to register the vSphere Replication Server to the VRMS. For instructions on how to do this, refer to the *Registering vSphere Replication Servers* section.

Registering vSphere Replication Servers

The deployed vSphere Replication Servers should be registered to the VRMS for them to be used to handle replication traffic. For instructions on how to deploy vSphere Replication Servers, read the *Deploying a vSphere Replication Server* section.

The following procedure will guide you through the steps required to register vSphere Replication Servers:

1. From the vSphere Web Client's **Home** page, click on **vSphere Replication** to bring up the vSphere Web Client's interface for vSphere Replication.

2. The vSphere Replication interface will list the vCenter the VRMS is registered to. Click on the toolbar item **Manage**, which should bring up the **Manage** tab for that vCenter Server with the **vSphere Replication** sub tab selected.

3. The **Replication Servers** view will display a list of registered VR servers. Click on the 📇 icon to bring up the **Register vSphere Replication Server** window:

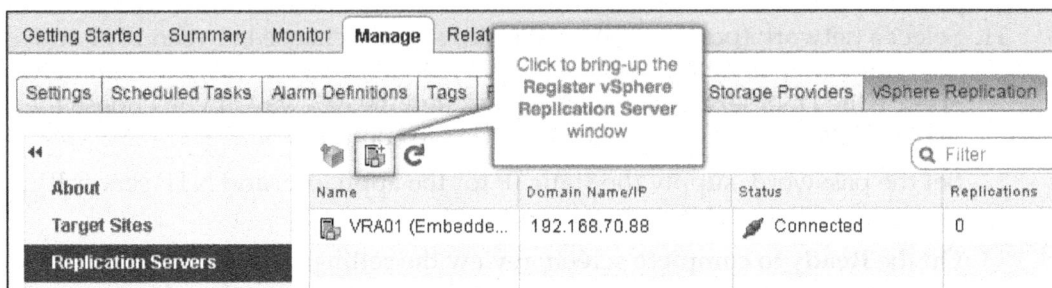

Getting Started	Summary	Monitor	**Manage**	Relat

Settings	Scheduled Tasks	Alarm Definitions	Tags			Storage Providers	vSphere Replication

Click to bring-up the Register vSphere Replication Server window

◀◀	🐚 📇 C	Q Filter
About	Name	Domain Name/IP	Status	Replications
Target Sites	📇 VRA01 (Embedde...	192.168.70.88	🔧 Connected	0
Replication Servers				

4. In the **Register vSphere Replication Server** window, browse through the vCenter inventory to locate the newly deployed VR appliance VM.

5. Click on the virtual machine to highlight and click on **OK** to confirm the selection:

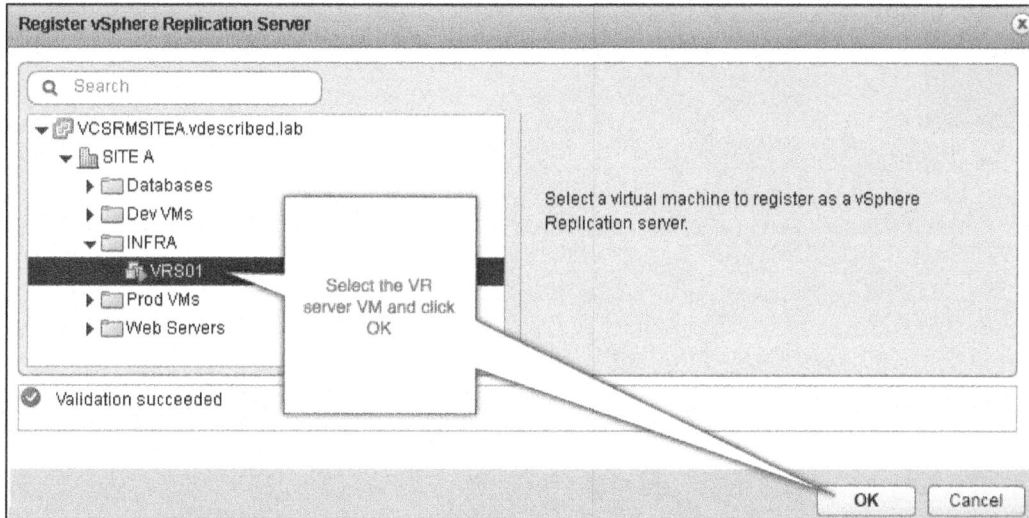

6. Once the registration is successful, it should be listed in the **Replication Servers** page:

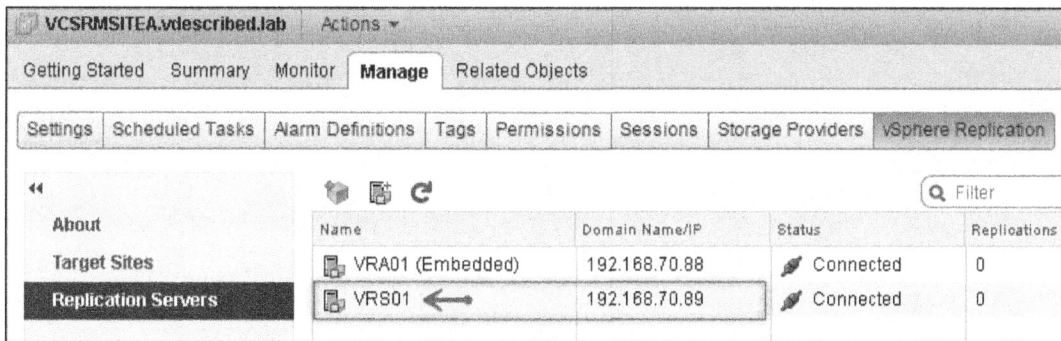

Summary

In this chapter, you learned what vSphere Replication is, its architecture, and the new features since version 5.5. You learned how to download, deploy, and configure the VRA. We covered the configuration of an external database hosted on a Microsoft SQL Server. Finally, you learned how to deploy and register additional VR. In *Chapter 5, Configuring and Using vSphere Replication 6.1*, you will learn how to replicate and recover virtual machines and how to orchestrate vSphere replication DR activities using SRM.

5
Configuring and Using vSphere Replication 6.1

In the previous chapter, you learned how to deploy the components required to form a vSphere Replication environment. Now, it is time to take the discussion further. In this chapter, you will learn how replication actually works and which configuration tasks are involved with the replication of a virtual machine.

Here is what we will be covering:

- Adding a remote site as a target
- Configuring replication for a VM to the local/remote site
- How does replication work?
- Using replication seeds
- Monitoring replication
- Reconfiguring replication
- Changing the target datastore
- Pausing an ongoing replication
- Stopping replication for a VM
- Moving replication to another VR Server
- Recovering virtual machines
- Configuring a Failback for virtual machines
- Using SRM with vSphere Replication

Adding a remote site as a target

A remote vCenter Server can be added as one of the targets. The pairing is mandatory when both the sites are managed by different vCenter Servers. This is because the VRM Server registered to the protected site vCenter can only see **vSphere Replication (VR)** Servers that are registered to it. You can deploy multiple VR Servers at either of the sites, but pairing can only be used if they are registered to its local VRM server. The pairing will not be possible if the vCenter Server managing the remote site does not have a VRMS registered to it.

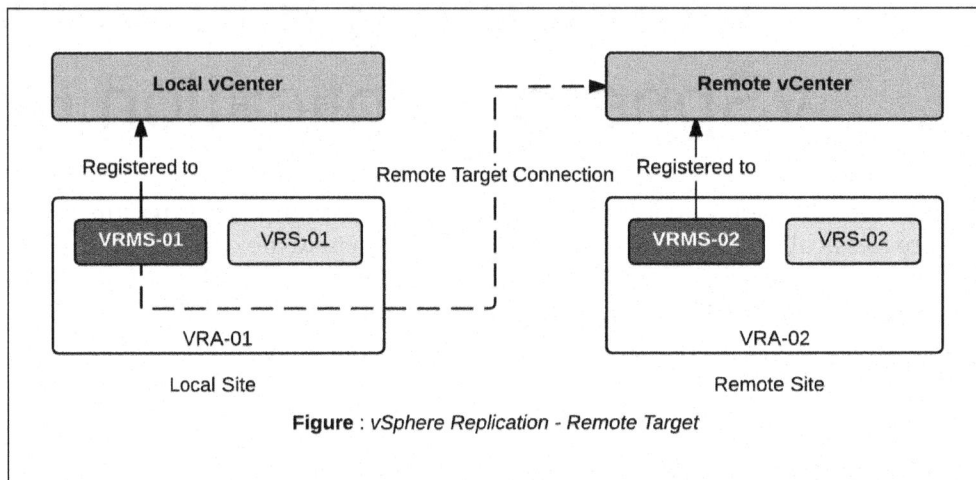

Figure : *vSphere Replication - Remote Target*

When adding a target site, you are prompted to specify the address (FQDN/IP) and connection credentials of the vCenter Server managing the target site. Most environments use separate accounts for connections between different vSphere components. The separate account can also be a service account corresponding to that component. In that case, you can use the service account corresponding to the vCenter Server that you are adding as a target site. Here the vCenter Server acts as a proxy to communicate with the VRM server registered to target site. Once the connection is successfully made, the VRM Server will be listed as the target site.

> The default site name of the VRM server is the name of the vCenter Server it is registered to. This can be changed in the VRA's web interface, under the configuration tab.

The following procedure will guide you through the steps required to add to a target site:

1. In the vSphere Web Client's **Home** page, click on **vSphere Replication** to bring up the vSphere Web Client's interface for vSphere Replication:

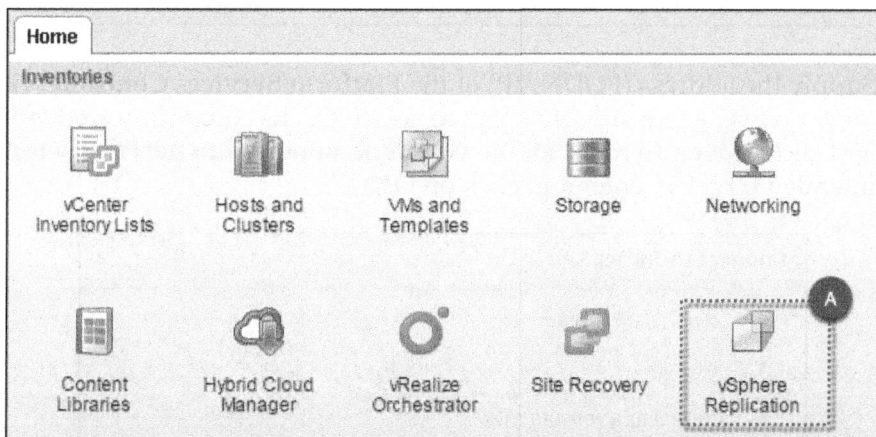

2. This page will list the vCenter Server the VRMS is registered to. Click on the toolbar item **Manage**, which should bring up the **Manage** tab for that vCenter Server with the **vSphere Replication** sub-tab selected:

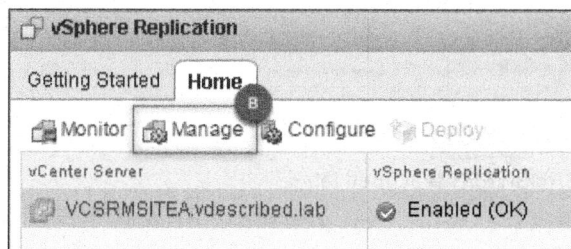

3. Click on **Target Sites** to list all the current target sites seen by the VRMS. In this case, there are none, because we have not added any sites yet. Click on the 🐟 icon to bring up the **Connect to Target Site** window:

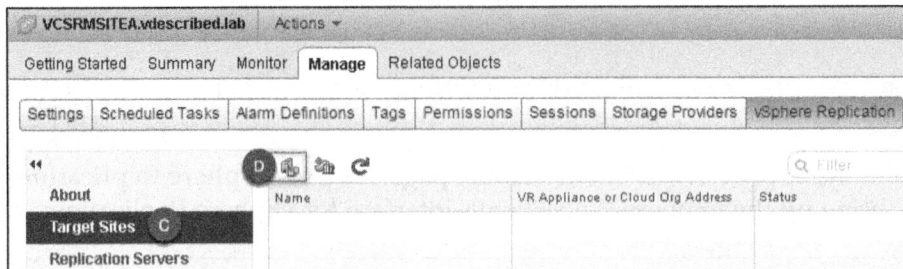

4. Supply the address (FQDN/IP) of the **Platform Services Controller** (PSC) the target vCenters are connected to, as well as its connection credentials and click on **Log In** to list all the vCenters connected to the PSC. Select the intended target vCenter and click on **OK**:

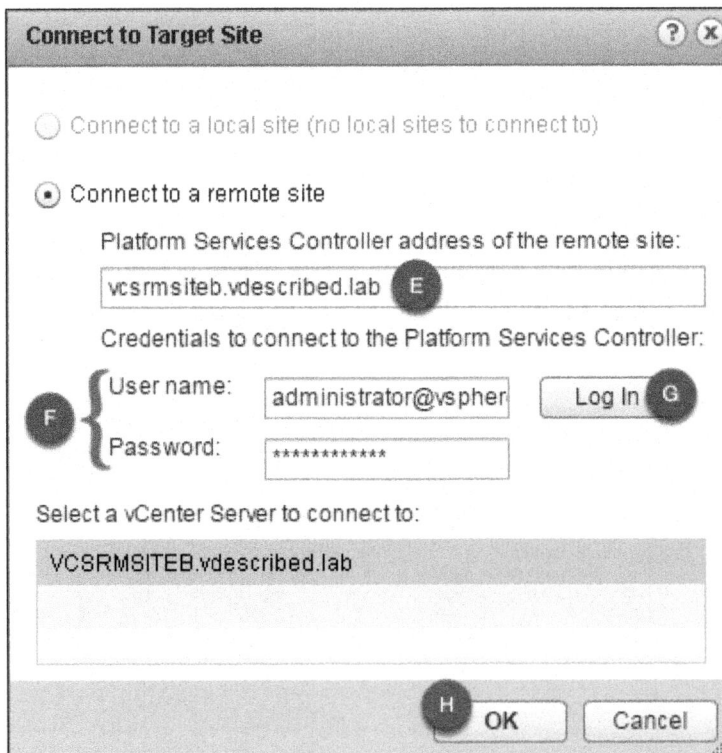

5. Once done, the VRM server registered with the added vCenter should be listed as a target site:

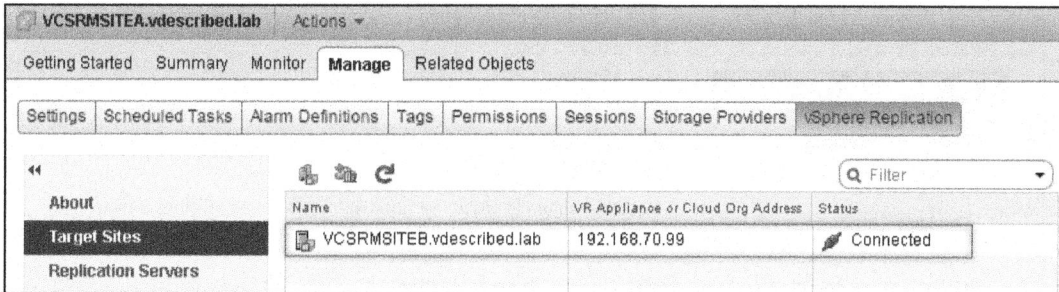

Configuring replication for a VM to the local/remote site

Replication can be across sites or at the same site. If you choose to replicate the VMs that you plan to protect, to a datastore at the same site, then you can use vSphere Replication to achieve the same.

Configuring replication requires the availability of a replication server (VRS) at the target site, be it *local* or *remote*. Since you have already deployed a vSphere Replication Appliance that includes both the VRMS and VRS components, there is no need for an additional step to get the replication working at the local site.

The following procedure will guide you through the steps required to configure replication for a VM to a local or remote vCenter site:

1. If you intend to replicate the virtual machine to a datastore managed by a remote site, then you will need to add the remote site vCenter as a target site. Refer to the *Adding a remote site as a target* section for instructions. Else, proceed directly to step 2.

2. Right-click on the intended virtual machine from the inventory and navigate to **All vSphere Replication Actions | Configure Replication** to bring up the **Configure Replication** wizard.

3. In the **Configure Replication** wizard, select the **Replicate to a vCenter Server** option and click on **Next** to continue:

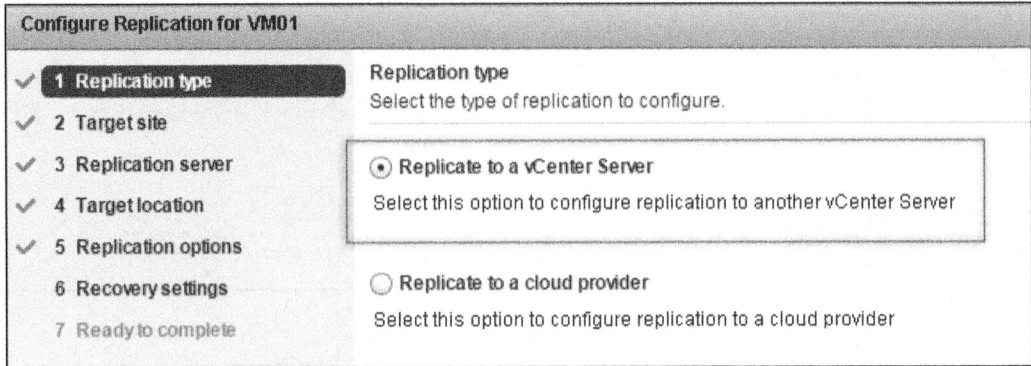

4. On the **Target site** screen, you will be presented with all the target sites, both *local* and *remote*. You also have an option to add remote sites as replication targets. Choose the intended (*local* or *remote*) site and click on **Next** to continue:

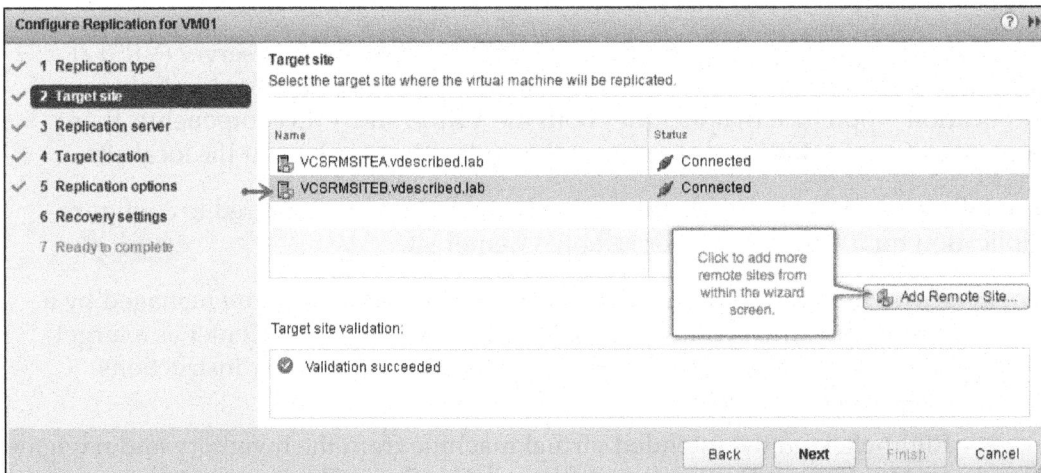

5. The **Replication server** screen will allow you to manually select a VR Server or select VRMS to auto-assign a VR server for replication:

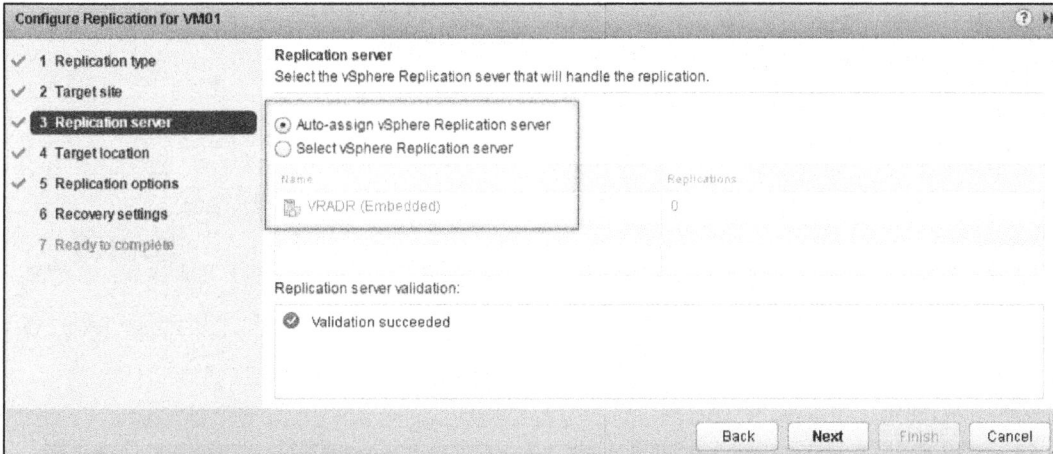

6. On the **Target location** screen, choose a datastore for the replica virtual machine that will be created. Click on **Edit** to bring up the **Select Target Location** window:

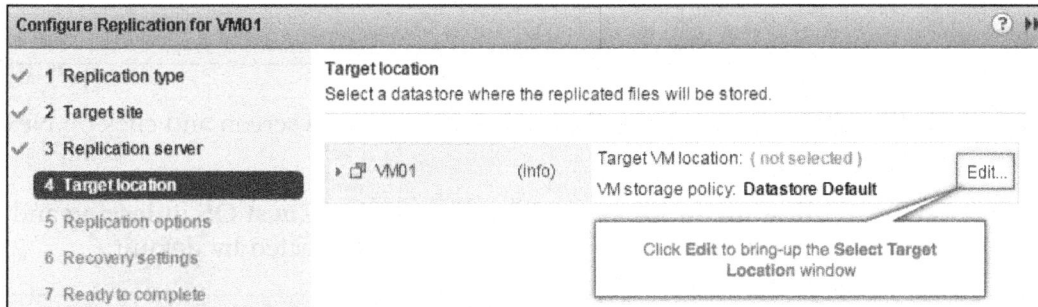

7. In the **Select Target Location** window, select the appropriate **VM Storage Policy** to filter down the list of datastores and choose a datastore:

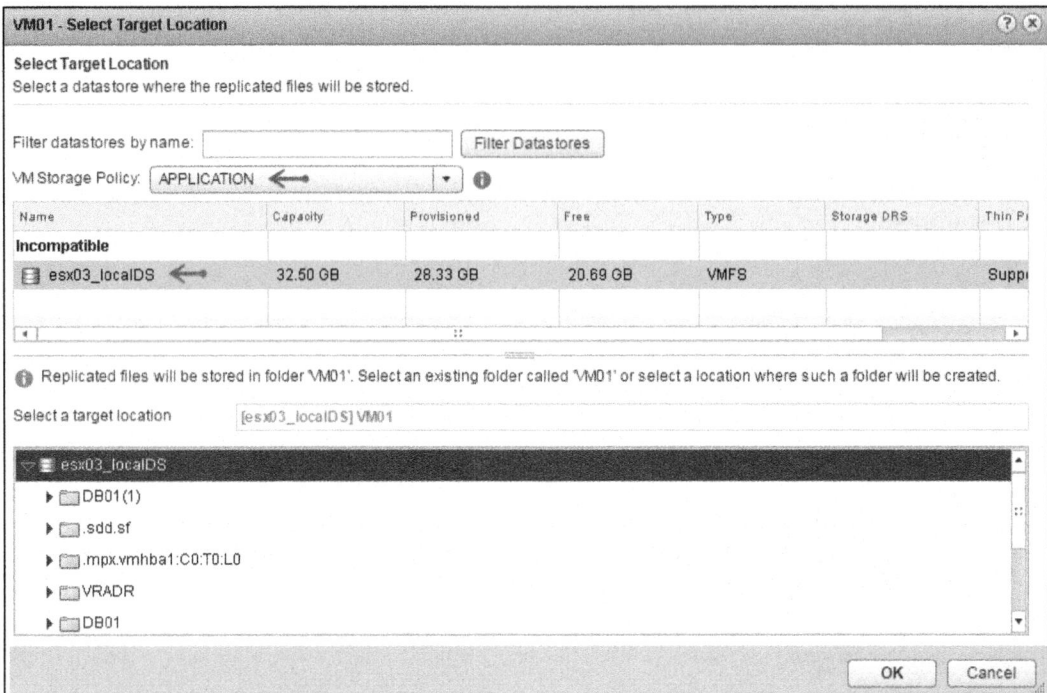

VM01 - Select Target Location						⑦ ⊗

Select Target Location
Select a datastore where the replicated files will be stored.

Filter datastores by name: [   ] [Filter Datastores]

VM Storage Policy: [APPLICATION ⟵   ▼] ❶

Name	Capacity	Provisioned	Free	Type	Storage DRS	Thin Pr
Incompatible						
🗎 esx03_localDS ⟵	32.50 GB	28.33 GB	20.69 GB	VMFS		Supp

❶ Replicated files will be stored in folder 'VM01'. Select an existing folder called 'VM01' or select a location where such a folder will be created.

Select a target location [[esx03_localDS] VM01]

▽ 🗎 esx03_localDS
  ▶ 🗀 DB01(1)
  ▶ 🗀 .sdd.sf
  ▶ 🗀 .mpx.vmhba1:C0:T0:L0
  ▶ 🗀 VRADR
  ▶ 🗀 DB01

[OK] [Cancel]

Click on **OK** to return to the **Target Location** wizard screen and click on **Next** to continue.

8. On the **Replication options** screen, you can enable **Guest OS quiescing** and **Network Compression**. Both the options are not selected by default:

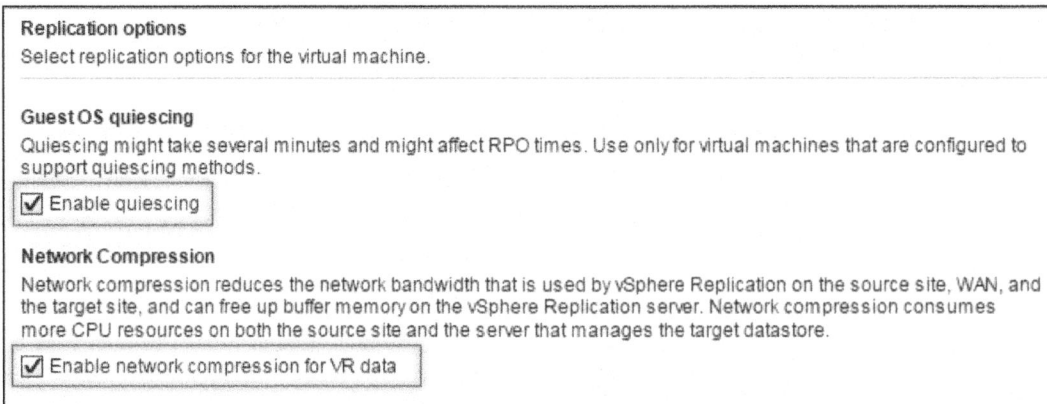

Replication options
Select replication options for the virtual machine.

Guest OS quiescing
Quiescing might take several minutes and might affect RPO times. Use only for virtual machines that are configured to support quiescing methods.
☑ Enable quiescing

Network Compression
Network compression reduces the network bandwidth that is used by vSphere Replication on the source site, WAN, and the target site, and can free up buffer memory on the vSphere Replication server. Network compression consumes more CPU resources on both the source site and the server that manages the target datastore.
☑ Enable network compression for VR data

Guest OS quiescing support includes both Microsoft VSS and Linux FS quiescing using VMware tools.

For details regarding VSS support refer to VMware KB – 2041909 from the following URL:

```
https://kb.vmware.com/selfservice/microsites/
search.do?language=en_US&cmd=displayKC&external
Id=2041909
```

9. On the **Recovery settings** screen, set a planned **Recovery Point Objective (RPO)** value. The default is **4 hours**, with the lowest possible being **15 minutes** and the highest **24 hours**. You can also choose to save point in time snapshots of the replication, by selecting the checkbox to enable it. By default, it creates 3 point-in-time instances and any such instances created during the last 5 days are retained. You can only retain a maximum of 24 point-in-time snapshots of the replication. Point-in-time snapshots are useful if you want to maintain multiple recoverable points for the virtual machine. Make a selection and click on **Next** to continue:

10. On the **Ready to complete** screen, review the settings and click on **Finish** to configure the replication.

11. The **Recent Tasks** pane should show a **Configure a virtual machine for replication** task completed successfully.

How does replication work?

Once VM replication is successfully configured, it first does an initial full sync of the source VMDKs to the target datastore. If you already have the base VMDKs precopied to the destination datastore, then only the changed blocks are replicated. The replication happens over the network using the **Network File Copy (NFC)** protocol. The changed blocks are transferred using ESXi's management VMkernel port group.

Once the initial sync is complete, the VR Agent tracks the changed blocks using the vSCSI filter driver. It tracks, writes, and maintains a bitmap of the changed blocks. Every time a replica is created, the data transferred is copied to a redo log file. This is done to make sure that a VM at the recovery site is not corrupted in the event of a network disruption. The redo log is committed to the base disk only after the changed blocks are fully copied, thereby making each replica crash consistent. When you configure replication for a VM you get to choose the RPO and the number of multiple point-in-time snapshots that you would like to maintain. The RPO ranges from 15 minutes to 24 hours, and you can have up to 24 point-in-time snapshots. This means you can have up to 24 historical point-in-time recovery points of the replicated VM. An RPO value of 5 minutes is possible if the virtual machine that is being replicated and its replica are on Datastores hosted by VSAN.

Both RPO and the number of point-in-time instances dictate the number of historical snapshots maintained for the VM. For instance, if you set an RPO of 2 hours, then you will retain 12 point-in-time recovery points for the VM each day. While the RPO is set to 2 hours, and if the number of point-in-time instances is set to 4, then you have only 4 snapshots for that VM. VR tries to keep the oldest of the recovery points created.

Once a replication has been successfully configured, the destination datastore is populated with the following files:

- `*.vmdk`: The base disk(s) to which the VM data is being replicated
- `hbrdisk.RDID-*`: This is the redo log file that has the latest replication data
- `hbrcfg*.vmx`: This is a shadow VMX file that will be used to register the VM, when a recovery is initiated

The following screenshot shows the contents of the replica VM's directory:

Name	Size	Modified	Type
hbrdisk.RDID-ede528d9-7094-4a00-b975-afe38fb8e241.4.22154...	1,024.00 KB	30/03/2016 13:...	Virtual Disk
VM01.vmdk	2,760,704.00 KB	30/03/2016 13:...	Virtual Disk
hbrcfg.GID-3d8cb202-d0e5-4095-a8a5-0cf9949d6daf.2.nvram.4	8.48 KB	30/03/2016 13:...	File
hbrcfg.GID-3d8cb202-d0e5-4095-a8a5-0cf9949d6daf.2.vmxf.3	3.18 KB	30/03/2016 13:...	File
hbrgrp.GID-3d8cb202-d0e5-4095-a8a5-0cf9949d6daf.txt	2.85 KB	30/03/2016 13:...	File
hbrcfg.GID-3d8cb202-d0e5-4095-a8a5-0cf9949d6daf.2.vmx.2	3.18 KB	30/03/2016 13:...	File

> If a VM being replicated is modified by adding a new VMDK to it, then the active replication will stop with an error. The replication should then be manually reconfigured by the administrator to include the new VMDK before resuming the replication.

Using replication seeds

When you configure replication on a virtual machine for the very first time, vSphere replication will need to make an initial copy of the VM's VMDKs. The initial copy can be bandwidth intensive and time consuming based on the size of the VMDKs. This can however be overcome by transporting the VMDKs to the intended location, prior to configuring the replication on the VM. The transport method can be of your choice, ideally couriered to the destination site, if remote.

> The copies of the VMDKs transported and placed at the destination datastore is referred to as a seed.

The following procedure will guide you through the steps required to use an available seed for a VM:

1. Power off the virtual machine at the source (protected) site, which you intend to replicate.

2. Copy the VM's folder to the target datastore. If it is in a different data center, then the files need to be transported to the data center first and then uploaded to the target datastore.

3. Power on the virtual machine at the source (protected) site.

4. Right-click on the virtual machine from the inventory and navigate to **All vSphere Replication Actions** | **Configure Replication**.

5. Select the **Replicate to a vCenter Server** option.

6. Select the intended target site and click on **Next**.

7. Choose a Replication Server or let VMRS auto select one for you. Make an intended selection and click on **Next**.

8. On the **Target Location** screen, click on **Edit...** to bring up the **Select Target Location** window:

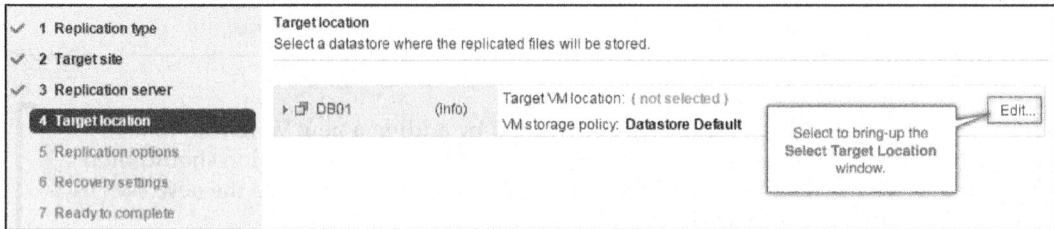

9. In the **Select Target Location** window, choose a datastore where you would like to place the replica of the virtual machine, and set *the folder corresponding to the copy of the source VM at the destination datastore* as the **Target Location**. Click on **OK** to confirm the section and return to the replication configuration wizard:

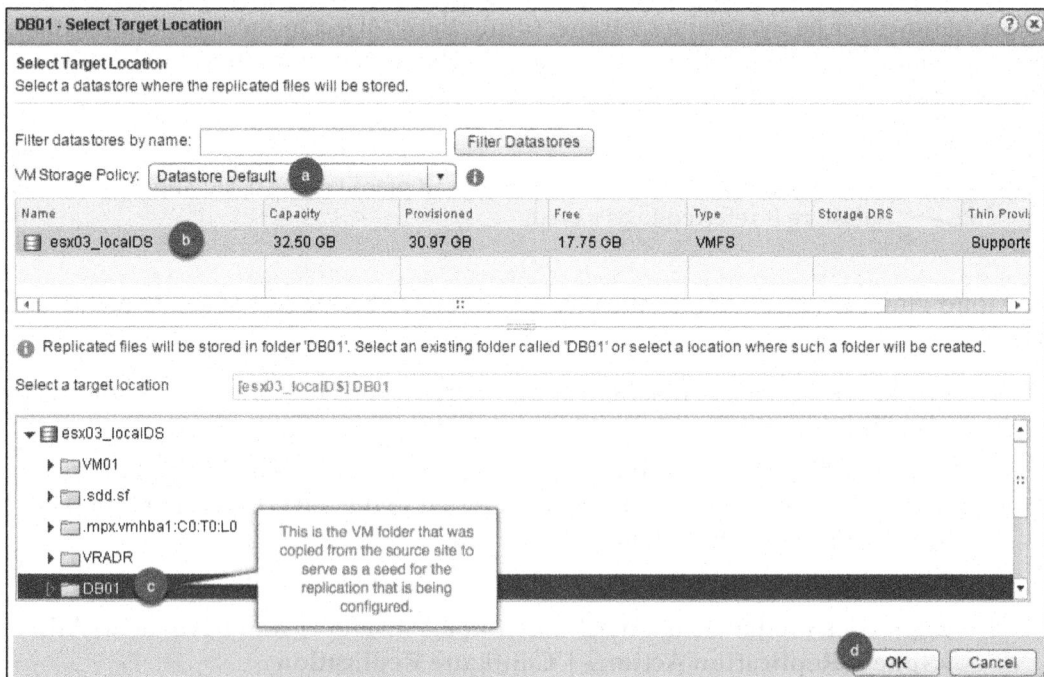

10. A **Folder Exists** warning prompting you to either use the existing folder or create a new one will appear. Click on the **Use existing** button to return to the **Configure Replication** wizard:

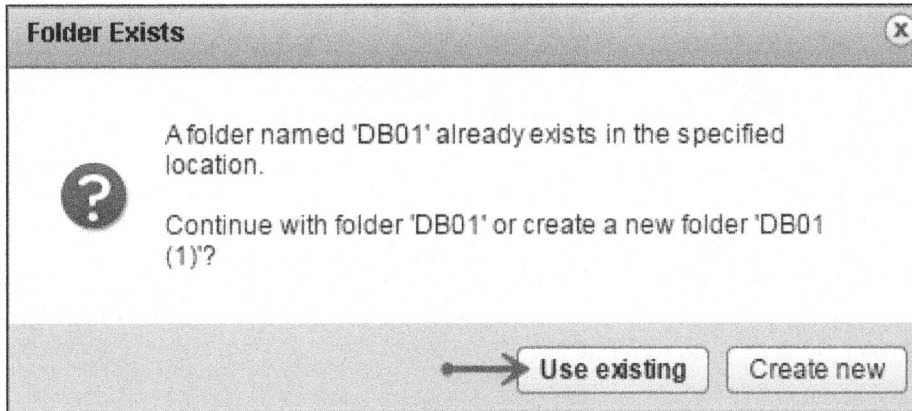

11. The **Target location** screen will now indicate that it has found seeds that can be used for the replication that is being configured. Here, each seed corresponds to a VMDK. Click on the VM to expand and review all the seeds found:

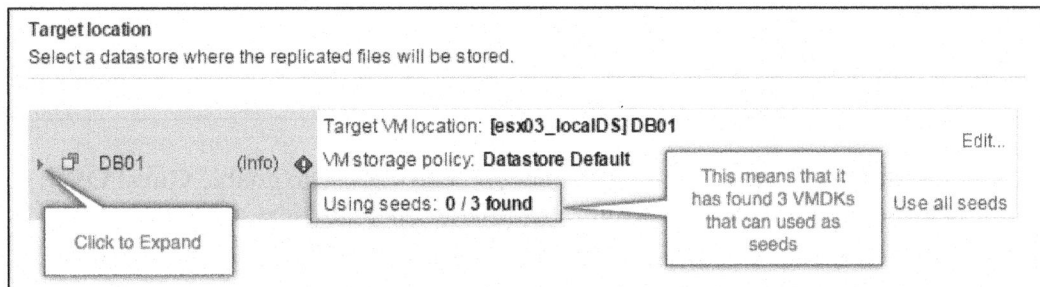

12. Once expanded, review all the found seeds and choose to either **Use all seeds** or selectively seed only the needed VMDKs. Click on **Next** to continue:

Target location
Select a datastore where the replicated files will be stored.

▼ ⊡ DB01 (info) ◆	Target VM location: **[esx03_localDS] DB01** VM storage policy: **Datastore Default**	Edit...
	Using seeds: **0 / 3 found** Replication enabled: **Yes**	Use all seeds Disable
⊟ Hard disk 1 (info) ◆	Target file location: Use the target VM location Disk format: Use existing disk Storage policy: Use the VM storage policy	Edit...
	Using seed: **No** Replication enabled: **Yes**	Use seed Disable
⊟ Hard disk 2 (info) ◆	Target file location: Use the target VM location Disk format: Use existing disk Storage policy: Use the VM storage policy	Edit...
	Using seed: **No** Replication enabled: **Yes**	Use seed Disable
⊟ Hard disk 3 (info) ◆	Target file location: Use the target VM location Disk format: Use existing disk Storage policy: Use the VM storage policy	Edit...
	Using seed: **No**	Use seed

---

13. On the **Replication options** screen, you can choose to enable **Guest OS quiescing** and **Network Compression** and click on **Next** to continue.

14. On the **Recovery settings** screen, set a desired RPO value and the number of point-in-time instances that you intend to retain and click on **Next** to continue.

15. On the **Ready to complete** screen, review the settings and click on **Finish** to configure the replication.

> Regardless of whether you choose to use a seed or not, vSphere Replication always initiates an initial full sync. When using a seed, the initial full sync will take considerably less time.

Monitoring replication

Replication configured on the VMs can be monitored for its current status. Replications can be incoming or outgoing.

The following procedure will guide you through the steps required to monitor a replication:

1. Connect to the vCenter Server and navigate to the inventory home.

2. Click on **vSphere Replication** to bring up the vSphere Replication **Home**.

3. Click on **Monitor** to go to the monitor tab with the **vSphere Replication** sub-tab selected:

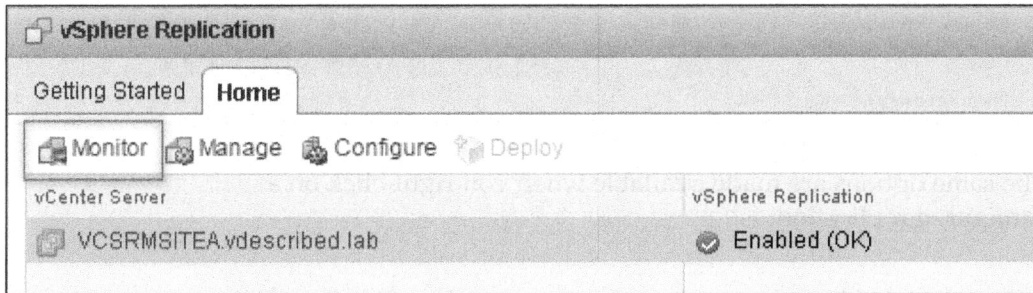

4. On the left-hand pane, you will find both **Outgoing Replications** and **Incoming Replications** selected. The **Outgoing Replications** section will show all the replications leaving the VR server at the current site. The **Incoming Replications** section will show all the replications arriving at the VR server at the current site:

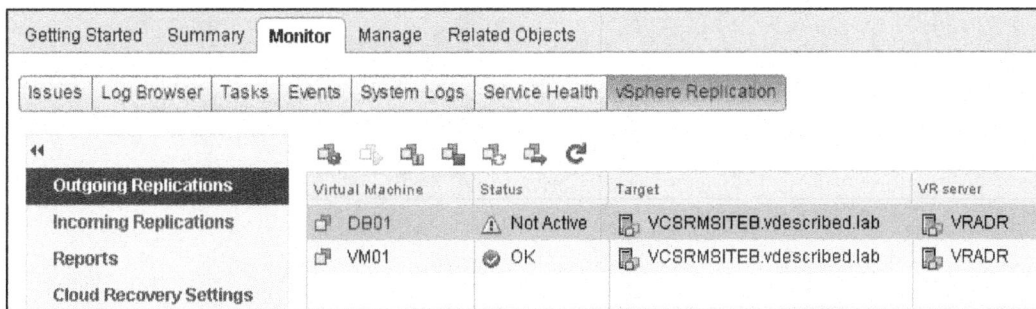

Here, you might have noticed a **Not Active** status on one of the replications. This is because the source VM was not powered on. VR requires the source VM to be powered on for the replication to begin.

Selecting either **Incoming Replications** / **Outgoing Replications** will list the names of the VMs being replicated and the current status of the replication.

It is at the **Monitor** tab, where you get options to **Reconfigure** 🔧, **Pause** 🔧, **Synchronize** 🔧, and **Stop** 🔧 or **Move** 🔧 an ongoing replication. More information on these task have been covered in separate sections of this chapter:

The same options are made available when you right-click on a configured replication:

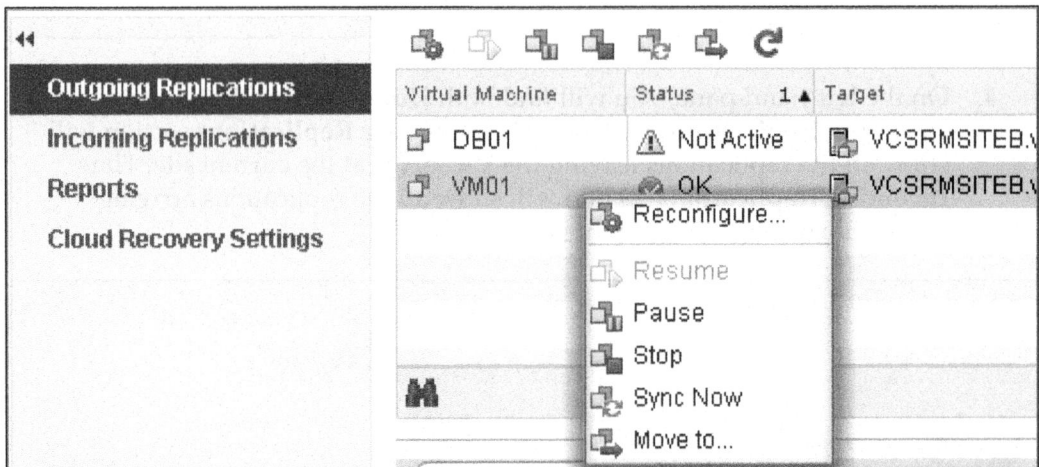

Reconfiguring replication

An Ongoing replication can be reconfigured. This is done if there is a need to change the replication server in use, the target datastore, or the recovery settings.

The following procedure will guide you through the steps required in reconfiguring a replication:

1. Connect to the vCenter Server and navigate to the inventory home.

2. Click on **vSphere Replication** to bring up the vSphere Replication home.

3. Click on **Monitor** to go to the monitor with the **vSphere Replication** sub-tab selected.

4. In the left-hand pane, you will find both **Outgoing Replications** and **Incoming Replications** selected. Make an appropriate selection depending on whether you are at the local or the remote vCenter Server.

5. Right-click on an intended replication and click on **Reconfigure** to start the reconfiguration wizard.

6. Change the replication server to handle the traffic, if intended. Click on **Next** to continue.

7. Select the new target location, if intended. Click on **Next** to continue.

8. Modify the replication options, if intended. Click on **Next** to continue.

9. Modify the recovery settings, if intended. Click on **Next** to continue.

10. Review the **Ready to complete** screen and click on **Finish** to initiate the reconfiguration.

Changing the target datastore

You can change the target datastore of an Ongoing replication by reconfiguring the replication. Doing so will result in the deletion of the files from the current destination datastore, and an initial full sync will be done again to the new target datastore location.

The following procedure will guide you through the steps required to change the target datastore of an ongoing replication:

1. Connect to the vCenter Server and navigate to the inventory home.

2. Click on **vSphere Replication** to bring up the vSphere Replication home.

3. Click on **Monitor** to go to the monitor with the vSphere Replication sub-tab selected.

4. In the left-hand pane, you will find both **Outgoing Replications** and **Incoming Replications** selected. Make an appropriate selection depending on whether you are at the local or the remote vCenter Server.

5. Right-click on the desired replication and click on **Reconfigure** to start the reconfiguration wizard.

6. Select a replication server to handle the traffic. In this case, we have selected the local VRA. Click on **Next** to continue.

7. On the **Target Location** screen, click on **Edit...** to bring up the **Select Target Location** window.

8. In the **Target Location** window, you will have to change the target location individually for the VM configuration file (.vmx) and the VMDKs and click on **OK**.

> Unlike version 5.5, wherein VR would do an initial full sync to the new location contributing to the loss of all the current replication instances, with version 6.1 vSphere Replication will move the selected replicated instances to the new target location.

9. Modify the **Replication options**, if needed. Click on **Next** to continue.

10. Modify the **Recovery Settings**, if needed. Click on **Next** to continue.

11. Review the **Ready to complete** screen and click on **Finish** to initiate the reconfiguration.

12. You should see a **Reconfigure virtual machine replication** task completed successfully in the **Recent Tasks** pane.

Pausing an Ongoing replication

An Ongoing replication can be paused regardless of the status it is in. Pausing a replication will stop the VR from tracking the changes to the VMDK files. The following procedure will guide you through the steps required in pausing an ongoing replication:

1. Connect to the vCenter Server and navigate to the inventory home.

2. Click on **vSphere Replication** to bring up the vSphere Replication home.

3. Click on **Monitor** to go to the monitor with the **vSphere Replication** sub-tab selected.

4. In the left-hand pane, you will find both **Outgoing Replications** and **Incoming Replications** selected. Make an appropriate selection depending on whether you are at the local or the remote vCenter Server.

5. Right-click on the replication that you want to pause and click on **Pause**.

6. Click on **Yes** on the confirmation window.

7. Once the replication has been successfully stopped, the status should read **Paused**.

On pausing an ongoing replication, the VR server will temporarily stop monitoring the source VM. A paused replication can then be resumed by following the same procedure, but by selecting **Actions | Resume** at the fifth step.

Synchronize Data Immediately

Synchronization is the process of transferring changed blocks from the source to the replica at the destination via the vSphere Replication Server component. vSphere Replication synchronizes the data based on the RPO setting. If the RPO is set to 4 hours, then the synchronization happens every 4 hours.

However, we do have an option to force an immediate synchronization, using **Synchronize Data Immediately**, without having to wait for the next scheduled sync. Although it is important to keep in mind that the amount of time required to perform the sync depends on the amount of changes to the source VM since the previous scheduled sync. This operation could potentially increase the network usage, owing to the amount of data that needs to be transferred.

The following procedure will guide you through the steps required to initiate an immediate data synchronization:

1. Connect to the vCenter Server and navigate to the inventory home.

2. Click on **vSphere Replication** to bring up the vSphere Replication home.

3. Click on **Monitor** to go to the monitor with the vSphere Replication sub-tab selected.

4. In the left-hand pane, you will find both **Outgoing Replications** and **Incoming Replications** selected. Make an appropriate selection depending on whether you are at the local or the remote vCenter Server.

5. Right-click on the replication that you want to Synchronize and click on **Sync Now** to perform the synchronization:

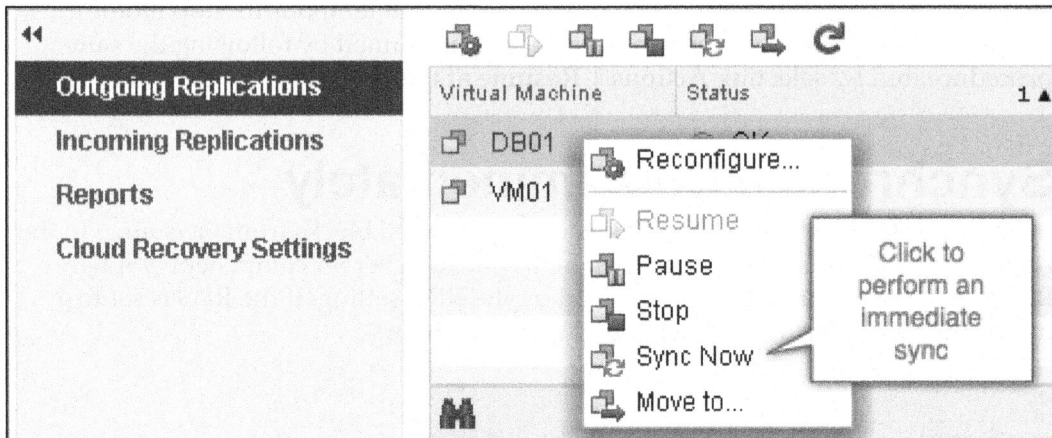

6. You should see a **Synchronize virtual machine** task completed successfully in the **Recent Tasks** pane.

Stopping replication on a VM

You can choose to stop the replication on a VM if there is a need to do so. *Stopping a replication will permanently stop the replication and delete all the replicas.* This is normally done to remove the replication for a VM.

The following procedure will guide you through the steps required to stop replication of a virtual machine:

1. Connect to the vCenter Server and navigate to the inventory home.

2. Click on **vSphere Replication** to bring up the vSphere Replication home.

3. Click on **Monitor** to go to the monitor tab with the vSphere Replication sub-tab selected.

4. Select **Outgoing Replications**, if at the protected site or **Incoming replications**, if at the recovery site; either can be selected if the VM is replicated to the same site as the source.

5. Select the replication, right-click on it, and click on the **Stop** menu item.

6. You will be prompted to confirm the action. Click on **Yes** to confirm. Keep in mind though that a replication can only be successfully stopped if both the source and the target sites are able to talk to each other. If, for whatever reason, the communication between source and target sites are disrupted, then you need to use the Force stop replication option to stop the replication at both the sites:

Stop Replication

? Permanently stop the replication for the selected virtual machine?

To stop the replication successfully, both sites must be accessible. If the remote site is not accessible, you can force stop the replication to remove it only from the local site.

☐ Force stop replication

OK   Cancel

7. The **Recent Tasks** pane will show an **Unconfigure virtual machine replication** task completed successfully.

8. The Outgoing/Incoming Replication sections will no longer list the stopped replication.

Moving replication to another VR Server

You can choose to move an active replication to another VR server if need be. This is generally done when you have multiple VR servers at the recovery site and you intend to distribute the replication load to those servers. Moving a replication to another VR Server requires a reconfiguring of the replication on the VM.

The following procedure will guide you through the steps required in moving the replication to another VR Server:

1. Connect to the vCenter Server and navigate to the inventory home.

2. Click on **vSphere Replication** to bring up the vSphere Replication home.

3. Click on **Monitor** to go to the monitor tab with the vSphere Replication sub-tab selected.

4. Select either **Outgoing Replications** or **Incoming Replications**.

5. Select the replication, right-click on it, and click on the **Move to...** menu item:

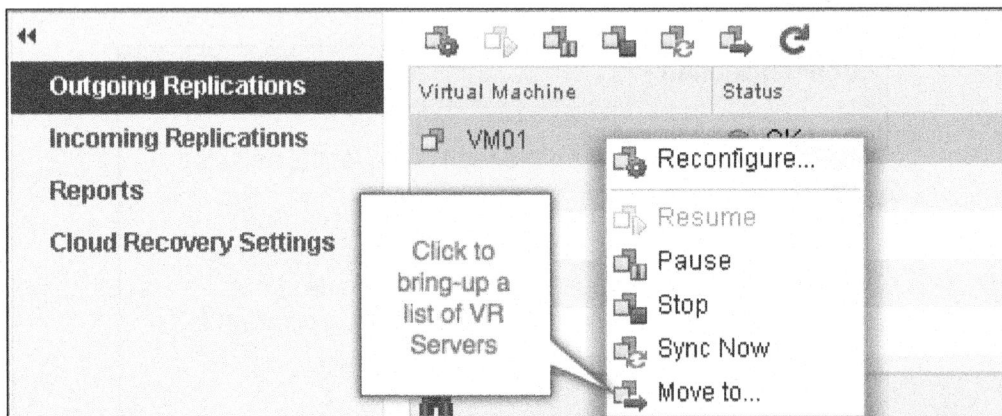

6. You should now be presented with a list of vSphere Replication servers registered to the site the VM is being replicated to. Make a selection and click on **OK**:

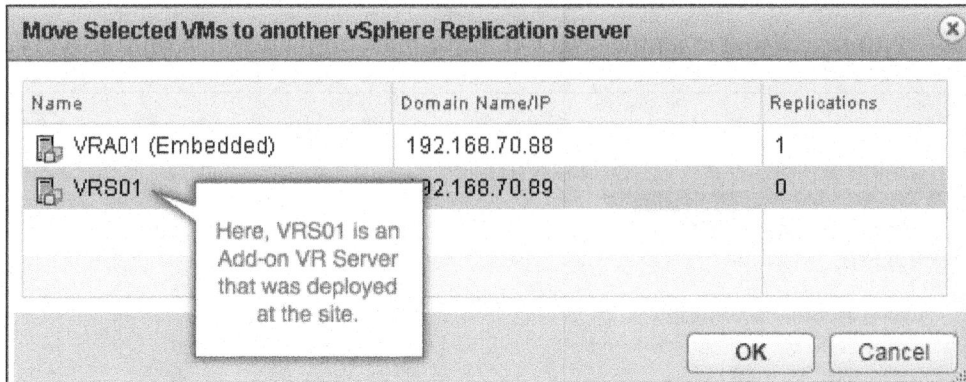

Move Selected VMs to another vSphere Replication server		
Name	Domain Name/IP	Replications
VRA01 (Embedded)	192.168.70.88	1
VRS01	92.168.70.89	0

Here, VRS01 is an Add-on VR Server that was deployed at the site.

OK   Cancel

7. The **Recent Tasks** pane should show the **Move replication to other vSphere Replication Server** task completed successfully and the status should read **OK**.

Recovering virtual machines

We have described how to configure replication for the virtual machines. The story will remain half-told, however, if we do not cover how to recover virtual machines using their replicas. You can perform a recovery only at the site target site. In other words, you will be presented with an option to initiate a recovery only at the site which has seen the incoming replication.

The following procedure will guide you through the steps required to perform a recovery:

1. Connect to the vCenter Server managing the remote site and navigate to the inventory home.

> If there is only one vCenter Server managing both the protected and recovery sites, then vSphere Replication's monitor tab will show both the outgoing and incoming replication for the virtual machine.

2. Click on **vSphere Replication** to bring up the vSphere Replication home.

3. Click on **Monitor** to go to the monitor tab with the vSphere Replication sub-tab selected.

4. Select **Incoming Replications** on the left-hand pane and select the virtual machine that you would like to recover.

5. With the virtual machine selected, right-click on it and click on **Recovery...**:

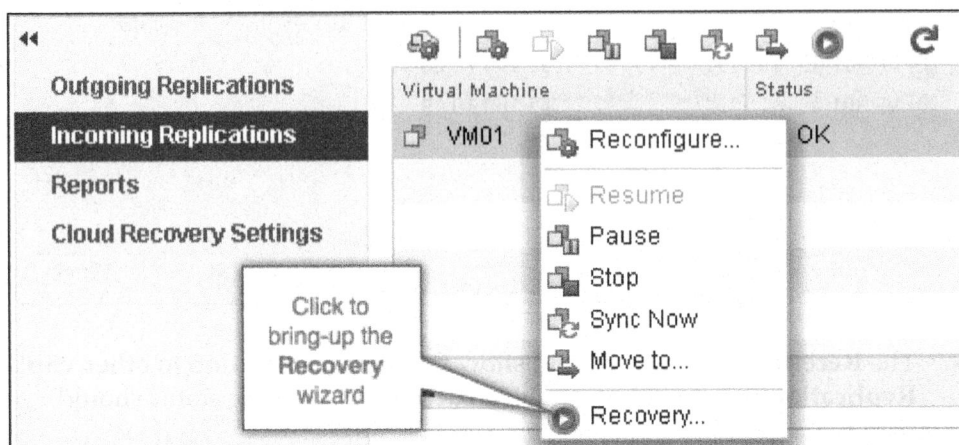

6. You will be presented with the **Synchronize recent changes** and **Use latest available data** recovery options. Choose the appropriate option and click on **Next** to continue. More insight on these options are included here:

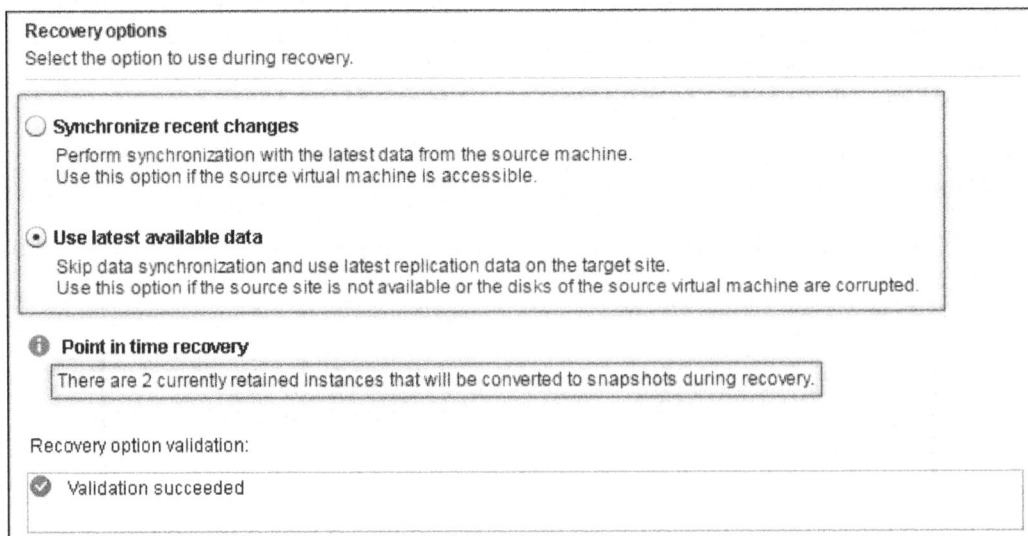

- ° **Synchronize recent changes**: This option will initiate an immediate synchronization to make sure that the VM after recovery has the latest data in it. This is not possible if the source VM is powered on. You will have to manually power off the VM if it is running.

- ° **Use latest available Data**: This option will recover using the most recent redo log that was created. In this case, you will lose all the changes that happened at the source VM since the last replication. The amount of data loss will not exceed the RPO set. For instance, if the RPO was set to 15 minutes, then you would only lose 15 minutes worth of data.

7. Select the data center/folder you intend to place the VM.

> Keep in mind that only the data center to which with the virtual machine was replicated to can be selected.

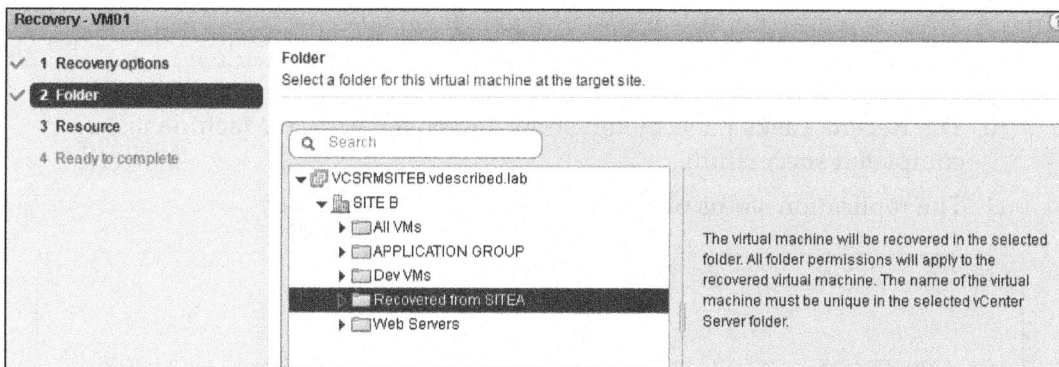

Recovery - VM01

✓ 1 Recovery options
✓ 2 Folder
3 Resource
4 Ready to complete

Folder
Select a folder for this virtual machine at the target site.

Q Search

- ▼ VCSRMSITEB.vdescribed.lab
  - ▼ SITE B
    - ▶ All VMs
    - ▶ APPLICATION GROUP
    - ▶ Dev VMs
    - Recovered from SITEA
    - ▶ Web Servers

The virtual machine will be recovered in the selected folder. All folder permissions will apply to the recovered virtual machine. The name of the virtual machine must be unique in the selected vCenter Server folder.

> You will not be able to place the recovered VM into the same inventory hierarchical level as that of the source VM. It is a general practice to create the folder under the data center level, to house the recovered VMs.

8. On the **Resource** screen, select the compute resource (cluster, host, or resource) and click on **Next** to continue.

9. On the **Ready to complete** screen, you can choose not to power on the recovered virtual machine, by unchecking the **Power on the virtual machine after recovery** checkbox. It is selected (checked) by default. Click on **Finish** to start the recovery:

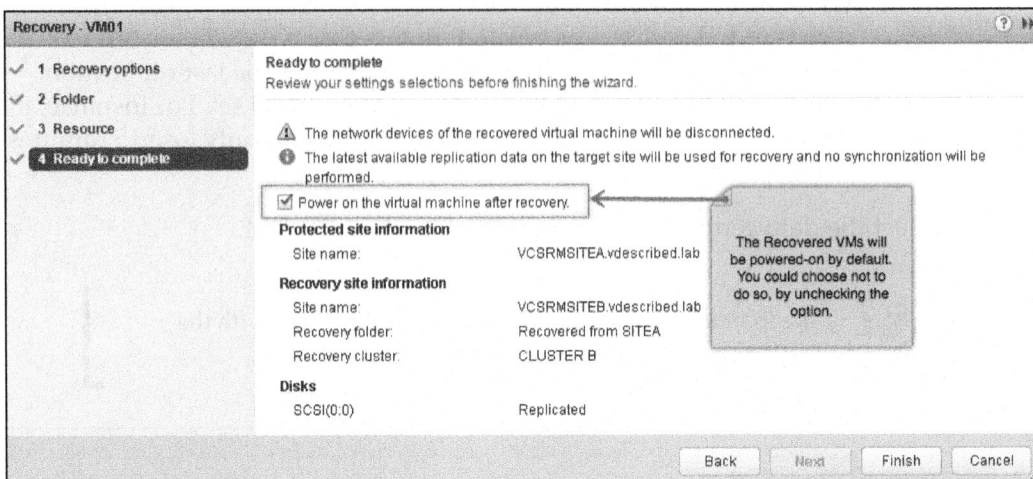

10. The **Recent Tasks** pane should show a **Recover Virtual Machine** task completed successfully.

11. The replication status of the VM will now be **Recovered**:

12. After a successful recovery, you should see the recovered VM powered on and running.

13. The VM's snapshot manager will show all the point in time instances as snapshots so that Revert-To-snapshot is possible:

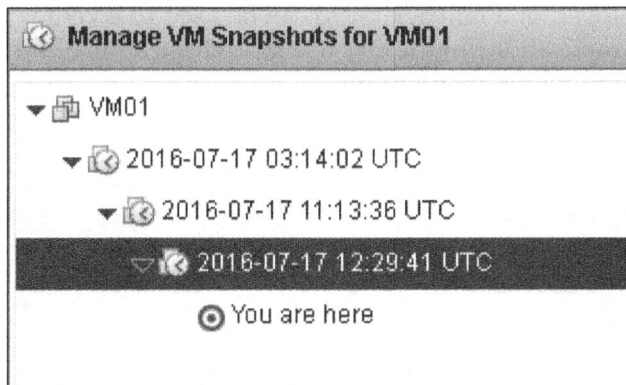

Configuring failback for VMs

With vSphere Replication, configuring failback for a virtual machine is a manual process. The following process will guide you through the steps required to perform a failback:

1. Recover the virtual machine to the recovery site. Refer to the *Recovering virtual machines* section for instructions.

2. Remove the virtual machine from the inventory at the protected site.

3. Configure an outgoing replication from the recovery site to the protected site. Refer to the *Configuring Replication for a VM to the local/remote site* section for instructions.

When configuring the replication from the recovery to the protected site, if the datastore at the protected site has the VM files, then those can be used as seeds; otherwise an initial full sync is performed.

A failover can be automated using SRM.

Using SRM with vSphere Replication

vSphere Replication as a standalone product has no ability to automate DR tasks such as a test, a failover, or a failback. SRM can be used to leverage vSphere Replication as the replication engine and use its orchestration ability to automate the DR tasks. Refer to following diagram:

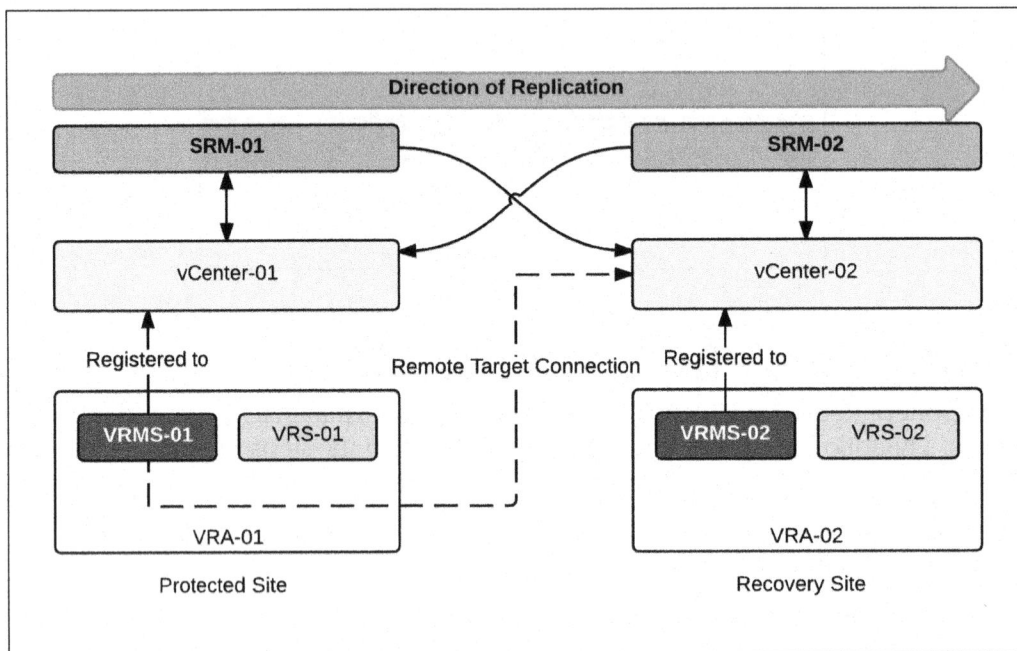

SRM relies on the concept of two sites replicating data between them with the help of a replication engine. So, you need two sites managed separately by two different vCenter Servers. Each of the vCenter Servers should have a VRMS instance registered to it. This means you need to deploy a **vSphere Replication Appliance (VRA)** at both the sites. Once the VRA is deployed, use the vSphere Web Client's vSphere Replication interface at the protected site to add the recovery site as the target site. For more information on how to add target sites, refer to the *Adding a remote site as a target* section. For SRM to detect the registered vSphere Replication Appliances at both the sites, you will need to install the vSphere Replication component bundled with the SRM installer. If you already have SRM installed, you can run the installer to repair the installer and install vSphere Replication components as well. Once you have installed the vSphere Replication component, the SRM interface should list vSphere Replication.

All the DR tasks that can be performed using SRM have been explained in the chapters that cover SRM's array-based replication. Although the DR tasks are notably similar, there are a few changes to the workflow.

We will cover the following tasks in this section:

- Creating a vSphere Replication protection group
- Creating a vSphere Replication recovery plan
- Testing a vSphere Replication recovery plan
- Performing a failover (recovery)
- Preforming a failback (re-protect and failover)

Creating a vSphere Replication protection group

You will need to create a protection group for the VMs that you would like to protect using vSphere Replication. Unlike array-based replication, you can select any replication-enabled virtual machine to become part of a protection group.

To do this, perform the following steps:

1. Navigate to the vCenter Server's inventory home and click on **Site Recovery**.
2. Click on **Protection Groups** in the left-hand pane.
3. Click on the create protection group icon 🛡 to bring up the **Create Protection Group** wizard.
4. In the wizard, set a name for the protection group and an optional description and click on **Next** to continue.

5. In the **Protection group type** window, select the **Protected site** and set the **Replication type** as vSphere Replication (VR) and click on **Next** to continue:

6. The next screen will provide you with a list of all the replication-enabled virtual machines. Choose the ones you want to include in the protection group and click on **Next** to continue.

7. On the **Ready to complete** screen, click on **Finish** to create the protection group.

You should see a **Create Protection Group** and a **Protect VM** task completed successfully in the **Recent Tasks** pane. At the recovery site, you should see a shadow virtual machine created for the VMs that we added to the protection group.

Creating a vSphere Replication recovery plan

Once the protection groups are created, the next step is to create recovery plans.

This is done by performing the following steps:

1. Navigate to the vCenter Servers inventory home and click on **Site Recovery**.

2. Click on **Recovery Plans** in the left-hand pane and click on the create recovery plan icon to bring up the **Create Recovery Plan** wizard.

3. Supply a recovery plan name and an optional description and click on **Next** to continue.

4. The remote site is chosen as the recovery site by default. Click on **Next** to continue.

5. Select a protection group of the type VR. Note that this window will also display protection groups of the type array-based, if there are any. So make sure that you select a protection group of the type VR and click on **Next** to continue.

6. Choose a Recovery Network and a Test Network. You can leave the Test Network at Auto, if you intend to use the temporary vSwitch and the port group that SRM creates for the test. Otherwise, you can choose another port group that you have create for the testing. Click on **Next** to continue.

7. On the **Ready to complete** screen, review the options and click on **Finish** to create the recovery plan.

You should see a Create Recovery Plan task completed successfully in the **Recent Tasks** pane.

Testing a vSphere Replication recovery plan

Any recovery plan that you create should be periodically tested to make sure that it is ready for a DR activity, should a need arise.

This is done by performing the following steps:

1. Navigate to the vCenter Server's inventory home and click on **Site Recovery**.

2. Click on **Recovery Plans** in the left-hand pane and choose a plan for a vSphere Replication protection group.

3. Click on the **Test** button to bring up the **Test** wizard.

4. By default, the **Replicate recent changes to recovery site** checkbox is selected. Leave it selected and click on **Next** to continue.

5. On the next screen, review the options and click on **Start** to begin the test operation.

The progress of the recovery steps can be monitored in the **Recovery Steps** tab.

> Make sure that you run a Cleanup after the Test is complete.

Performing a recovery or a planned migration

In the event of a disaster at the protected site, or if there is a need for a planned migration, we can use SRM's Recovery option to run the recovery plan to perform either of the tasks. A planned migration and a recovery are different in terms of whether or not the replication of the recent changes is necessary. A planned migration cannot proceed without being able to replicate recent changes. A Disaster Recovery will attempt to replicate the recent changes, but will continue even if it is unable to replicate the changes.

The procedure is the same regardless of the replication engine in use. Refer to the *Performing a planned migration* and *Performing a disaster recovery (failover)* sections from the *Chapter 3, Testing and Performing a Failover and Failback* chapter.

A Recovery is always from the recovery site. Once initiated, a new sync is initiated to replicate the recent changes. Once done, the protected virtual machine is powered off, and the replication status is changed to Recovered.

Preforming a failback (re-protect and failover)

After a failover, you can enable protection of the VMs in the reverse direction, which is achieved by running a Reprotect operation. Refer to following diagram:

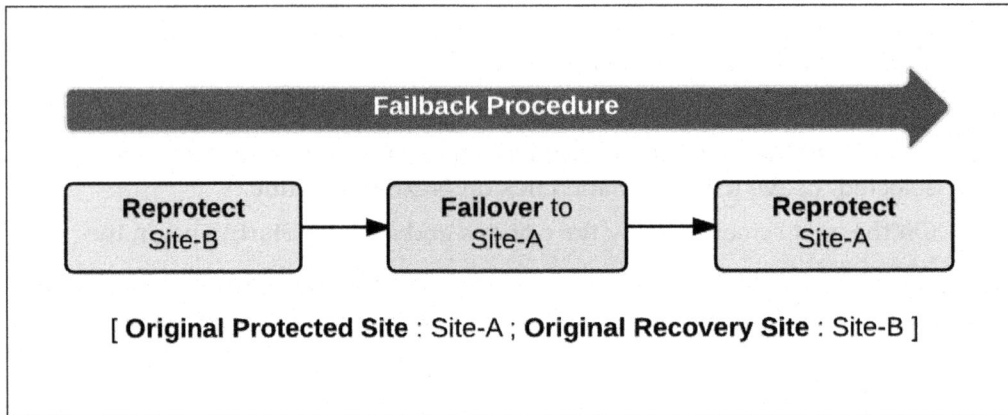

A Reprotect will reverse the direction of the replication. Now, after the original protected site becomes operational you can choose to failback to the original site. This is achieved by issuing a failover after a successful re-protect operation. Once the failover is complete, the replication status would be set to Recovered and there is not active replication. To re-enable replication in the original direction, you should run a Reprotect operation again.

Summary

In the previous chapter, you learned how to set up a vSphere Replication environment, and then use it to configure a replication on virtual machines. We also learned how to stop or pause an ongoing replication and how to move the replication load onto another vSphere Replication Server. More importantly, we learned how to recover a virtual machine from a replica. Most of the replication-related activities that we have discussed in the chapter are done on a per VM basis, and that is all you can do with vSphere Replication when implemented as a standalone solution. We then learned how to configure vCenter Site Recovery Manager to leverage the vSphere Replication and perform the disaster recovery tasks.

6

Using vRealize Orchestrator (vRO) to Automate SRM and vSphere Replication

From the previous chapters, you learned how to use SRM to leverage vSphere Replication and/or array-based replication to protect virtual machine workloads to make them available in a Disaster Recovery situation. While SRM orchestrates most of the DR activities which otherwise would require a lot of manual work, it still needs an administrator to hop between many GUI elements to perform the tasks. In this chapter, you will learn how to deploy and configure vRealize Orchestrator for use with SRM and vSphere Replication. What we will not cover is creating custom workflows using vRealize Orchestrator as that is beyond the scope of this book. This chapter also covers a brief topic on Troubleshooting SRM and vSphere Replication.

Here is what we will be covering:

- Deploying and configuring vRealize Orchestrator
- Installing the vRO plugins for SRM and vSphere Replication
- Troubleshooting SRM and vSphere Replication

Deploying and configuring vRealize Orchestrator

vRealize Orchestrator is a vSphere task automation tool that is available with your vCenter Standard License. It has access to the entire vSphere API, making it a very powerful tool. The vRO plugin for SRM/vSphere Replication will enable some prebuilt workflows that can be readily used. vRO can also be used to create custom workflows for commonly performed tasks.

It is important to download a version of vRO that is compatible with the version of the solution whose tasks you intend to automate.

Here are a few charts from the VMware Product Interoperability Matrix online tool:
`https://www.vmware.com/resources/compatibility/sim/interop_matrix.php`

	VMware vRealize Orchestrator							VMware vCenter Orchestrator	
	7.0.1	7.0.0	6.0.4	6.0.3	6.0.2	6.0.1	6.0.0	5.5.3	5.5.2
VMware Site Recovery Manager 6.1.1	✓	✓	✓	✓	✓	✓	✓	—	—
VMware Site Recovery Manager 6.1	—	—	✓	✓	✓	✓	✓	—	—
VMware Site Recovery Manager 6.0	—	—	✓	✓	✓	✓	✓	✓	—
VMware Site Recovery Manager 5.8.1	—	—	—	—	—	—	—	—	✓
VMware Site Recovery Manager 5.8.0	—	—	—	—	—	—	—	—	✓

VRO's compatibility with all supported versions of SRM

	VMware vRealize Orchestrator							VMware vCenter Orchestrator			
	7.0.1	7.0.0	6.0.4	6.0.3	6.0.2	6.0.1	6.0.0	5.5.3	5.5.2	5.5.1	5.5
VMware vCenter Server 6.0.0 U2	✓	✓	✓	✓	✓	✓	✓	—	—	—	—
VMware vCenter Server 6.0.0 U1	✓	✓	✓	✓	✓	✓	✓	—	—	—	—
VMware vCenter Server 6.0.0	✓	✓	✓	✓	✓	✓	✓	✓	—	—	—
VMware vCenter Server 5.5 U3	✓	✓	✓	✓	✓	✓	✓	✓	—	—	—
VMware vCenter Server 5.5 U2	✓	✓	✓	✓	✓	✓	✓	✓	✓	—	—
VMware vCenter Server 5.5 U1	✓	✓	✓	✓	✓	✓	✓	✓	✓	✓	—
VMware vCenter Server 5.5	✓	✓	✓	✓	✓	✓	✓	✓	✓	✓	✓

VRO's compatibility with vSphere versions dating back to vCenter 5.5

VMware vRealize Orchestrator	7.0.1	7.0.0	6.0.4	6.0.3	6.0.2	6.0.1
VMware vSphere Replication 6.1.1	✓	✓	✓	✓	✓	✓
VMware vSphere Replication 6.1	—	—	✓	✓	✓	✓
VMware vSphere Replication 6.0	—	—	✓	✓	✓	✓

VRO's compatibility with all supported versions of vSphere Replication

Downloading vRealize Orchestrator

At the time of writing, vRealize Orchestrator 7.0.1 was the latest version available, and it is compatible with SRM 6.1.1 and vSphere Replication 6.1.1. It is available for download in the OVA format.

The following URL will take you to the download page for VRO 7.0.1:

```
https://my.vmware.com/web/vmware/details?productId=490&downloadGroup=
VROVA_701
```

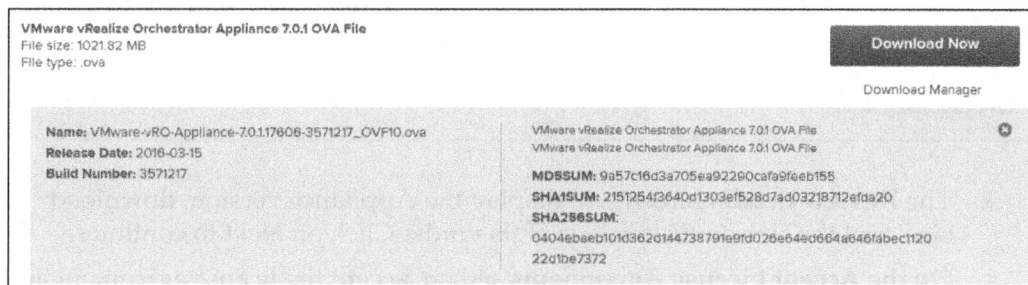

Deploying vRealize Orchestrator

The following procedure will guide you through the steps required to deploy vRealize Orchestrator from an OVA:

1. Log in to the vCenter Server using vSphere Web client and initiate the **Deploy OVF Template** wizard from the right-click context menu of the vCenter Server:

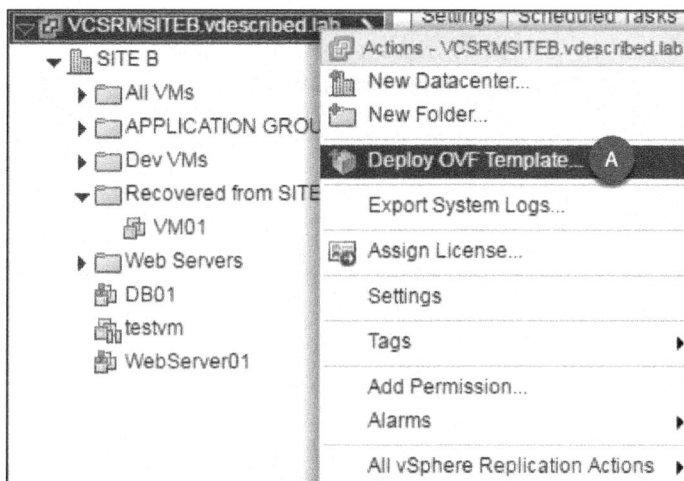

2. In the **Deploy OVF Template** wizard, browse and locate the vRO OVA file and click on **Next** to continue:

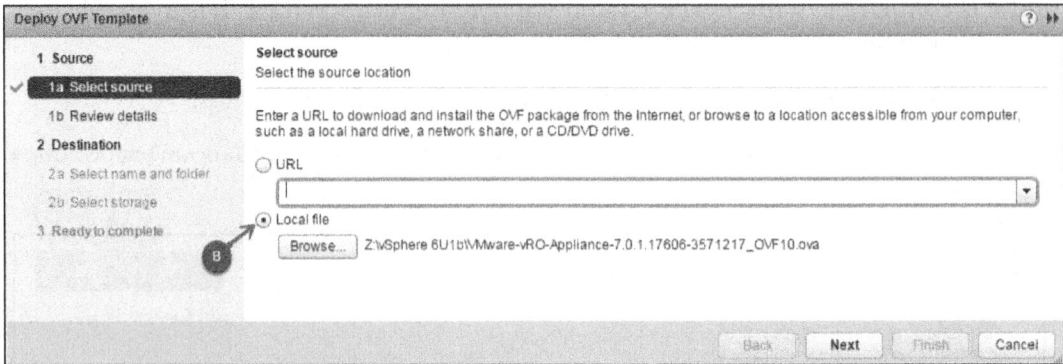

3. The **Review details** screen will display the Appliance version, download size, and the size on disk values of its vmdk. Click on **Next** to continue.

4. On the **Accept License Agreements** screen, accept the license agreement and click on **Next** to continue.

5. On the **Select name and folder** screen, supply a name for the appliance virtual machines and select a virtual machine folder. Click on **Next** to continue:

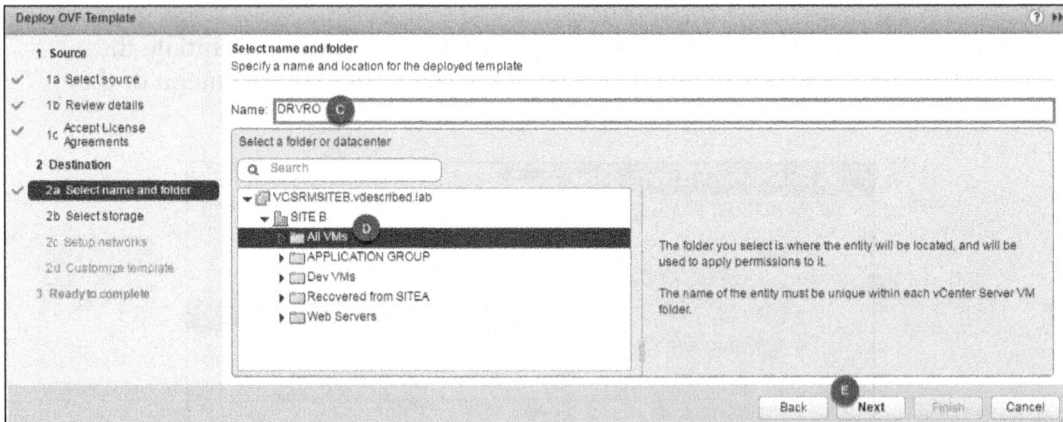

6. On the **Select storage** screen, select the intended VMDK format, **VM Storage Policy** policy, and then a datastore to put the virtual machine files on. Once done, click on **Next** to continue:

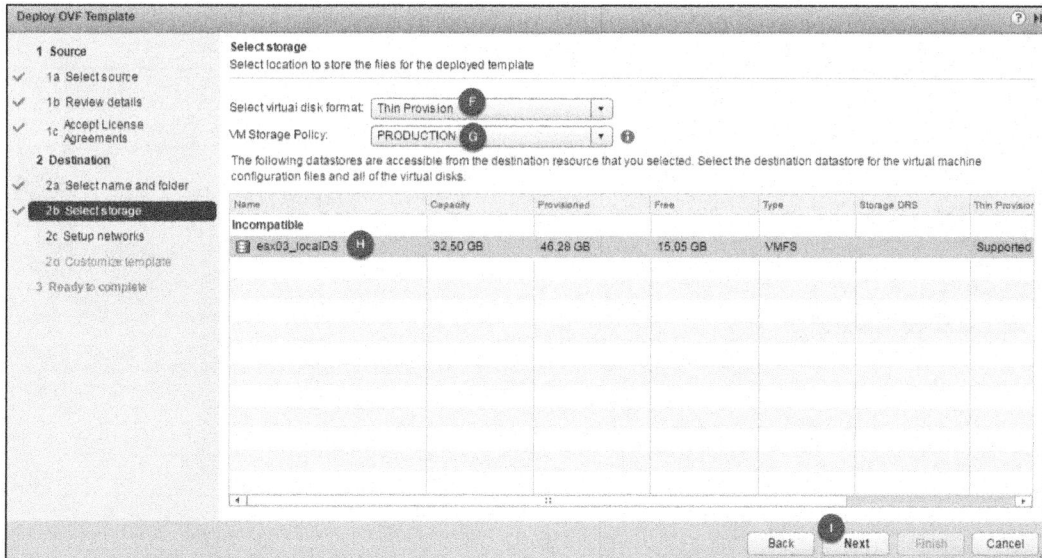

7. On the **Setup networks** screen, select a virtual machine port group for the appliance's vNIC and set the **IP protocol** to **IPv4**. Once done, click on **Next** to continue:

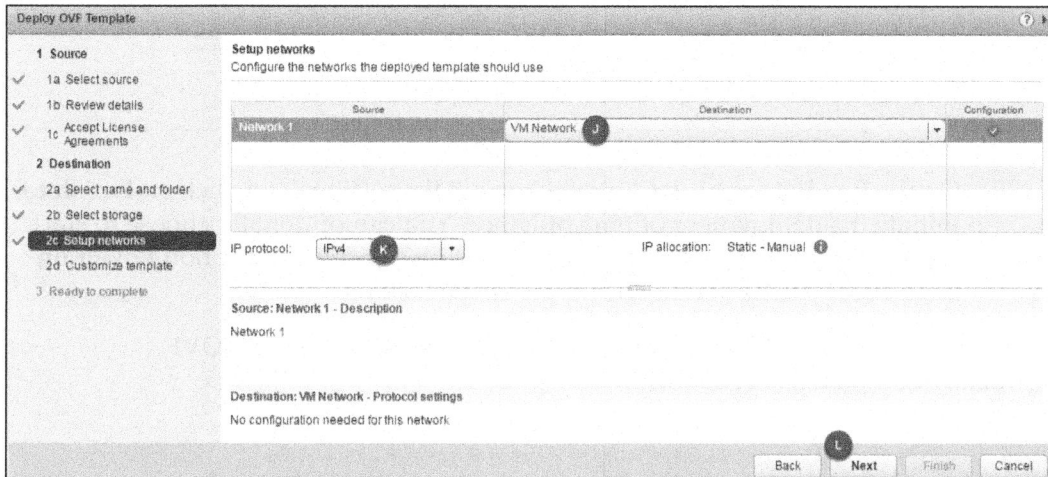

8. On the **Customize template** screen, set an initial root password for the appliance. Optionally enable SSH, supply a hostname, and IP configuration details. It is recommended that you make sure that a DNS record is created for the appliance using the supplied hostname and IP address before you proceed further. Once done, click on **Next** to continue:

9. On the **Ready to complete** screen, review the settings and click on **Finish** to initiate the deployment of the appliance. You can optionally choose to start the virtual machine after the deployment by selecting the option **Power on after deployment** before hitting the **Finish** button.

You should see two tasks—Initialize OVF deployment and Deploy OVF template—completed successfully.

Using the vRealize Orchestrator client

Before we proceed further, let's review the types of vRO client available. The vRO client is available as a standalone client that can be downloaded from the vRO server or as a Java JNLP client. In this example, we will use the standalone client application. But keep in mind that both require the latest Java Runtime Environment installed.

> To download the latest version of Java, go to www.java.com/download.

Both the clients are available from the vRealize Orchestrators home page. The home page URL has the following syntax:

```
https://FQDN or IP of vRO Server:8281/vco/
```

At the home page, you get an option to either start the Orchestrator client or download load the standalone version of the client:

The **Start Orchestrator Client** link will download a `clinet.jnlp` file, which can be launched to web start the orchestrator client.

The **Download Orchestrator Client Installable** option has client versions for Windows, Linux, and Mac OS X. Unlike what the description says, it is not really an installer. It is a ZIP archive containing a directly launchable version of the client. The name of the client file is vROWorkflowDesigner:

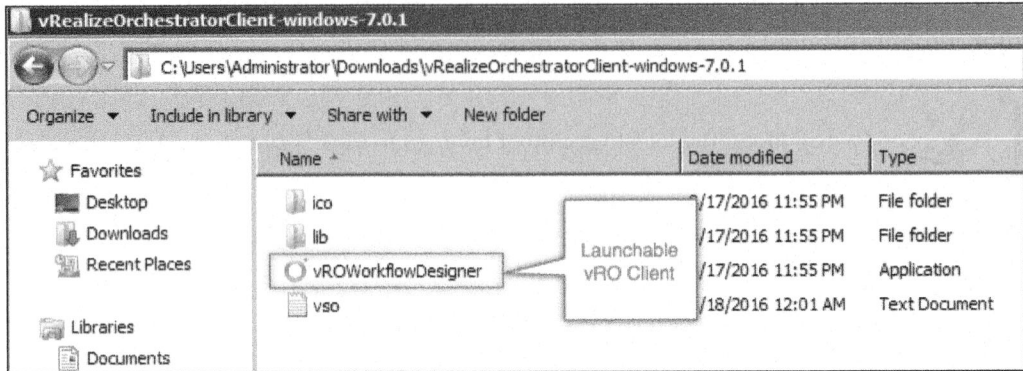

Configuring vRealize Orchestrator

Once installed, the vRO Server must be prepared and configured to orchestrate the vCenter instances using one of its built-in workflows. vRO can be configured using the Orchestrator Control Center. The URLs for this can be learned from the vRO virtual machines console:

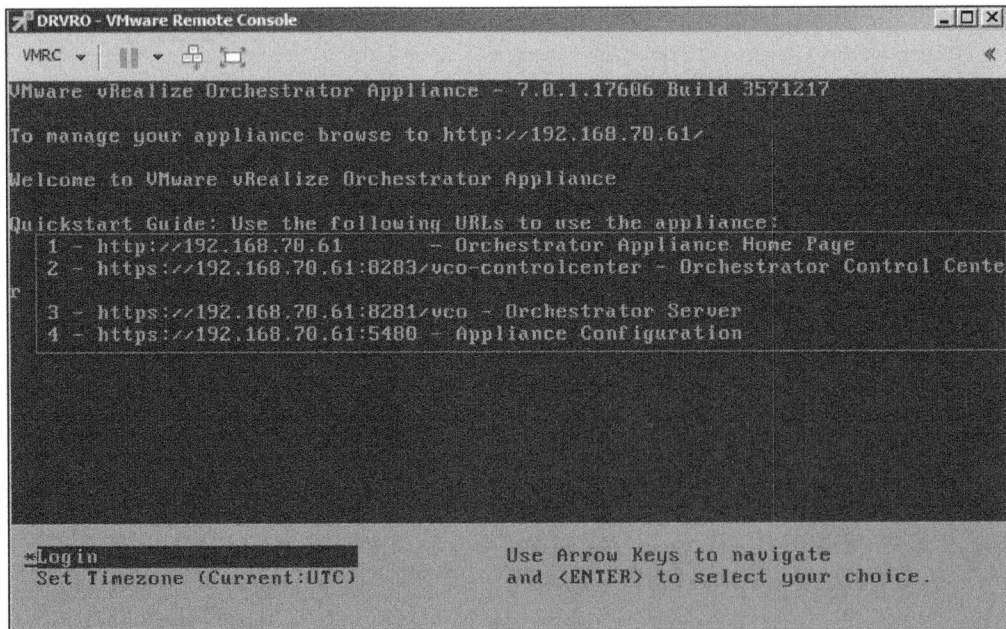

The configuration is a two step process:

- Configure vRO database
- Configure authentication provider

Configure vRO database

The following procedure will guide you through the steps required to configure the vRO database:

1. Connect to the vRO Control Center using the following URL:
   `https://<vRO IP or FQDN>:8283/vco-controlcenter`

2. Use the root user password that was supplied by the Deploy OVF template wizard.

3. In the **Control Center**, switch to **Configuration View** and click on **Configure Database**:

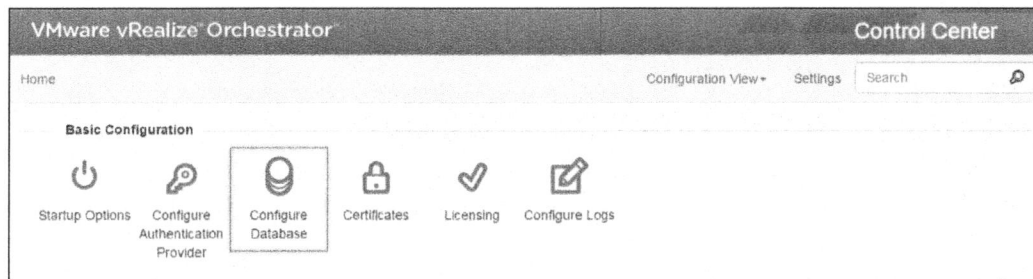

4. On the **Configure Database** screen, set the database type accordingly. In this case, I will be using an embedded PostgreSQL database. Set the database credentials. The default database name and username should not be modified.

   The defaults are as follows:

   - database name: **vmware**
   - username: **vmware**

       °   Password: a blank password

> vRO does support external SQL, Oracle databases, and an in-process Apache Derby DB as well.

5. Click on **Save Changes** to configure the DB.

Configure authentication provider

The vRO must be configured to connect to a vCenter instance for the plugins to work. This is done by letting it connect to the corresponding vCenter Single Sign-On Server or the Platform Services Controller.

The following procedure will guide you through the steps required in configuring vRO to connect to vCenter Server:

1. Connect to the vRO Control Center using the following URL: `https://<vRO IP or FQDN>/vco-controlcenter`

2. In the **Control Center**, click on **Configure Authentication Provider**:

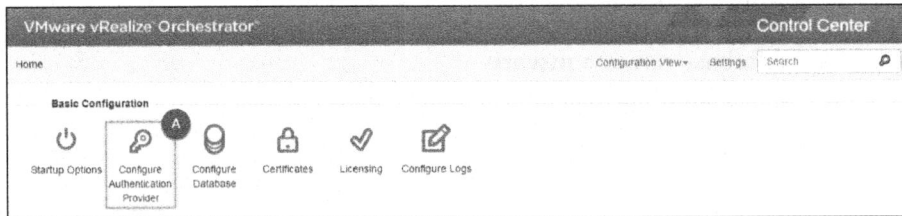

3. On the **Configure Authentication Provider** screen, change the **Authentication mode** to **vSphere** and supply the FQDN of the SSO Server or PSC in the **Host address** field. Doing so will autogenerate an https URL to the VMware Component Manager. Click on **Connect**:

> Post this configuration change, the vCenter SSO becomes the authentication provider.

4. You will be prompted to accept the SSO/PSC server certificate for the connection to go through. Click on **Accept Certificate**:

5. Now, you will be prompted for the SSO username and password. Supply the SSO credentials, select the **Configure licenses** checkbox and click on **Register**:

Authentication Provider	Test Login

Configure the authentication provider.

Warning: Required parameters are missing: username and/or password

Authentication mode   vSphere ▾

Host address   vcsrmsiteb.vdescribed.lab

URL   https://vcsrmsiteb.vdescribed.lab/cm

Identity service

   User name   administrator@vsphere.local G

   Password   •••••••••••• H

   Configure licences   I ☑

   Default tenant   vsphere.local J

   K
   Register

Cancel	Save Changes

6. You will then be prompted for the **Admin group**. Click on the **Search** button for a drop-down list of user groups. Choose a user group which has administrator rights at the vCenter Server. In this example, I have selected the **vsphere.local\Administrators** group:

Authentication Provider   Test Login

Configure the authentication provider.

Warning: Required parameters are missing: adminGroup and/or adminDomain

Authentication mode   vSphere ▾

Host address   vcsrmsiteb.vdescribed.lab   Unregister

URL   https://vcsrmsiteb.vdescribed.lab/cm

Admin group   L Search

vsphere.local\DCAdmins
vsphere.local\LicenseService.Administrators
vsphere.local\ActAsUsers
vsphere.local\Administrators ← M
vsphere.local\CAAdmins
vsphere.local\DCClients

Default tenant   vsphere.local

Cancel   Save Changes

7.   With the **Admin group** selected, click on **Save Changes**:

Authentication mode   vSphere ▾

Host address   vcsrmsiteb.vdescribed.lab   Unregister

URL   https://vcsrmsiteb.vdescribed.lab/cm

Admin group   vsphere.local\Administrators   Change

Default tenant   vsphere.local

Cancel   Save Changes N

8. Once the configuration has been successfully saved, you will be instructed to restart the Orchestrator Server for the changes to take effect. Click on the hyperlink **Startup Options** to navigate to the **Startup Options** page:

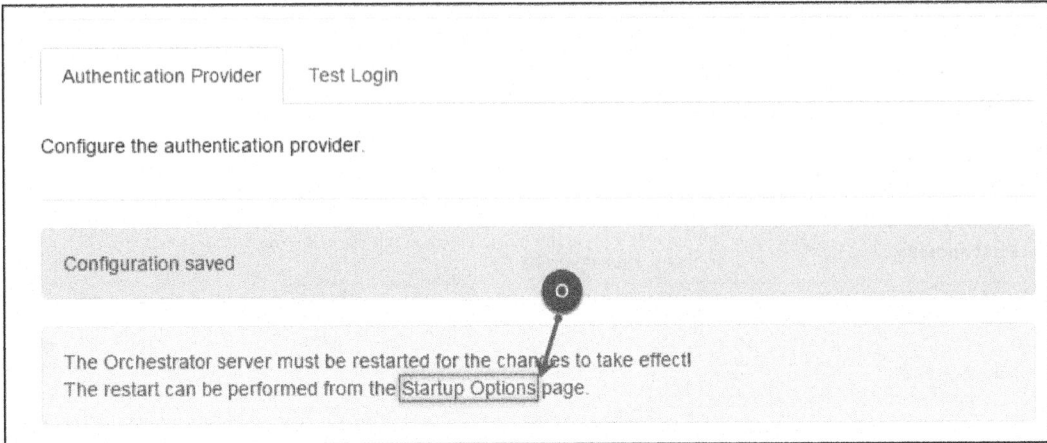

Authentication Provider   Test Login

Configure the authentication provider.

Configuration saved

The Orchestrator server must be restarted for the changes to take effect!
The restart can be performed from the Startup Options page.

9. In the **Startup Options** page, click on **Restart** to bounce the Orchestrator server service. You can see the progress of restarting the service in the gray area below the **Start/Stop/Restart** buttons:

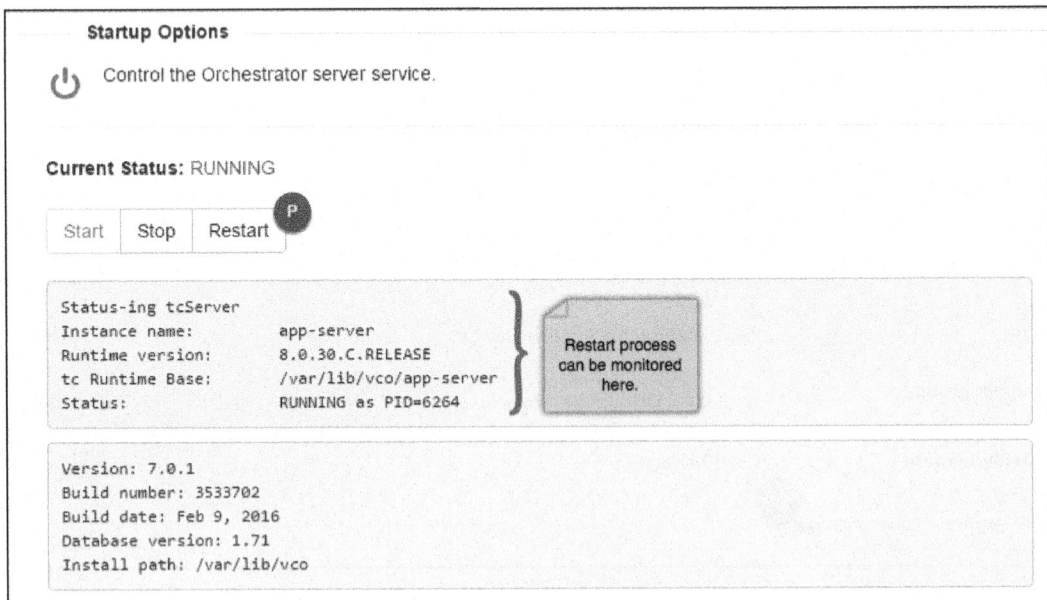

Startup Options

Control the Orchestrator server service.

Current Status: RUNNING

Start   Stop   Restart

```
Status-ing tcServer
Instance name:        app-server
Runtime version:      8.0.30.C.RELEASE
tc Runtime Base:      /var/lib/vco/app-server
Status:               RUNNING as PID=6264
```

Restart process can be monitored here.

```
Version: 7.0.1
Build number: 3533702
Build date: Feb 9, 2016
Database version: 1.71
Install path: /var/lib/vco
```

10. Navigate back to the Control Center Home and click on **Validate Configuration**:

11. On the **Validate Configuration** screen, if you see a green tick mark against all the components, then you are good to go:

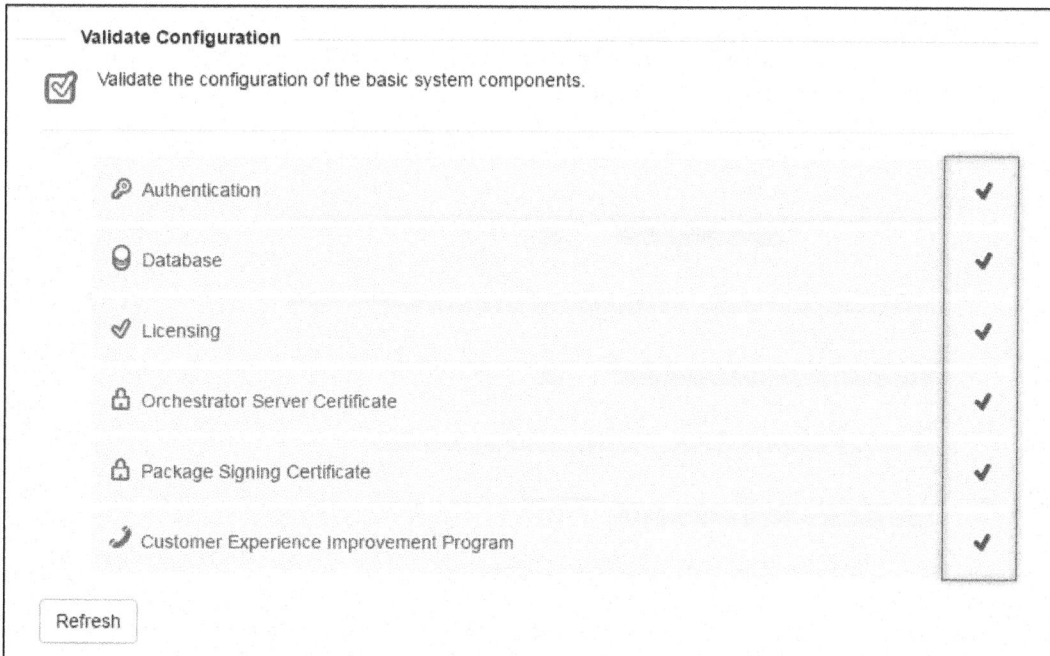

Enabling vRealize Orchestration for a vCenter

Now that we have configured the vRO server, the next step is to tell the vRO server which vCenter instance we intend to orchestrate and make the plugin available via the vSphere Web client.

This a two step process:

- Adding a vCenter Server instance to vRO
- Registering vRO as a vCenter Server Extension

Adding a vCenter Server instance to vRO

The following procedure will guide you through the steps required to add a vCenter Server instance to vRO:

1. Start the vRO Client and supply the username and password that correspond to a user in the Admin group, specified when configuring vSphere as the Authentication provider for vRO. Refer to the *Configure authentication provider* section in this chapter for more details:

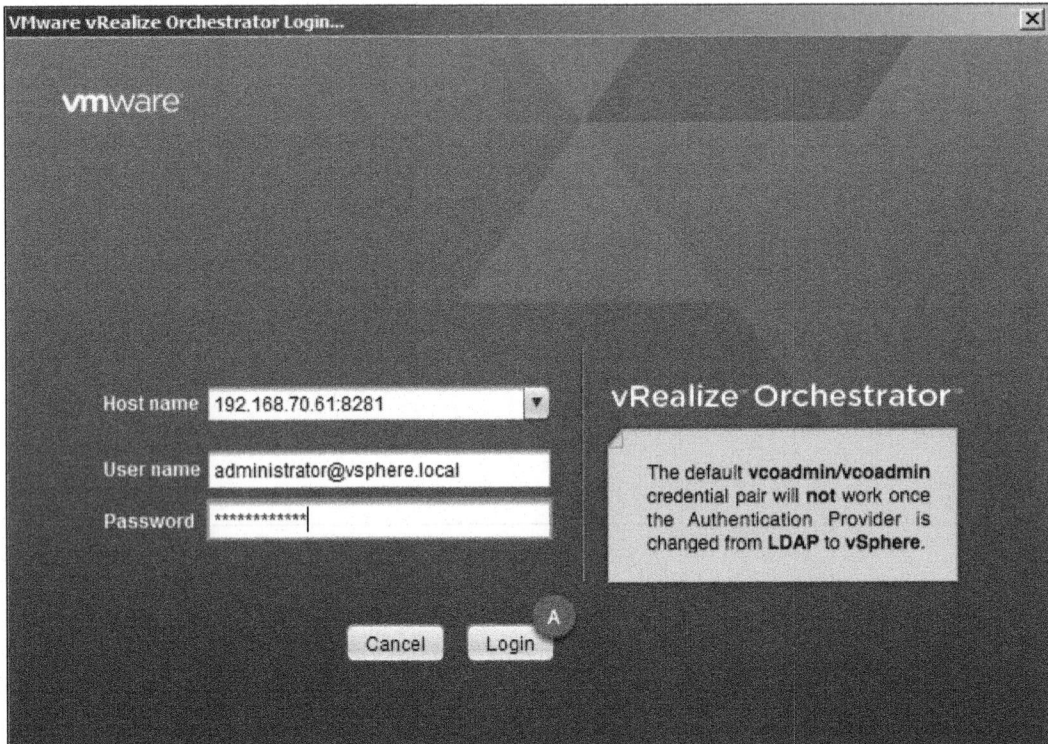

Keep in mind that the default username/password for the vRO client connection is vcoadmin/vcoadmin. This username/password cannot be used to log in to the orchestrator once the authentication provider has been changed from LDAP to vSphere.

2. Once you have logged into the vRO server, click on the ⬛ icon to navigate to the workflows tab.

3. In the workflows tab, navigate to **Library | vCenter | Configuration** and select **Add a vCenter Server instance**:

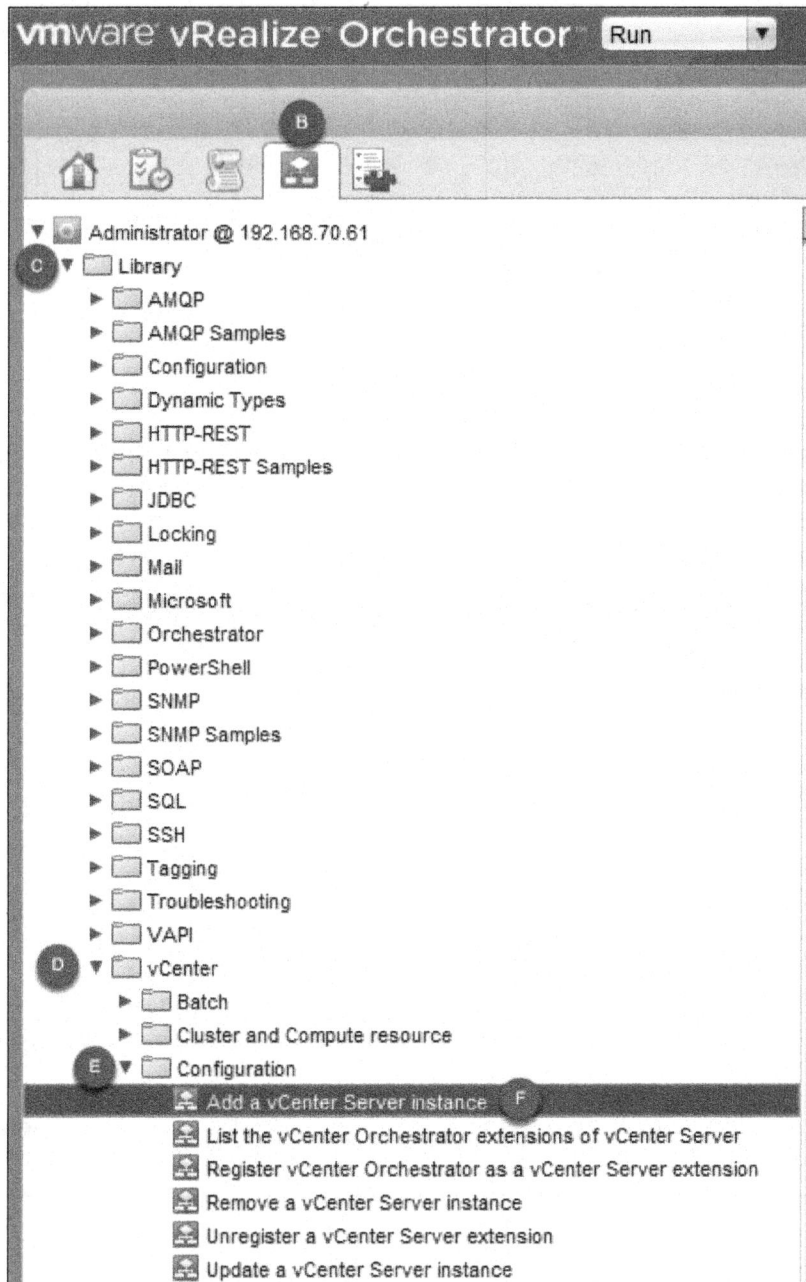

4. Right-click on the **Add a vCenter Server instance** workflow and click on **Start workflow...**:

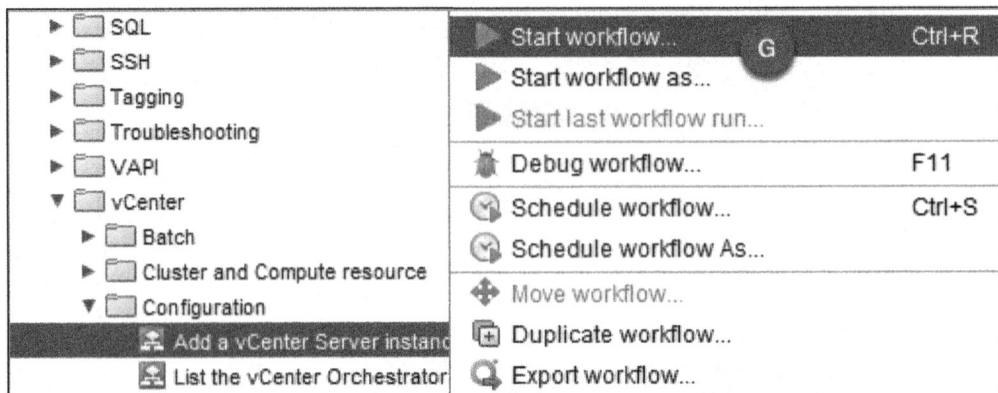

5. In the **Start Workflow: Add a vCenter Server instance** window, supply the IP address or the FQDN of the vCenter Server that you intend to add. Leave the port and the SDK location unmodified. Select **Yes** to orchestrate the instance. You could also choose to ignore the certificate warning:

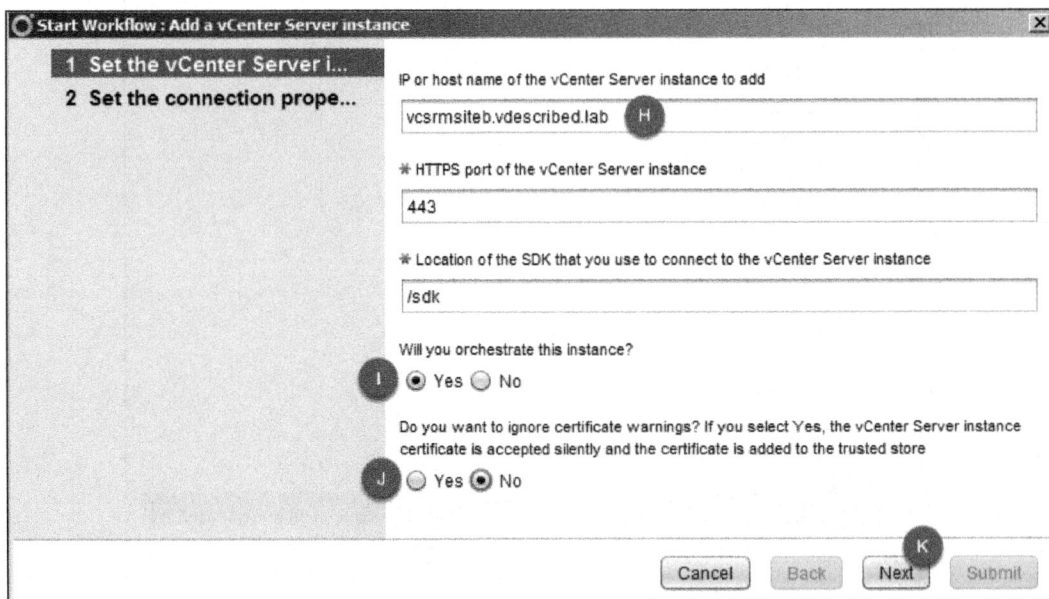

6. In the **Set the connection properties** screen, supply user credentials for the vCenter Server. On this screen you could choose to spawn only a single unique share connection to the vCenter. By default, vRO will use a separate session per user. Once done with all the necessary inputs in the window, click on **Submit** to run the workflow:

7. If there are no errors, you should see the workflow completed successfully.

Registering vRO as a vCenter Server extension

Once the vCenter is added to the vRO, the next step is to install the vRO plugin to the vSphere web client. This is achieved by running the Register vCenter Orchestrator as a vCenter Server extension workflow:

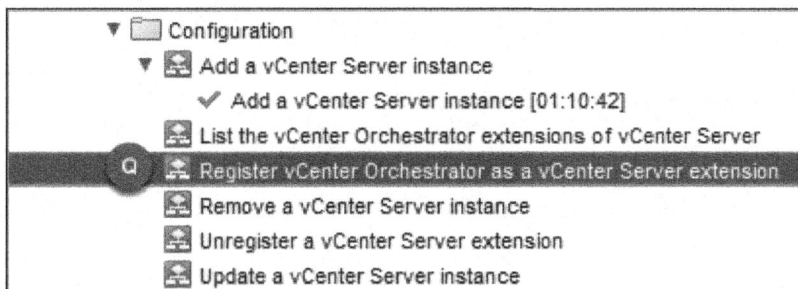

1. Right-click on the extension and click on **Start Workflow** to bring up the **Register vCenter Orchestrator as a vCenter Server extension** window.

2. In the **Register vCenter Orchestrator as a vCenter Server extension** window, you will need to select the vCenter to register with. To do this, click inside the search box to bring up the **Select (VC:SdkConnection)** window:

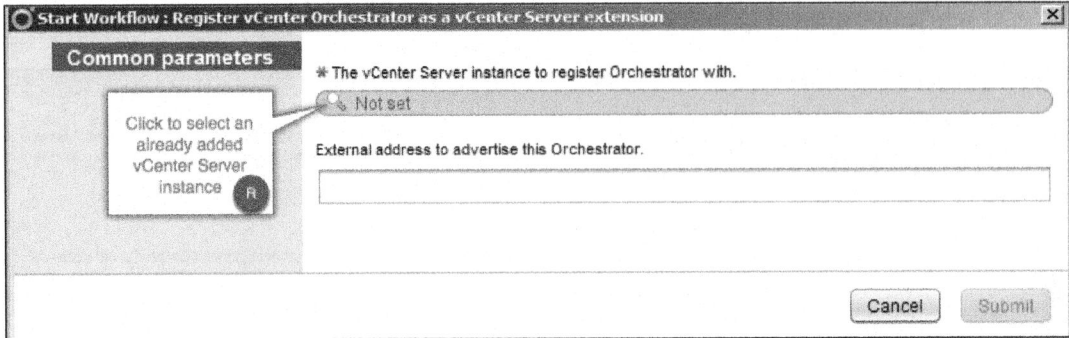

3. In the **Select (VC:SdkConnection)** window, highlight the vCenter instance and click on **Select**:

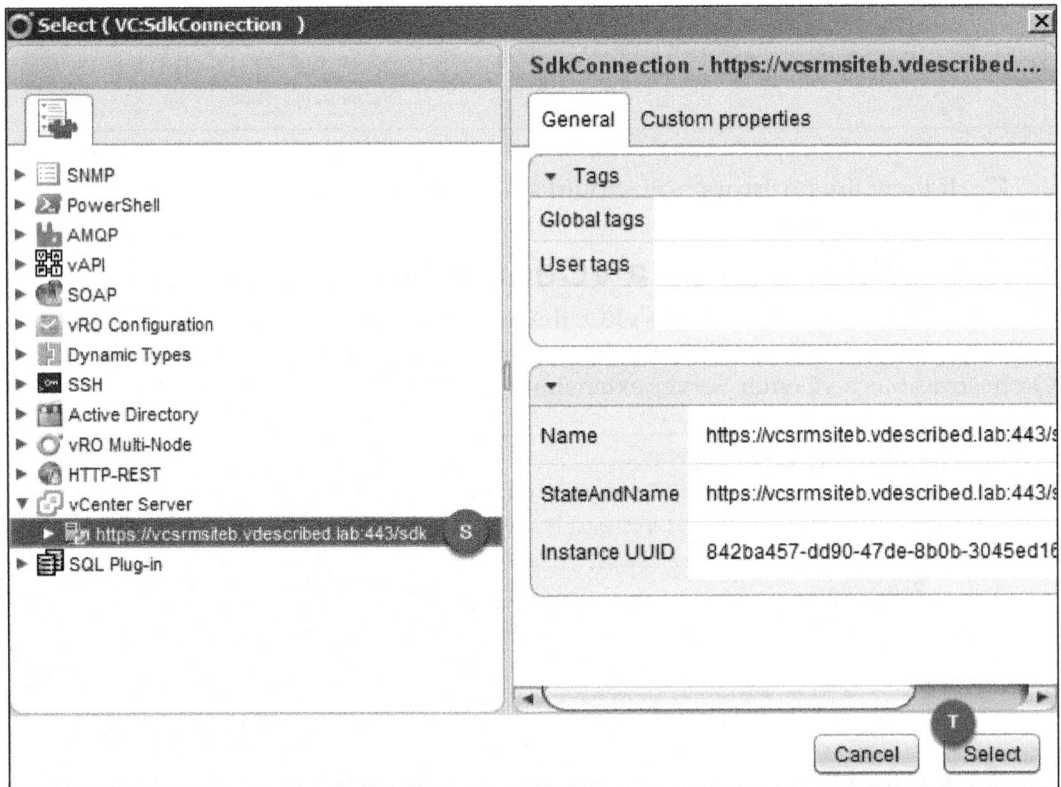

4. Once you are back at the **Register vCenter Orchestrator** window, click on **Submit** to run the workflow.

5. If there are no errors, you should see the workflow complete successfully.

6. Close the current vSphere Web client session and reconnect to select **vRealize Orchestrator** from the vSphere Web client's Inventory **Home**:

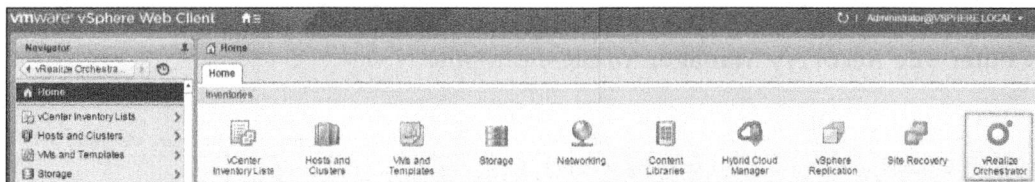

7. The **Summary** tab of **vRO Home** will show the vRO registered to this vCenter:

So, this completes the procedure of Registering a vRO server to a vCenter Server instance to enable orchestration. In the next section, you will learn how to enable the use of SRM and vSphere Replication vRO plugins.

Install vRealize Orchestrator plugins for SRM and vSphere Replication

In addition to the default plugin for the vCenter Server, VMware provides separate plugins for Site Recovery Manager and vSphere Replication. In this section of the chapter, you will learn how to download, install, and enable these plugins.

Downloading the vRO plugins for SRM and vSphere Replication

The vRO plugins can be downloaded from the following URL:

`https://www.vmware.com/support/pubs/vco_plugins_pubs.html.`

At the **vRealize Orchestrator Plugin Information** page, select the Plugin Product as **vCenter Site Recovery Manager** for SRM plugins:

Select a plug-in: | vCenter Site Recovery Manager ▼ |

vRealize Orchestrator Plug-In for vCenter Site Recovery Manager

6.1.1 Released	6.1 Released	6.0 Released	5.8.1 Released	5.8.0.1 Released	5.8 Released
26 May 2016	10 Sep 2015	12 Mar 2015	16 Sep 2016	09 Apr 2015	09 Sep 2014
Download	Download	Download	Download	Download	

Select **vSphere Replication** for VR plugins:

Select a plug-in: | vSphere Replication ▼ |

vRealize Orchestrator Plug-In for vSphere Replication

6.1.1 Released 26 May 2016	6.1 Released 10 Sep 2015	6.0 Released 9 Apr 2015
Download	Download	Download

The downloaded files will be of the `.vmoapp` extension:

Name ▲	Date modified	Type	Size
vr-6.1.0.vmoapp	8/18/2016 2:17 AM	VMOAPP File	11,841 KB
VMware-srm-vcoplugin-6.0.0-2580226.vmoapp	8/18/2016 2:16 AM	VMOAPP File	6,786 KB

Installing vRO plugins

The following procedure will guide you through the steps required to install vRO plugins:

1. Connect to the vRO Control Center using the following URL:
   `https://<vRO IP or FQDN>:8283/vco-controlcenter`.

2. In the **Control Center**, switch to the **Configuration** view and click on **Manage Plug-Ins**:

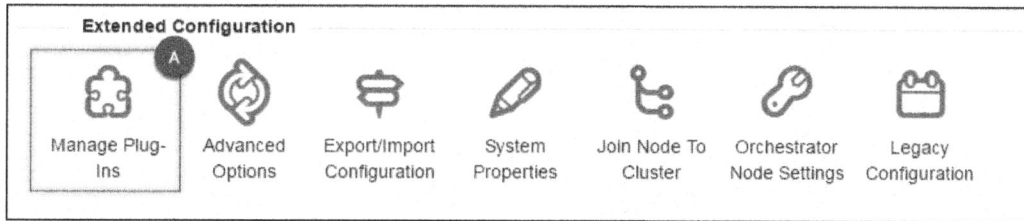

3. In the **Manage Plug-Ins** page, click on **Browse...** and locate the `.vmoapp` file and click on **Install**:

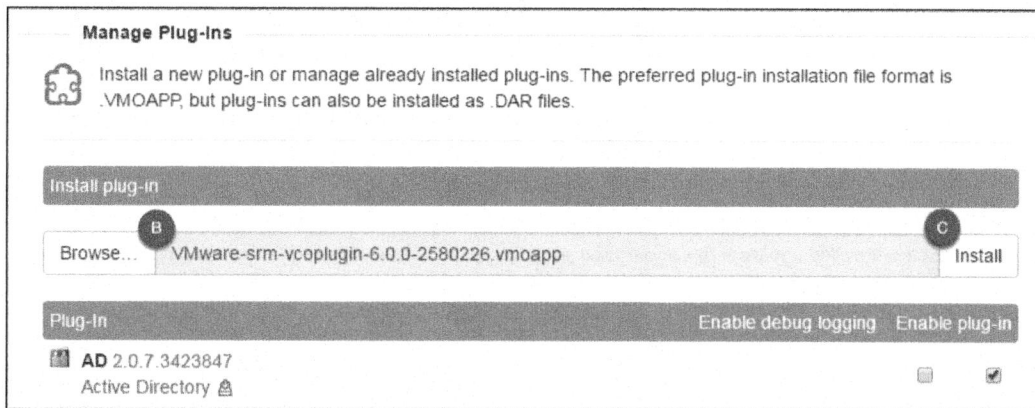

4. Accept the **EULA** and click on **Install** to begin the installation:

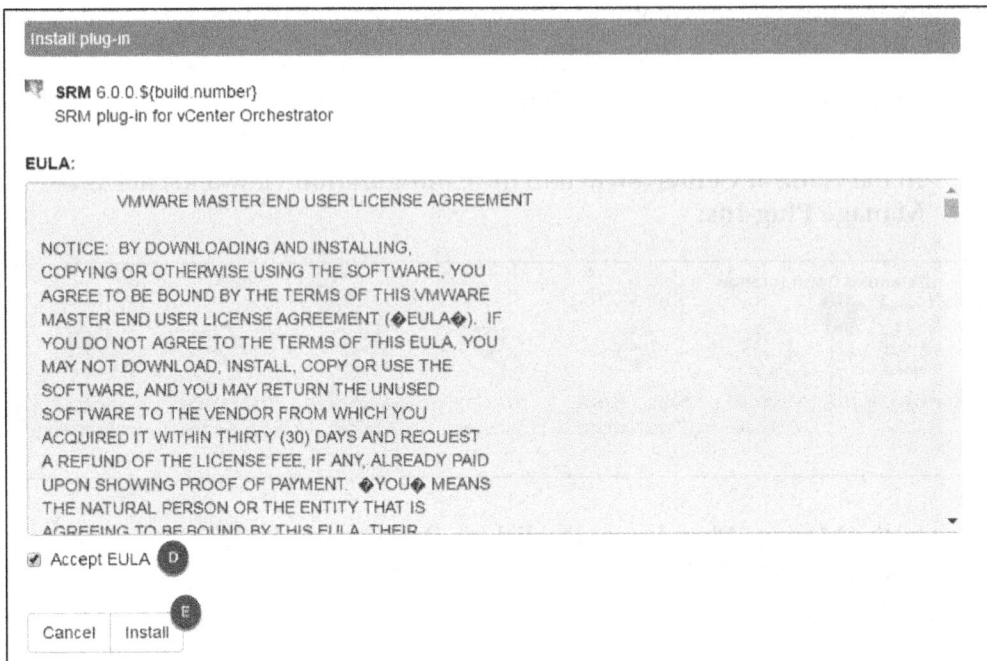

5. Once the install is complete, you will be instructed to restart the Orchestrator Server for the changes to take effect:

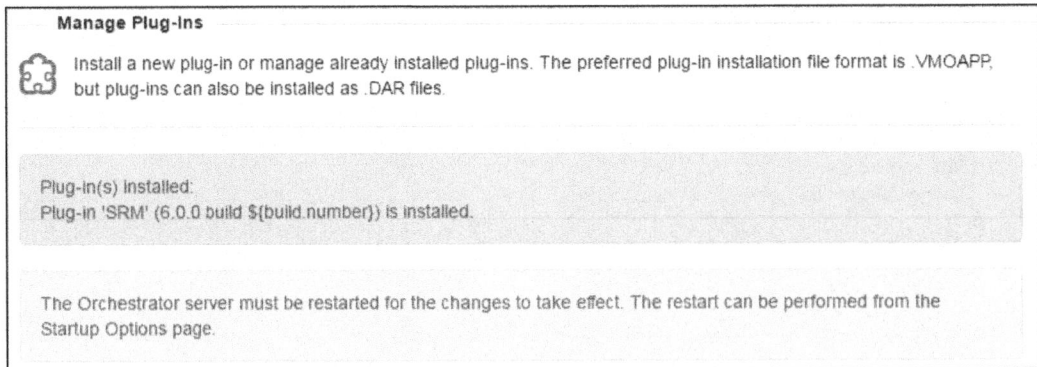

6. Go to **Startup Options** and **Restart** the Orchestrator service.

7. Repeat steps 1-6 to install the vSphere Replication plugin as well.

8. If successfully installed, the SRM and vSphere Replication workflows will be made available in the Workflow library:

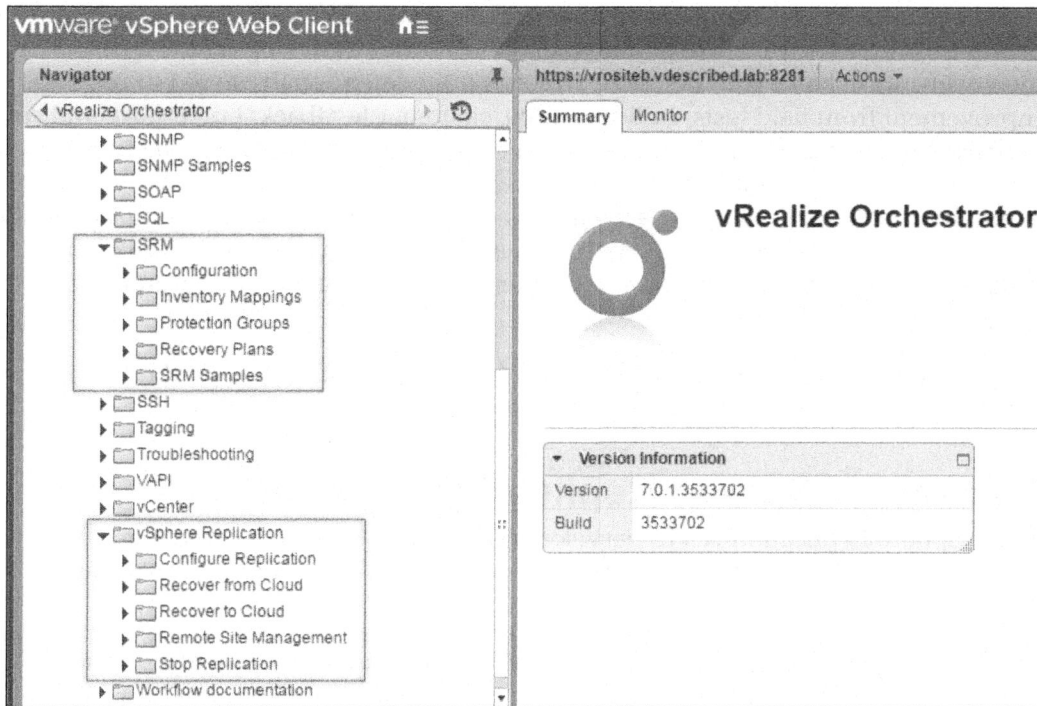

Troubleshooting SRM and vSphere Replication

Like with any other software product, you will unavoidably run into issues that are product configuration issues, bugs or operational gotchas and so on. The section of the chapter will help you to get to SRM and vSphere Replication logs and also provide you with troubleshooting references.

Getting to the logs

To understand why a software functionality failed or exhibited abnormal behavior, it is important to know what exactly transpired during that occurrence. Although most modern software will expose events/errors in the GUI, it is impractical to present a more detailed view of the events/errors in the graphical user interface. Hence, all software products maintain logs. Logs are not just generated when something goes wrong but are constantly maintained. Logs might show errors and warnings even when everything is working fine.

The important fact is that not everything in the logs would make sense or help an administrator to troubleshoot an issue. Some entries in the logs could be developer-infused and very detailed, which is done intentionally to aid in product improvement from field tests, in-house tests, customer feedback, bug report, and so on. However, the good thing here is that, such unnecessary details can be suppressed by what is referred to as a log level. Log level dictates as to what type of events/error should be generated in the log files. There is generally an advanced setting to modify the logging levels. It is also quite possible that a single software product maintain multiple log files stored at different locations and corresponding to different components of the software.

In this section of the chapter, you will learn how to get to the log files of both Site Recovery Manager and vSphere Replication.

Analyzing vSphere Replication logs

Since vSphere Replication is a hypervisor-based replication engine, the logs pertaining to replication can be found both on the ESXi host and on the vSphere Replication Appliance.

The following are the log files to refer to during the troubleshooting of a vSphere Replication issue:

Host	vSphere Replication Appliance
`/var/log/vmkernel.log`	`/var/log/vmware/hbsrv.log`
	`/var/log/vmware/hms.log`

Now that we know the log files, how do we go about using them to troubleshoot an issue? Since, vSphere Replication is enabled on a per-virtual machine basis the replication can be tracked based on its Group-ID. We use the vSphere API command `vim-cmd` to send instructions to the host management service (`hostd`) to perform the actions. The `vimcmd` has several command spaces — `vmsvc`, `hostsvc`, `vimsvc`, `hbrsvc`, `proxysvc`, `internalsvc`, and `solo`. We will be using `vmsvc` and `hbrsvc`.

The following procedure will guide you through the process of tracking the replication of a virtual machine:

1. Connect to the ESXi host running the virtual machine using an SSH client such as putty. Log in as root.

2. Now, to the get the VMID of the running virtual machine, issue the following command:

   ```
   vim-cmd vmsvc/getallvms
   ```

The command will list all the virtual machines registered to the ESXi host. The first column is the VMID

3. The next step will be to list the replication job details corresponding to the virtual machine. The input for this command will be the VMID procured from the output of the previous command:

```
vim-cmd hbrsvc/vmreplica.getState VMID
```

The command will retrieve the VM running replication state and a Group ID

4. You can now check the vmkernel.log file for instances corresponding to the GID procured from the previous command output.

5. You can use the same GID to track events corresponding to the replication in the appliance logs hbsrv.log and hms.log.

Analyzing SRM logs

Since SRM is installed on a machine running a supported Windows server operating system, the log files are maintained under the ProgramData directory structure.

Here is the full path to log file location:

\ProgramData\VMware\VMware vCenter Site Recovery Manager\Logs\.

Name	Date modified ▾	Type	Size
vmware-dr-89.log.gz	9/26/2016 10:42 PM	GZ File	233 KB
vmware-dr-90	9/26/2016 11:01 PM	Text Document	432 KB
vmware-dr-88.log.gz	9/26/2016 6:57 PM	GZ File	288 KB
vmware-dr-87	9/26/2016 3:29 PM	Text Document	3 KB
vmware-dr-87.log.gz	9/26/2016 3:29 PM	GZ File	1 KB
vmware-dr-86.log.gz	9/26/2016 3:29 PM	GZ File	167 KB
vmware-dr-85.log.gz	9/26/2016 3:29 PM	GZ File	1 KB
vmware-dr-84.log.gz	9/26/2016 1:45 PM	GZ File	143 KB
vmware-dr-83.log.gz	8/18/2016 9:27 PM	GZ File	256 KB
vmware-dr-82.log.gz	8/18/2016 7:00 PM	GZ File	258 KB
vmware-dr-81.log.gz	8/18/2016 3:08 AM	GZ File	281 KB
SRAs	3/26/2016 6:03 PM	File folder	

The `vmware-dr` log files is where all the SRM events are logged. All SRA events are logged in separate log files. For the location of the SRA log files, refer to the Storage vendor's SRA documentation.

Increasing the logging level for SRM

Sometimes it becomes necessary to capture more events/warnings/errors to get to the crux of an issue. You can change the logging level of SRM from **Advanced Settings**.

The following procedure will guide you through the steps required to change the logging level of SRM:

1. Navigate to **Site Recovery Manager Home** and click on Sites to list the paired sites.

2. Select the site you intend to increase the logging level on, navigate to **Manage | Advanced Settings**, and select **Log Manager** from the left pane to view the log settings. Click on **Edit** to bring up the **Edit Advanced Settings** window:

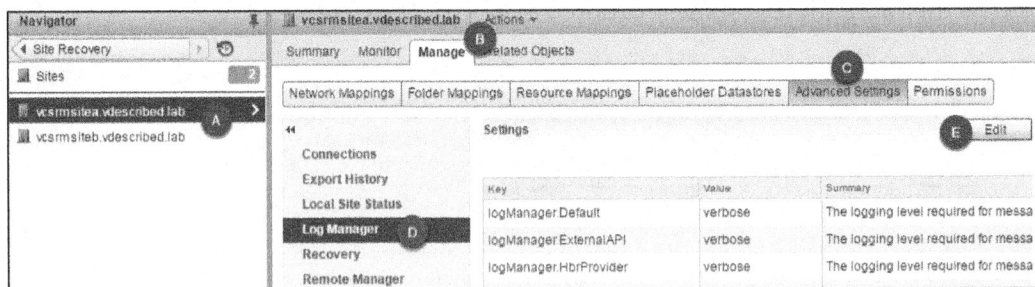

3. In the **Edit Advanced Settings** window, select the first entry `logManager.Default` and use the drop-down box to set a desired logging level:

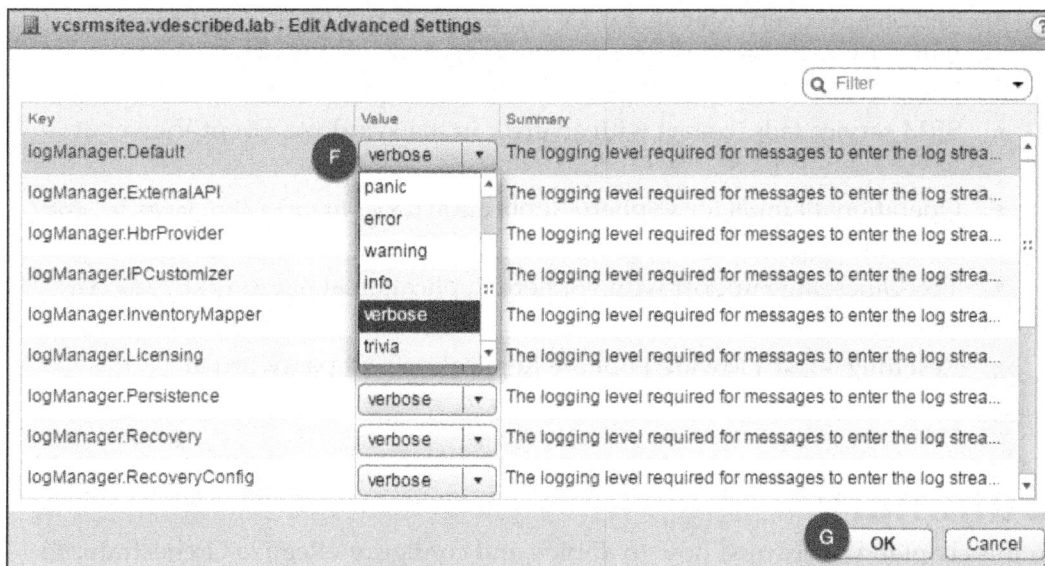

[A restart of the SRM service is not necessary for the changes to take effect.]

For more details regarding the logs level, read the *Change Logging Settings* section at page 135 of the *SRM 6.1 Administration Guide*, available at `http://bit.ly/ SRM61AdminGuide`.

Troubleshooting references

As mentioned earlier, the intention of this section is to provide you with guidelines on how to find the information you need to troubleshoot an issue. The following list of references could aid you during troubleshooting:

- Collecting diagnostic information for Site Recovery Manager at `http://kb.vmware.com/kb/1009253`

- Collecting the VMware vSphere Replication logs at `http://kb.vmware.com/kb/2013091`

- Solutions for common vSphere Replication Problems at page 93 of the vSphere Replication 6.1 Administration Guide at `http://bit.ly/ VR61AdminGuide`

- Troubleshooting SRM at page 169 of the SRM 6.1 Administration Guide at `http://bit.ly/SRM61AdminGuide`

- The Site Recovery Manager 6.1.x service stops running during a test failover for a protection group containing multiple virtual machines at `http://kb.vmware.com/kb/2145559`

- SRM service fails to start with an error in the Windows Event Viewer at `http://kb.vmware.com/kb/2050400`

- Operational Limits for vSphere Replication 6.x at `http://kb.vmware.com/kb/2102453`

- VSS Quiescing Support with vSphere Replication at `http://kb.vmware.com/kb/2041909`

- Resetting a lost VMware vSphere Replication root password at `http://kb.vmware.com/kb/2062059`

Summary

In this chapter, you learned how to deploy and configure vRealize Orchestrator to enable orchestration of tasks on vCenter Server instances. You also learned how to install vRO plugins for SRM and vSphere Replication. Since creating custom workflows is beyond the scope of this book, I would recommend that you read *Using VMware vRealize Orchestrator Plug-Ins* and *Developing with VMware vRealize Orchestrator* available at the vRealize Orchestration documentation home page: `https://www.vmware.com/support/pubs/orchestrator_pubs.html`. You also learned how to get to the log files of both SRM and vSphere Replication. You also learned how to change the logging level of SRM logs. The chapter also included additional references to troubleshooting articles.

Index

A

active replication
  switching, to vSphere Replication(VR)
      server 146, 147
array-based replication
  enabling 7, 8
array managers
  adding 19-25
array pairs
  enabling 19-25

D

data
  synchronization 143, 144
datastore groups 43, 44
Disaster Recovery (DR) 3
disaster recovery (failover)
  performing 73-75
Discover Devices operation 25
Distributed Power Management (DPM) 65
Dynamic Host Configuration
      Protocol (DHCP) 85

E

ESXi hosts
  zonning, at protected and recovery sites 8

F

failback
  configuring, virtual machine (VMs)
      used 151
failback (re-protect and failover)
  performing 156, 157

folder mappings
  about 33
  configuring 34
  creating 30-36
forced recovery
  Advanced Settings 76
  enabling, for site 76, 77
  performing 76
  running 78, 79

G

guest OS customization support matrix
  reference 83

I

IPv4 customization rules
  about 82
  creating 83-85

J

Java
  URL, for downloading 165

L

logs
  level, increasing Site Recovery
      Manager (SRM) used 186, 187
  level, increasing vSphere
      Replication used 186, 187
  obtaining 183, 184
  references, troubleshooting 187
  Site Recovery Manager (SRM) logs,
      analyzing 185

vSphere Replication logs,
  analyzing 184, 185

N

Network File Copy (NFC) protocol 134
network mappings
  about 37
  configuring 37
  creating 30, 37-40
Node Storage Module (NSM) 24

O

Ongoing replication
  pausing 143

P

placeholder datastores
  configuring 26-29
planned migration
  performing 69-73, 156
Platform Services Controller (PSC) 128
protected site 111
protection group
  about 44, 45
  creating 46-51
  creating, vSphere Replication used 153, 154
  storage policy based protection groups 46
PSC 3

R

recovery migration
  performing 156
recovery plan
  about 54
  background 65, 66
  cleanup, performing after test 66-69
  creating 54-57
  creating, vSphere Replication used 155
  testing 59
  test, running 61-64
  test workflow 60
references
  troubleshooting 187

remote site
  adding, as target 126-129
remote vCenter Server
  adding, as target 126-129
replication
  configuring, for virtual machine to local
    vCenter site 129-133
  configuring, for virtual machine to remote
    vCenter site 129-133
  monitoring 139, 140
  reconfiguring 141
  stopping, on virtual machine 145, 146
  switching, to VR server 146, 147
  working 134
replication seeds
  using 135-138
resource mappings
  about 30
  configuring 30
  creating 30-32

S

Site Recovery Manager (SRM)
  about 3
  architecture 3
  Array Manager 4
  components 3
  installing, on protected and recovery sites 8
  IP customization rules, using 85, 86
  logs, obtaining 183, 184
  troubleshooting 183
  used, for vSphere Replication 152
Site Recovery Manager (SRM) logs
  analyzing 185
SQL database
  configuring, for VRMS 112-119
SRM environment
  configuration activities, listing 6
  storage, preparing for array-based
    replication 7, 8
SRM installation
  performing 9-15
SRM Instance 3

SRM site
failback, performing 82
pairing 16-18
reprotecting 79-81
Storage Replication Adapter (SRA)
about 4-6
downloading 19
installing 19
swap files
cons 41
pros 41

T

target datastore
modifying 141, 142
target location 136

V

vCenter SRM. *See* **Site Recovery Manager (SRM)**
Virtual Appliance Management Interface (VAMI) 110
Virtual IP (VIP) 24
virtual machine
replication, configuring to local vCenter site 129-133
replication, configuring to remote vCenter site 129-133
replication, stopping 145, 146
virtual machines (VMs)
about 3
data, using 149
recovering 147-151
synchronize recent changes 149
used, for configuring failback 151
virtual machine swap file location
about 40
datastore, separating 41
swap files, storing in VM's working directory 41
VMware KB - 2041909
reference link 133

VM recovery properties
configuring 86, 87
IP customization 88-90
post power on steps 95
pre power on steps 95
priority group 91, 92
recovery properties 90
shutdown action 94
startup action 95
VM dependencies 92-94
vPostgres database 112
VRA hostname
setting, for VRA 110
vRealize Orchestrator (vRO)
authentication provider, configuring 168-173
client, used 165, 166
configuring 160, 166
database, configuring 167
deploying 160-164
downloading 161
enabling, vCenter used 173
logs, obtaining 183, 184
plugins, downloading Site Recovery Manager (SRM) used 180
plugins, downloading vSphere Replication used 180
plugins, installing 181, 182
plugins, installing Site Recovery Manager (SRM) used 179
plugins, installing vSphere Replication used 179
registering, as vCenter Server extension 177-179
vCenter Server instance, adding 173-177
vRealize Orchestrator (vRO) plugins
URL, for downloading 180
VRM site name
setting, for VRA 110, 111
VRO 7.0.1
URL, for downloading 161

vSphere Replication
about 4, 98, 126
architecture 99, 100
bundle, downloading 101
configuring, VM used to local vCenter site 129-134
configuring, VM used to remote vCenter site 129-134
failback (re-protect and failover), performing 156
logs, obtaining 183, 184
monitoring 139,140
planned migration, performing 156, 157
protection group, creating 153, 154
reconfiguring 141
recovery plan, creating 154, 155
recovery plan, performing 156, 157
recovery plan, testing 155
Site Recovery Manager (SRM), used 152, 153
SRM, used 152, 153
seed, using 135-138
stopping, on VM 145, 146

troubleshooting 183
used, for creating protection group 153, 154
used, for creating recovery plan 154, 155
used, for testing recovery plan 155
version upgrades 98
working 134, 135
vSphere Replication 6.1
features 98, 99
vSphere Replication Appliance (VRA) 152
deploying 102-109
working 109, 110
vSphere Replication logs
analyzing 184, 185
vSphere Replication Management Server (VRMS)
about 109
SQL database, configuring for 112-119
vSphere Replication Server
active replication, switching 146, 147
deploying 119-121
registering 122
replication, switching to 146, 147

Lightning Source UK Ltd.
Milton Keynes UK
UKOW05f1444290917

310109UK00004B/76/P

9 781785 886096